TRÜBNER'S COLLECTION

OF

SIMPLIFIED GRAMMARS

OF THE PRINCIPAL

ASIATIC AND EUROPEAN LANGUAGES.

EDITED BY

REINHOLD ROST, LL.D., Ph D.

IV.

MALAGASY.

BY G. W. PARKER.

TRÜBNER'S COLLECTION OF SIMPLIFIED GRAMMARS OF THE PRINCIPAL ASIATIC AND EUROPEAN LANGUAGES.

EDITED BY REINHOLD ROST, LL D., Ph D.

I.

HINDUSTANI, PERSIAN, AND ARABIC.
By the late E. H. Palmer, M.A.
Price 5s.

II.

HUNGARIAN.
By I. Singer.
Price 4s. 6d.

III.

BASQUE.
By W. Van Eys.

IV.

MALAGASY.
By G. W. Parker.

V

MODERN GREEK.
By E. M. Geldart, M.A.

VI.

ROUMANIAN.
By R. Torceanu.

Grammars of the following are in preparation.—
Albanese, Anglo-Saxon, Assyrian, Bohemian, Bulgarian, Burmese, Chinese, Cymric and Gaelic, Danish, Finnish, Hebrew, Malay, Pali, Polish, Russian, Sanskrit, Serbian, Siamese, Singhalese, Swedish, Tibetan, Turkish.

London : TRUBNER & CO.. Ludgate Hill.

A

CONCISE GRAMMAR

OF THE

MALAGASY LANGUAGE.

BY

G. W. PARKER.

LONDON:

TRÜBNER & CO., 57 AND 59, LUDGATE HILL.

1883.

LONDON ·
PRINTED BY GILBERT AND RIVINGTON, LIMITED,
ST. JOHN'S SQUARE.

PREFACE.

THE language spoken by the various tribes which inhabit Madagascar was essentially a spoken language, no symbols or pictures of the nature of writing having been found, until the early part of the present century; since which time the English Missionaries, by degrees, reduced it to its present alphabetic form. The characters chosen for it were those of our own English alphabet, with the exception of the five letters *c, q, u, w, x,* which have no corresponding sounds in Malagasy: but some, or all, of these (especially *w*) seem likely to be incorporated into the Malagasy language along with foreign words which require their use.

With regard to the place which Malagasy occupies among languages, there can be no doubt at all that it belongs to the Malayo-Polynesian group, or that it seems to have the closest affinity to the Malay proper and the Eastern Polynesian; although it is still a puzzle why the Malagasy people, who are chiefly of African origin (with the exception of the Hova tribe), should use a Malay language.

The use of *infixes* is a feature which the Malagasy language possesses in common with other languages of the Malayo-Polynesian group; and on this subject Mr. Keane has kindly given the following valuable information:—" The infix syllable *om* (*um, am, om*) is a feature which Malagasy has in common with Khmêr

(Cambojan), Javanese, Malay, Tagala (Philippine Archipelago), and, no doubt, other members of the Malayo-Polynesian family.

Ex. Khmêr: *slap*, dead; *samlap*, to kill.
    Javanese: *hurub*, flame; *humurub*, to inflame.
    Malay: *pilih*, to choose; *pamilihan*, choice.
    Tagala: *basa*, to read; *bumasa*, to make use of reading.

Originally a prefix, as it still is in Samoan (ex. *moto*, unripe; *momoto*, to die young), this particle seems to have worked its way into the body of the word by a process of metathesis analogous to the transposition common to most languages (compare Anglo-Saxon *thridda* with *third*)."

Briefly stated, the influence of foreigners upon the Malagasy language is as follows :—

(1) The influence of the *Arabs* is seen in the names of the days of the week, the Hova names for the months, and in many terms connected with dress, bed, money, musical instruments, &c.

(2) The influence of the *English* and of the *French* is seen in many abstract scientific, theological, and architectural terms, and in the names of modern weapons. Above all, the Malagasy people have gained much by the reduction of their language to the condition of a written tongue, and by the translation of the Bible into Malagasy— for which benefits they are more especially indebted to the labours of the English Missionaries.

G. W. PARKER.

MALAGASY GRAMMAR.

Letters.—The Malagasy Alphabet contains the same letters as the English Alphabet, with the exception of *c, q, u, w,* and *x.*

Vowels and Diphthongs.—These are pronounced as follows :—

> *a* as *a* in psalm ; example, *tùna,* (a) chamæleon.
> *e* ... *a* ... date ; ... *èny,* yes.
> *i* ... *ee* ... weep ; ... *hìdy,* (a) lock.
> *o* ... *oo* ... too ; ... *òny,* (a) river.

These are the usual sounds of the four vowels.

> *ai, ay* }
> *ei, ey* } pronounced like *i* in might.
>
> *ao* ... ... *ow* ... now.

These two sounds are the only true diphthongs.

Y represents the same sound as *i,* but is used at the ends of words, has a lighter sound, and becomes mute in certain cases ; while, in the translation of the New Testament, *y* is used in the body of words taken from the Greek to represent the letter *upsīlon :* thus, *sỳnagògy,* synagogue.

O, when used as the sign of a vocative case, or in names introduced from another language (as *Rajòna,* John), has the sound of *o* in ' no.'

In *writing*, all Malagasy words are written in full, except when the first of two words is a noun followed by its possessive case, or a verb in the passive or relative voice followed by its agent.

In *speaking*, each vowel must be clearly pronounced, because often a single vowel is the only means of distinction between two words dissimilar in meaning.   Examples :—

òlona, a person.	*mànana*, to possess.	*manènina*, to regret.
òlana, twisting.	*mànina*, to long after.	*manènona*, to weave.

An *elision* occurs in speaking usually when a final *a*, not accented, precedes a word beginning with any other vowel ; also when final *o* precedes a word beginning with *o*.

Euphonic Letters.—These are *h* and *i*. Euphonic *h* is generally inserted (both in speaking and writing) in a derivative, when two vowels would otherwise come together, of which one would be the first letter of the root, and the other the last letter of the prefix ; thus, *ihaviany* (instead of *iaviany*), from root *àvy*. Euphonic *i* is pronounced (but neither written nor printed) when *i* or *y* precedes *g*, *h*, *k*, *ng*, or *nk ;* thus, *mikàsa*, 'to intend,' is pronounced *mikiasa*.

Apparent Diphthongs.—The double vowels *eo*, *io*, found often, are not true diphthongs, because the sound of each vowel can be distinguished, unless they are pronounced too quickly : moreover, in forming passive verbs, the accent passes on to the second vowel.   Thus, *lèo* makes passive imperative *alèovy ;* *dìo* makes passive imperative *dìòvy*.

Sometimes, too, the diphthongs *ai* and *ao* are resolved into their component vowel-sounds ; thus, *aìdina*, 'poured out ;'

aòrina, 'built.' In these cases the *a* is a prefix, the rest of the word being a root.

The following combinations of vowels are less often found : *ia, oa, oi* (or *oy*), *oe, aoe,* and *oai.*

Final *a* is changed into *y* when a word ending in -*na,* -*ka,* or -*tra,* is followed either by the article *ny* or by certain proper nouns which do not admit of the article : this change softens and shortens the sound of the final syllable, and also serves to mark the genitive and ablative cases.

Ex. *Nỳ sàtroky nỳ lèhilàhy,* the hat of the man. ⎫
Andrìamànitry Jakòba, the God of Jacob. ⎬ *Nouns.*
Fàntatry nỳ òlona, known by the people.— *Verb.*

The third example shows that verbs in -*na,* -*ka,* or -*tra,* also follow this rule.

Final *a* is left unchanged, in order that the sense may not be doubtful, when a word ending in -*na,* -*ka,* or -*tra,* is *not* followed by another word in the genitive or in the ablative case.

Ex. *Fàntatra nỳ òlona,* known (are) the people, *i e.* the people are known.

Consonants.—The consonants are pronounced as in English, with the following exceptions :—

g is always hard, as in ' gold.'

j as *dz,* in ' adze.'

s before *e* and *i* is pronounced as a soft *sh* (ex. *mìsy* pronounced *mìsh*); otherwise it is always pronounced as *s* in ' sun ' (ex. *ìsa,* one).

z as *z,* in ' zone.'

The *s* and the *z* are never confounded in Malagasy as in the English word *surprise*.

Double Consonants.—The following are commonly used:—

dr, dz (or *j*), tr, and ts.   These have the force of single letters, and may begin a syllable or a word.

ng, mb, mp, also used often to begin words, seem to have arisen out of the fuller forms *ang*, *amb*, and *amp*, which still survive among other dialects than that of the Hovas : ex. Sihànaka, *ambàmy* = Hova, *mbàmy* ('together with, including ').

n and *m* are often used to close syllables :—

n is so used before *d, t, dr, dz* (or *j*), *tr, ts, g*, and *k*.

m   ...   .   *b* or *p*.

Hence the RULE : when *n* or *m* in the body of a word (*not* a compound) is followed by another consonant, the *n* or *m* is the closing letter of the preceding syllable.   With this one exception *all syllables end in a vowel*.

As *n* will combine only with *d, g, k,* and *t,* and *m* only with *b* or *p,* the only combinations of consonants allowable in the Malagasy language are the following :—

dr, dz (or *j*).

tr, ts.

mb, mp.

nd, ndr, ndz (or *nj*) ng, nk, nt, ntr, nts.

Hence the following euphonic changes among consonants become necessary :

f is replaced by *p*	*r* is strengthened by *d*, becoming *dr*.	
h .. .. *k* or *g*.	*s* .. .. *t*, .. *ts*.	
l .. .. *d*.	*z* .. .. *d*, .. *dz*	
v .. .. *b*.	(or *j*).	

These euphonic changes among consonants are required:—

(1) In forming derivatives that take a prefix ending
in *n* or *m*.

(2) When *n* or *m* is inserted between two words as
the sign of an indefinite possessive or ablative
case.

(3) In contracting words ending in -*na* by throwing
away the final *a*, so shortening the word by one
syllable.

But no euphonic change is needed (1) when the *whole*
syllable -*na* is rejected before a word beginning with *m or
n*; thus, *manàmpina-màso* becomes *mànampi-màso*: or
(2) when the *n* of possession (short for -*ny*) is similarly
rejected before a noun beginning with *m* or *n*; thus, *ràno-
màso*, "eye-water" (*i.e.* tears).

The final syllables -*na*, -*ka*, and -*tra* are contracted
sometimes by rejection of the final syllable. When one of
the changeable consonants follows a word so contracted, it is
changed according to rule (*see* p. 8), as if the letter *m* or *n*
closed the preceding syllable. These final syllables (if not
contracted) are always sounded lightly, although they
become almost mute when the accent falls on the antepenult.
When followed by a consonant, the sound of final *a* is
always kept.

When a word ending in -*na*, -*ka*, or -*tra*, is joined
with another word beginning with a vowel, the final *a* is
replaced by an apostrophe; thus, *sàtrok' òlona*, 'some-one's
hat.'

From the fondness of the Malagasy for contractions, the

relationship of the second of two contracted words to the preceding word may be any one of these ten things :—

(1) It may be a *possessive case;* as, *akànim-bòrona (akàny, vòrona),* ' a bird's nest.'

(2)   .   ...   *the agent of a passive or relative verb;* as, *tìam-bàdy (tìana, vàdy),* ' loved by one's wife.'

(3) ...   ...   *the object of a verb;* as, *manòso-dòko (manòsotra, lòko),* ' to smear with paint.'

(4) ...   ...   *a limiting accusative;* as, *tsàra-fanàhy (tsàra, fanàhy),* ' good as regards disposition.'

(5) ...   ...   *a noun in apposition;* as, *andrìan-drày àman-drèny (andrìana, rày, àmana, rèny),* ' the nobles (who are as) father and mother.'

(6) ..   . .   *a subject;* as, *ìtatàram-poza (tàtatra, fòza),* ' crabs are the things for which people cut channels.'

(7) ...   ...   *a predicate;* as, *nỳ fonòsin-dò (fonòsina, lò),* ' the thing that is wrapped up is putrid.'

(8) ...   ...   *an adjective;* as, *zàva-tsòa (zàvatra, sòa),* ' good things.'

(9) ...   ...   *a verb in the infinitive mood;* as, *nasàinanaò (nasàina, nanaò),* ' bidden to do.'

(10) ...   ...   *an adverb;* as, *mipètra-pòana (mipètraka, fòana),* ' to sit about idly.'

ROOTS.

In any language the study of the *roots* of the words is important, but this is more especially the case with the Malagasy language, because the derivatives, though regular, are very varied. These roots are chiefly verbs (active and passive), nouns, and adjectives; but some of the pronouns, adverbs, prepositions, conjunctions, and interjections may also be considered as roots, as they have not yet been traced to simpler forms.

The two classes of Malagasy roots are as follows:—

Primary roots; consisting of one, two, or three syllables; with the accent on the *first* syllable. The few apparent exceptions to this rule about accentuation (as *lalàna*, from the French *la loi; mizàna*, from the Arabic *mizán*, &c.) are explainable by a foreign derivation, or by assuming that the syllable preceding that which is accented was originally a monosyllabic primary root: ex. *lalaò* (i.e. *lao* reduplicated, 'play, playthings').

Secondary roots; formed from primary roots by the addition of a class of special monosyllabic prefixes, which differ from all the prefixes and affixes used in the formation of other words. These secondary roots are treated exactly like the primary roots in making verbs, &c. from them; and their accent is always on the *second* syllable.

Of these prefixes, *kan-*, *san-*, and *tan-* are treated like the active prefix *man-;* q.v. Besides these, we find an *infixed* syllable *om* inserted into a root of either kind immediately after the first consonant, apparently only the transposed form of a prefix *mo* (= *ma*); thus, *tàny, tomàny*.

TABLE OF THE CHIEF VARIETIES OF THESE PREFIXES.

PREFIX.	PRIMARY ROOT.	SECONDARY ROOT.
A. An	zàra	anjàra.
B. Bo	sesìka	bosesìka.
D Da	bòboka	dabòboka.
Do	nèndrina	donèndrina.
F. Fa	rìtsoka	farìtsoka.
Fo	rehitra	forèhitra.
G. Gɔ	ròbaka	goròbaka.
K. Ka	ràzana	karàzana.
Kan	tòvo	kantòvo.
Ki	fàfa	kifàfa
Ko	fèhy	kofehy.
L. Lah	àsa	lahàsa.
M. Mo	kòko	mokòko.
N. Ngo	ròdana	ngoròdana.
P. Po	ròtsaka	poròtsaka.
R. Re	hètra	rehètra (?).
Ro	àhana	roàhana.
S. Sa	fìdy	safìdy
San	làva	sandàva (-ny).
T. Ta	fòtsy	tafòtsi (-ny).
Tan	làpa	tandàpa
Ton	hìlana	tongìlana.
Tsi	laìnga	tsilaìnga.
Tsin	gàla	tsingàla.
V. Va	hìhy	vahìhy.
Z. Za	tòvo	zatòvo.

Reduplication of a root, whether primary or secondary, expresses the repetition, *or* the diminution, *or* the increased force, of the idea which the root in its single form expresses: hence, many roots may appear in a fourfold form. It is only the primary root which is thus doubled, for the prefixes and affixes remain unaltered.

Some roots occur only in the reduplicate form; as, *làolào*

(or *lalào*), ' play ;' *sàlasàla*, ' doubtful.' With regard to roots which end in syllables other than -*ka, -na, -tra*, no contraction occurs, but the root is simply reduplicated, with sometimes an *n* inserted, especially when the root begins with a vowel.

Ex.   *Fòtsy*, white ; *fòtsyfòtsy*, whitish.

     Tòro, crushed , *tòrotòro*, crushed into pieces.

     Ampy, sufficient ; *manàmpinàmpy*, to keep on adding. ⎫

     Mandà, to deny ; *mandàndà*, to deny repeatedly. ⎬ With inser-

     Zòky, elder ; *zòkinjòky*, still older. ⎭ tion of *n*.

Dissyllabic roots ending in -*ka, -na*, or -*tra*, may be either simply repeated or contracted ; thus, in *mitànatàna*, ' to be open ' (as the mouth), the root is repeated, while in *mitàntàna*, ' to hold,' the root is contracted.

Trisyllabic roots ending in -*ka, -na*, or -*tra*, accented on the antepenult, are contracted according to the rules for forming euphonic changes.

N.B.—As trisyllabic roots seem all to end in -*ka, -na*, or -*tra*, it is probable that these terminations are only affixes to primary roots of one or two syllables, as the following facts seem to show :—

(1) They are sometimes disused, especially in dialects other than the Hova ; as, *irày* and *iraìka*, and *ìsa* and *isaha*, for ' one '

(2) They are interchangeable in certain words ; as, *pòtsika* and *pòtsitra*.

(3) Dissyllabic roots, used in a sense allied to that of the longer forms, are not rare. Thus, dissyllabic root *rìa* ; trisyllabic words, *marìa, rìaka, rìana* ; tetrasyllabic words, *tsorìaka, korìana*.

RULE.—In reduplicating a word, remember (1) that the prefix is never altered; (2) that the primary root alone is reduplicated; and (2) that when the accent advances one syllable, owing to the addition of an affix, the first part of the word (*i.e.* prefix and primary root) is never altered, all changes occurring in the *last* part of the word. Thus :—

Primary root	*dìo,*	*fòtotra.*
Ditto, with prefix . . .	*madìo,*	*afòtotra.*
Do., with prefix reduplicated,	*madìodìo,*	*afòtopòtotra.*
Do., with prefix reduplicated, with accent shifted . .	*madìodìovy,*	*afòtopotòrana.*

Contracted adjectives and some verbs with active prefixes keep the *m* or *n* of the present or past tenses, when reduplicated, either instead of, or in addition to, the first letter of the root. Thus :—

> *Màrina, adj.* root *àrina,* becomes *màrimàrina.*
> *Manao, verb* ... *tao,* ... *manàonào.*

Or an *n* is inserted, especially when the root to be reduplicated begins with a vowel.

> Thus :—*Manèso,* root *èso,* becomes *manèsonèso.*

Derivatives in Malagasy, which are very numerous, are formed regularly from *any* kind of root (single, reduplicated, primary, or secondary) by appending to the root (1) a prefix, or (2) an affix, or (3) both prefix and affix. Thus :—

root	*zàra.*
root with prefix .	*mizàra.*
root with affix . .	*zaràina.*
root with both . .	*izaràna.*

Sometimes it is difficult to find out the root, owing (1), to the loss of its first consonant; or (2), to a change in its vowel; or (3), to a change in the consonant of its final syllable.

Brief Rules for Accentuation.

I. *Roots*, both primary and secondary, seem always to have the accent on the first syllable of the primary root, whether the root be two-syllabic or three-syllabic.

N.B.—A secondary root may be regarded as a primary root *plus* a monosyllabic prefix, which does *not* alter the place of the accent.

Reduplicated roots.—As only the primary root (and not a prefix) is reduplicated, the above rule still holds good in these cases, whether there be, or be not, any contraction of the reduplicated word.

N.B.—Only tri-syllabic roots ending in -*ka*, -*na*, or -*tra*, are contracted when reduplicated, although they may sometimes be reduplicated *without* contraction. No change of letters in the reduplicated word alters the place of the accent.

II. *Derivatives.*—No prefix alters the place of an accent; but affixes always cause the accent to advance one syllable nearer to the end of the word (generally bringing the accent on to the antepenult).

N.B.—A few roots (chiefly monosyllabic) do not allow the accent to shift at all; and in a few cases the accent (apparently contrary to the above rule) goes off the root on to the first syllable of the affix (as in the word *ànka-toàvina*, from root *to*).

But even in these cases the accent still rests on the

antepenult, in accordance with the apparently invariable
RULE for *all* pure Malagasy words, that *the accent must
never be further from the end of a word than the antepenult.*

VERBS.

The Malagasy Verb has three voices, the *active,* the
passive, and the *relative;* each voice has only two moods,
the *indicative* and the *imperative;* and each mood has the
three simple tenses, *present, past* and *future.* No changes
are made for gender, number, or person.

Of these two moods, the indicative serves for *every* mood,
except these three, viz. the imperative, the subjunctive, and
the optative, for which three the imperative itself serves.

ACTIVE VOICE.

Table of Active Verbs.

NAME.	EXAMPLES.	MEANING.
(1) Root, primary . . .	hòmana	to eat
.. secondary . .	homehy (*hèhy*) . . .	to laugh.
(2) .. with tafa-.		
.. primary. . .	tàfalàtsaka (*làtsaka*)..	fallen down.
.. secondary . .	tàfatsimbàdika (*ìddika*)	overturned.
(3) .. with simple active prefix.		
Mi, with primary root,	milàtsaka (*làtsaka*)	} to fall down.
Mi, with secondary root,	mìanjèra (*zèra*) . . .	
Miha	mìhatsàra (*tsàra*) . .	to become better.
Man	maneso (*èso*)	to taunt.
Maha.	mahàro (*àro*) . . .	to be able to protect.
(4) Causative of (3) . .	màmpilàtsaka (*làtsaka*)	to cause to fall down.
(5) Reciprocal of (3) . .	mìfaneso (*èso*) . .	to taunt one another.
(6) Reciprocal causative of (3)	màmpifanèso (*èso*) . .	to ask permission of one another.
(7) Causative reciprocal of (3)	mifàmpièra (*èra*) . .	to cause (people) to taunt one another.

Table of the chief Active Prefixes.

For the signs of causality and reciprocity look *up and down* the Table : for the simple forms, look *across* it.

SIMPLE.	CAUSATIVE.	RECIPROCAL	CAUSATIVE RECIPROCAL.	RECIPROCAL CAUSATIVE
Mi-	m-amp-i-	... ...	. ...	m-ifamp-i-.
Miha- (*progressive verbs.*)	m-amp-iha-	... ..	... ...	m-ifamp-iha-.
Maha- (*potential verbs*)	m-amp-aha-	... ...	... ...	m-ifamp-aha-.
Ma-	m-amp-a-	m-if-a	. ...	m-ifamp-a-.
Man-	m-amp-an-	m-if-an	m-ampif-an-	m-ifamp-an-.
Mana-	m-amp-ana-	m-if-ana	m-ampif-ana-	m-ifamp-ana-.
Manka	m-amp-anka-	m-if-anka-	m-ampif-anka-	m-ifamp-anka-.

Notice (1) that *amp* is the sign of causality, and *if* of reciprocity ; and (2) that the causative-reciprocal sign *ampif*, and the reciprocal-causative sign *ifamp*, are only combinations of these two.

Tafa-, prefixed to a root, gives the idea of completeness, but differs slightly from our perfect tense, in that it may be used of something altogether past ; in this respect it resembles rather the *pluperfect* of some languages. Père Webber says, (1) that *tàfa* gives the right answer to an intransitive imperative (as, *Mipetràha hianaò,* sit down ; *tàfapètraka àho,* I am seated) ; and (2) that while the prefix *vòa* implies the operation of an external agent, *tàfa* usually implies internal agency. Sometimes, however, these two prefixes seem interchangeable.

B

Mi-, *Man-*, and *Màha-*, are the three most common active prefixes.

Mi- (contracted into *M-* before *i*) forms chiefly intransitive verbs, but forms also a few transitive verbs when prefixed to a primary root.

Man- forms verbs of either kind, but chiefly transitive verbs. *Man-* and *Mana-* (a longer form) both seem contracted forms of the verb *manaò*, 'to do, or make,' used as a prefix.

Màha- (contracted into *Mah-* before a vowel) is a contracted form of the verb *Mahày*, 'to be able.' This is the most widely used prefix in the Malagasy language, as it may be added to almost any word or phrase.

Màha- is used to express (1) power to perform an action, (2) that which makes a thing what it is.

N.B.—*Mana-* and *Maha-* are often confounded; but their difference is well shown by the following example, where the same root (*tsàra*, 'good') produces a verb with each of the prefixes :—

Mànatsàra, to do some action for the improvement of a thing ; to render good ; to make good.

Màhatsàra, possessing the power to make a thing good ; possessing some quality showing or proving its intrinsic goodness.

Rules for the formation of the Verbs with the prefix 'man-.'

a. If the root begins with a vowel or with the consonants *d*, *g*, *j* ; simply apply the prefix, and make no change.

b. If the root begins with any consonant except one of these three :—

The first consonant of the root is rejected :–*k, s, t, tr, ts,* and sometimes *h,* are rejected.

or, The first consonant of the root is changed :—*h* sometimes becomes *g*; *l* becomes *d*; *r* becomes *dr*; *z* becomes *j* (*dz*).

or, The first consonant of the root is rejected *and the prefix changed* (*from* man- *to* mam-) before *b, v, f,* or *p.*

But sometimes *v* is changed into *b,* or *b* itself is kept.

Before *m* or *n,* the prefix is contracted into *ma-.*

Ma- (or *M-,* before vowels) is a shorter form of *Man-,* which forms a few transitive verbs, but a large number of adjectives usable as verbs.

Rules for the formation of the Imperative Mood of Active Verbs.

(1) Affix -*a,* unless the word already ends in *a.*

(2) Shift the accent one syllable forward, unless the root is a monosyllabic diphthong; *or,* unless the root is two-syllabic, but with the accent on the *last* syllable; *or,* unless the root is two-syllabic, but ending in -*ka,*-*na,* or *tra-.*

(3) Sometimes also one or other of the following changes are necessary :—

Change of a consonant preceding the final *a*: this occurs only in roots ending in -*ka,* -*na,* or -*tra,* where *k* becomes *h* or *f, tr* becomes *t, r,* or *f,* and *n* becomes *m.*

Insertion of a consonant (*s*, *v*, or *z*) before the final *a* : there are a few exceptions to this.

Vowel-changes, usually taking place among the vowels of the accented syllable, viz. *i* (or *y*) into *a* or *e*.

Vowel-changes, usually taking place among the vowels of the accented syllable, viz. *ai* into *e*.

The government of cases by Malagasy verbs is often puzzling, because, while many verbs govern direct accusatives, others require the preposition *àmy* to be inserted between them and the cases they govern; while others, again, have both constructions. Thus, *mitèny àminy*, ' to speak to him ;' *mitèny àzy*, ' to reprove him ' (*i.e.* to speak *at* him).

Again, many Malagasy verbs take *two* accusatives, which may refer to person and thing, instrument and object, or limiting accusative and object.

PASSIVE VOICE.

Table of the various forms of the Passive Voice.

NAME	EXAMPLE.	MEANING.
1 Root passive	tàpaka	cut off.
2. Passive in *voa-*....	vòasàsa (sàsa)	washed.
3. .. .. *-ina.*		
.. from primary root .	zaraìna (zàra)	divided.
.. secondary root,	tsìnjaraìna (zàra)	divided into lots.
.. abstract noun..	hàtsaraìna (tsara)	made good.
.. compound preposition	àmpoìzina (fò)	expected.
retaining *an-* of verb in *man-* ..	àntsakaìna (tsàka)	fetched (of water from a well).
	ànavaràtina (avàratra)	moved northwards.
.. *anka-* of verb in *manka-* ..	ànkahalaìna (hàla)	hated.

NAME.	EXAMPLE.	MEANING.
Passive retaining *amp-* of causative verb in *mamp-*......	àmpilazaìna (làza)	... caused to tell *or* to be told.
.. .. *ampif-* of causative-reciprocal verb in *mampif*	àmpifàndahàrina.. (làhatra)	caused to plead against one another.
4. Passive in *-ana* (*from roots only*)	fotsìana (fòtsy) ..	whitened.
5. .. .. *-ena*..........	vonjèna (vònjy) ..	saved, helped.
6. .. .. *a-*.............	asèho (sèho)	shown.
7. Transposed passive	tinàpaka (tàpaka).	cut off.

Root-passive means a root-word containing a passive idea and usable as a passive verb.

The difference (usually existing) between a root-passive and a passive in *a-*, *-ana*, or *-ina* is that the former usually calls attention to the idea contained, leaving the agent almost out of consideration, while the latter calls attention to the agent as well as to the act.

The imperative mood of a root-passive (like the imperative mood of an adjective) has usually an optative meaning : as *sitràna,* ' may (*he*) be healed.' But *sitràno,* the imperative passive of the verb *màna̧sìtrana* (from *sitrana*) has an imperative, not an optative, meaning.

Vòa (literally *struck*) is a root-passive used as a prefix. Often *vòa-* and *tàfa-* are equally suitable as prefixes, but generally *tàfa-* implies self-agency, *vòa-* the agency of another ; but both give almost a " pluperfect " idea.

-ina is the usual ending of most passive verbs. Of these varieties of passives the only kind at all troublesome to distinguish is the passive in *-ina* formed from an abstract

noun ; with regard to this, remember that *the abstract noun ends in* ana, *while the passive verb ends in* ina. Example :— *hàtsaràna* (*abstract noun*), goodness ; *hàtsaraìna* (*passive verb*), made to possess goodness, made good.

As regards causative verbs, the *i* of the affix is the *only* visible distinction between their passive and their relative voices Example :—passive, *àmpanolòina ;* relative, *àmpanolòana,* root *sòlo.*

The passive in *a-* (which is very common) calls attention principally to the position or state of the object.

Rule for distinguishing the use of the passive in *a,* from the use of the passive in *-ana :*—When a verb governs two accusatives, the one of the object acted on, the other of the instrument or means with which the action is effected, the *latter* is made the nominative of a passive in *a-,* the *former* of a passive in *-ana.*

Example :—*manòso-tsòlika àzy,* ‘to anoint it with oil ; ’ *ahòsotra àzy nỳ sòlika* (the oil is here the nominative of the verb *ahòsotra*) ; *hosòrana sòlika izy* (the thing anointed is here the nominative of the verb *hosòrana.*)

N.B.—“ The non-observance of this rule may lead the foreigner into gross absurdities,” says the Rev. W. E. Cousins.

Passives in *a-*change their accent only in their imperative mood ; thus, root *hàro, ahàro* (indicative), *àharòy* (imperative). Transposed passives are formed by prefixing *ni-* or *no-* to a root, and then transposing the *n* and the first letter of the root, as, *tàpaka, nitàpaka, tinàpaka.*

Rule.—in forming the passives in *a-, -ana,* and *-ina,* the relatives, and the imperative mood in verbs of all voices and classes, one or *all* of the following five changes are necessary :—

1. Append the characteristic termination—

-*ina,* -*ana,* or -*ena,* for the indicative mood passive voice ; -*ana,* and -*ena,* for the indicative mood relative voice.

-*o* (or -*y,* if *o* is already contained in the root) for the imperative mood of all relative verbs and of passives in *a-,* -*ina,* and -*ana.*

-*a* (in a few cases -*e*) for the imperative of a root, and for all active imperatives.

2. Move the accent one syllable forward. Exceptions :— when the root has one syllable only ; when the root has two syllables, the second being accented ; when the root has two syllables, the second ending in -*na,* -*ka,* or -*tra.*

3. For roots in -*na,* -*ka,* and -*tra,* a change occurs in the consonant preceding the characteristic termination : *k* becomes *h* or *f; tr* becomes *r, t,* or *f; n* (often) becomes *m.*

4. Insert *s, v,* or *z,* before the characteristic termination.

5. Alter a vowel, usually of the accented syllable ; as, *i* (or *y*) into *a* or *e,* and *ai* into *e.*

ia (that is, *i* of the root and *a* of the affix) are sometimes contracted into *e* ; as, root *vonjy,* passive *vonjiana* contracted into *vonjèna.*

` Rule for choosing which voice* (active or passive) *is to be used :*—When " *the agent and his act* " are most in your thoughts, choose the active voice ; when " *the result of the* *act "* is most in your thoughts, choose the passive voice. The Malagasy usually prefer the passive voice.

Rule for the use of the passive voice of verbs which govern two accusatives :— Either accusative may be made the nominative of a passive verb.

N.B.—When two passives exist from the same root (viz. in *a-* and *-ina*) take care to choose the *right* one.

RELATIVE VOICE.

The relative voice is one which is peculiar to the Malagasy language; and, although somewhat puzzling at first, its use is very convenient. It is a *blending* of the two other voices, both in form and in construction; and expresses some *relationship* between the agent of a verb and the object.

Rule for forming the relative voice (from the active voice) :—1. Omit the *m* of the active prefix. 2. Affix *-ana,* or *-ena,* for the indicative mood; and *-o,* or *-y,* for the imperative mood; then treat the word (as regards changes) as if it were a passive in *-ana.* The *government* still remains that of the active verb, but the *agent* is expressed by the suffix pronoun, as if the verb were really passive.

Some relative verbs are also used for the passive voice, and their meaning must be found from the context. Also, what has been said of the twofold meaning of active verbs in *maha-* is equally true of relative verbs formed from them.

Table of the chief characters of the subject of a
Relative Verb.

1. (*As in English*) the nominative case of an active
verb is its agent, and that of a passive verb its direct
object.

2. The Nominative may have any of the following degrees
of relation :—

    (*a*) Direct object considered partitively.

    (*b*) Indirect object (*i.e.* one which would be preceded
        by the preposition *amy* if it followed a verb,
        whether active or passive).

    (*c*) An adjunct of time (point, duration, *or* repetition).
       ... ... place (in, towards, *or* from).
       ... ... mode (manner, *or* measure).
       ... ... cause (cause, *or* occasion ; reason ;
             means, *or* instrument; price).

Tenses of Verbs.

The indicative mood alone has any tenses ; these tenses
are the three simple tenses—*present, past,* and *future.* As
with Malagasy adjectives, so with the tenses of Malagasy
verbs, *n* is the sign of the past, and *h* of the future.

TABLE SHOWING HOW TO FORM THE TENSES OF VERBS.

NAME.	CHANGE REQUIRED.	EXAMPLE.		
		PAST.	PRESENT.	FUTURE.
1. Roots (with or without prefix) *tafa-* or *voa-* . . .	no change for the past; *ho* for the future . . .	fia	fia	*hò fia.*
2. Verbs with any active prefix . .	change *m* of the prefix into *n* for the past, and *h* for the future . .	misòlo	nisòlo	hisòlo.
3. { All Relatives . . . All Passives with prefix *a-* . . All Passives beginning with a vowel and ending in *-ana, -ena,* or *-ina* . .	prefix (to their present) *n* for the past, and *h* for the future . .	alaina asòlo	nalaina nasòlo	halaina. hasòlo.
4. All Passives beginning with a con-sonant . . .	prefix (to their present) *no* for the past, and *ho* for the future .	lazaina	nolazaina	holazaina.

Use and force of *èfa.*—As the Malagasy language has no exact equivalents for the perfect, pluperfect, and future perfect tenses, the nearest equivalents are got by using the auxiliary verb *èfa* (literally, *done*). It may be used before any tense of any voice, and conveys the idea of more or less 'completeness.'

Examples :—*Èfa manaò,* is doing, has begun to do and is still doing (*incomplete present*). *Èfa nanào,* was in the act of doing (*incomplete perfect*) ; *or,* had done (*completed perfect, pluperfect*). *Èfa hanaò,* is just about to do, is on the point of doing (*incomplete future*).

Compound Future Tense.—This is formed by putting *ho* before a past tense ; as, *nanào hò nànkatỳ,* 'he intended to come (*or* to have come) here.'

The various uses of the Infinitive Mood.

The indicative mood may be used in any voice or tense ; (1) as an adjective or as a participle, especially when a noun is left to be understood ; as, *nỳ mànana,* 'the (men) ; possessing,' the possessors, *i. e.* the rich ; *nỳ natào,* 'the (deed) done ;' *nỳ hàndidìana,* the (instrument, &c.) for cutting. (2) It may be used where in other languages an infinitive would be required, viz. either as a noun, usually with the article ; as, *nỳ mangàlatra,* 'stealing,' *or* 'the thieves.'

(N.B.—In such cases the meaning must be made clear by the context, or else it remains doubtful) :—or as dependent on another verb ; as, *asaìko manào,* 'is bidden by me to do (it).'

The dependent verb, and that on which it depends, are not necessarily of the same voice or of the same tense; but, among the many possible combinations made in this way, the following two *Rules* should be remembered : (1) A past can only be used as dependent on a past. (2) The future is more often used in this dependent manner than either the past or the present.

An *Imperative* can be followed by a present or a future of any voice.

The *Conditional* mood is expressed by the indicative mood preceded by a conditional conjunction (*ràha, nòny,* &c.).

The *Hortative* mood is expressed either by an imperative passive with the suffix pronoun, as *anàrontsìka,* 'let him be reproved by us' (*i.e.* let us reprove him) ; or by an indicative future preceded by *aòka* or *andèha,* as *aòka,* or *andèha, hihìra isìka,* 'let us sing.' (N.B.—Of these two, *aòka* is never followed by any other tense than the future; *andèha,* usually by the future, but sometimes by the present, as in the phrase *andèha màka ràno,* 'go (and) fetch (some) water.')

A *prohibition* is expressed, not by the imperative mood, as in many languages, but by the indicative mood preceded by *àza.* In this case the verb (in the indicative) may belong to any of the three voices. Ex.: *àza mitèny hìanào,* 'do not speak. (N.B.—As there is no exact equivalent for the verb "to be" in Malagasy, *àza* may be used prohibitively with adjectives also; thus, *àza tèzitra hìanào,* 'do not (be) angry.')

Defective Auxiliary Verbs.

Of these there are five in common use, viz.,

EXAMPLES.

Mahàzo, implying practicability.	*tsy mahàzo manào*, not able to do (because hindered).
Mahày, implying ability *or* skill.	*tsy mahày manào*, not able to do (absence, or deficiency, of skill).
Mèty, implying consent, willingness,	*tsy mèty manào*, not willing to do (absence of consent).
Tìa, implying desire, wish.	*tsy ta-hanào*, not desirous to do (absence of wish).
Mìsy, implying existence.	*tsy mìsy*, there is none (non-existence).

N.B.—*Mìsy* is the nearest equivalent to our verb "to be."

Table of Defective Auxiliary Verbs.

TENSE.	ACTIVE.	PASSIVE.	RELATIVE.
Indicative	mahàzo	àzo	ahazàana.
Imperative.	màhazòa		ahazòy.
Indicative	mahày	hày	ahàizana.
Imperative.	mahàiza		ahàizo.
Indicative	mèty		etèzana.
Imperative.	metèza		etèzo.
Indicative	tìa (ta-, te-)	tìana	itìavana.
Imperative.	tiàva	tiàvo	itiàvo
Indicative	mìsy (pronounced *mish*)		isìana.
Imperative.	misìa		isìo.

(The Imperative Relative of these is seldom used.)

Rule for the contraction of *tìa* (into *te-* or *tà-*) :—*Tìa* is not contracted when a suffix pronoun will be affixed, even when a future tense will follow; as, *tìako hatào izàny,*

'I wish that to be done.' Otherwise *tia* is contracted into *ta-* before a future beginning with *ha-* (*hamp-, han-,* &c); as, *tà-hanào izány àho,* 'I wish to do that :' or into *tè-* before a future beginning with *hi-* or *ho ;* as, *tè-hilàza,* ' wish to tell ;' *te-ho fàty,* 'wish to be a dead body' (*i.e.* wish to die).

The active and relative forms of *mahàzo, manào,* and *mèty,* must be followed by an active voice ; but the passive forms *àzo* and *haỳ,* take either a passive or a relative after them, *not* an active. The pronoun is generally affixed to the auxiliary verb ; as, *àzoko soràtana,* 'able by me to be written' (for nothing hinders).

Partitive force of mìsy.—*Mìsy* often serves to show that the verb which it precedes applies only to *some* of the persons or things indicated by the subject. Ex.: *mandaìnga nỳ òlona,* 'the people tell lies' (all, or some ?); *mìsy mandaìnga nỳ òlona,* ' some of the people tell lies.'

NOUNS.

TABLE OF NOUN-FORMS.

NAME.		EXAMPLE.	MEANING.
Single root	primary	*màso* . . .	(an) eye.
	secondary	*kofehy (fèhy)*	cord.
Redup. root	primary	*rèharèha* .	overbearing conduct.
	secondary	*kiràzìràzy* .	(a) joke.
Verbal noun in *-ana*		*vonδana (vδno)*.	murder.
Habitual noun of agent		*mpamòno (vòno)*	one who often kills.
„ noun of manner		*famòno (vòno)* .	usual way of killing.
„ relational noun		*famonδana* .	usual place of killing.
Abstract noun in *ha-*		*halàlina* ⎫	
„ „ in *ha-ana*		*hàlalìnana* ⎬ (*làlina*), depth.	
„ „ in *fàha-*		*fàhalalina* ⎬	
„ „ in *faha-ana*		*fahalalìnana* ⎭	
Negative noun .		*tsi-finδana (ìno)* . .	unbelief.
Compound noun		*fòto-kèntra (fòtotra, hèvitra)*.	principle.

The verbal noun in *-ana* follows the same rules as the passive verbs in *-ana*.

The habitual nouns (*f* and *p* convey the idea of habituality) are verbal in form, meaning, and government. The habitual nouns of manner, or 'modal nouns,' are so-called because they *may* be used to express the mode of the action indicated by the verbs from which they are derived. They are usually preceded by a qualifying adjective (as, *tsara-filàza*, 'good as to the way of speaking,' having a good delivery); and also may denote the customary instrument, agent, or object.

Relative Noun.—*f* prefixed to a relative *verb* changes it into a relative *noun*; and as the meaning is still as wide

as before (*f* only adding the idea of *habit*) another noun
is often put before it, to limit its meaning; as, *tràno-fivavà-
hana*, 'a house for prayer.'

N.B.—Do not use the habitual noun of the agent (which
always begins with *mp-*) for an agent not necessarily
habitual. Ex.: *mpamòno*, 'a man who *often and habitually*
murders,' a regular assassin; *mamòno*, 'a man who perhaps
only once murders.'

The abstract nouns in *ha-* and *faha-* are really *habitual
modal* nouns derived from verbs in *màha-*; they are similar
in meaning, and are seldom used without the suffix pronoun -*ny*.

The difference in meaning between these abstract nouns,
according to Père Webber, is as follows :—

   hatsàra shows *intrinsic* goodness, worth.
   hàtsaràna shows *extrinsic* goodness, or goodness em-
        bodied in deeds, good conduct.
   fàhatsaràna shows goodness as the source or principle
        of good deeds.

Cases of Nouns.

There are no declensions in the Malagasy language, so
that where the case of a noun is not left to be found out
from the context, one or other of the following case-
indications are necessary :—

   For an accusative case, its position immediately after or
        close to its verb.

   For an accusative case, the particle *àny* (which precedes
        all proper names and some pronouns).

For a possessive or an ablative case :—

(*a*) When the noun is made definite by the article *nỳ*, the governing word (whether noun or verb) takes the suffixed pronoun *-ny* (or *n'*); as, *trànon' nỳ sakaìza*, 'house of the friend'. *Or*, if the governing word end in *-na, -ka*, or *tra*, the final *-a* is changed into *-y*; as, *fàntatry nỳ òlona*, 'known by the people'.

(*b*) When the noun is *not* made definite by the article, either *m* or *n* (regardable as contracted forms of the suffix pronoun *-ny*) is inserted; as, *hàlam-bahòaka*, 'hated by (the) people'; *or*, if the governing word end in *-na, -ka*, or *-tra*, a contraction occurs with some euphonic change among the consonants. [See *Euphonic changes among consonants.*]

For a vocative case :—the omission of the article ; as, *Rainaỳ izaỳ àny an-dànitra*, 'Our Father who (art) in heaven '; *or*, the use of *rỳ* (*ràry*, or *rèy*) before the vocative case, or *ò* after it.

Special uses of the Nominative and Accusative Cases.

The nominative is often used absolutely, at the beginning of a sentence, where we might say ' *as to* ' or ' *in reference to*'.

The accusative, besides indicating the object, may be (adverbial) used as an adverb of time or of place; (instrumental) used of an instrument, as *namèly sàbatra anào izy*, 'he struck you (with) a sword'; (limiting) used to limit the meaning of an adjective or a verb (which verb may be in any of the three voices). This last is a very common use of the accusative case.

c

ADJECTIVES.

TABLE OF ADJECTIVE FORMS.

NAME.		EXAMPLE.	MEANING.
Single root	primary	tsàra	good.
	secondary ..	sahìrana (hìrana) ..	perplexed.
Reduplicated root	primary.. ..	tsàratsàra	tolerably good, goodish.
	secondary ...	sahìrankìrana (hìrana)..........	slightly perplexed.
Adjective in ma-, uncontracted,		madìtra (dìtra) ...	obstinate.
Ditto, contracted.. (a combining with the following o or i to form a diphthong).		maòzatra (òzatra)..	sinewy, tough.
Adjective in m-, before a or e		màrina (àrina).....	level, true.
Ditto, before ha- or he-		màfy (hàfy).	hard.
Reduplicated adjective in ma- or in m-...............		madìodìo (dìo).....	rather clean.
Negative adjective		tsi-màrina (arina) ..	not level, untrue.
Adjective with limiting accusative		tsàra-bìka........	good as regards shape.
Antithetic compound adjective		kèli-malàza	little (but) famous.

The scarcity of true adjectives in the Malagasy language is supplied in various ways, viz. by the free use of verbs as adjectives or participles, as already said; by the use of words which are verbal in form but practically adjectives; as, *vavàna* (root *vàva*), talkative, literally '*mouthed*'.

N.B.—In English we have the very same form, '*mouthed*', '*mouthing*', both from '*mouth*'.

By the use of nouns for our adjectives of material; as, *tràno hàzo*, 'a house (of) wood', i.e. a wooden house.

By the use of the auxiliary verb *àzo* for our adjectives in -*able* and -*ible*; as, *àzo hànina*, 'able (to be) eaten', i.e. eatable.

Comparison of Adjectives.

Reduplication of an adjective nearly always lessens its meaning; as, *fòtsy*, ' white '; *fòtsifòtsy*, ' whitish '. But repetition of an adjective, with the insertion of *dia* in the interval, always intensifies its meaning; as, *fòtsy dia fòtsy*, ' very white '.

No changes are made in the form of an adjective to show the degrees of comparison. A comparative degree is known by *nòho*, *kòa nòho*, *kokòa nòho*, or *làmitra nòho*, following the adjective; a superlative degree, by *àmy* or *indrìnda àmy*.

Or, by the omission of *nòho* or *àmy*, any of these forms may be used absolutely, the compared object being supplied mentally; as, *tsàratsàra kokòa io*, ' that is better ' (than some other).

Or the simplest form of the adjective may be used as a superlative, *nò* (the emphatic and discriminative particle) being put after it; as, *iza no tsàra?* ' which (is the) good (one)?' *i.e.* which is the best?

Another idiom is what the Rev. W. E. Cousins calls "the conditional superlative", a term which is best explained by the following examples:—

(a) From Fable XII.: *màfy kòa ràha màfy*, ' hard, if (there be anything) hard'. (*Adjective.*)

(b) From Luke xxii. 15: *Nanìry koa ràha nanìry Aho*, ' desired, if I desired '; or, as our Authorized Version says, *With desire have I desired.* (*Verb.*)

Table of Degrees of Comparison of Adjectives.

DEGREE.	EXAMPLE.	MEANING.
A. Positive	tsàra	good
Comparative	{ tsàra kokòa } { tsàratsàra kokoa } . . .	better.
Superlative..	{ tsaɪa ɪndrìndra } { tsàɪa dìa tsàra } . . .	best.
B. Comparative..	tsàra nòho	better than.
	{ tsàra kokòa nòho . . . } { tsàratsàra kòa (or kokòa) nòho }	a little better than.
	tsàra làvitra nòho . . .	far better than.
Superlative..	tsàra àmy nỳ — rehètra. .	best of all.
	tsàra indrìndra àmy nỳ . .	very best of all.

Tenses of Adjectives.

The Rule for forming the tenses of adjectives is as follows :—

Adjectives in *ma-* uncontracted, make *na-* in the past, and *ha-* in the future.*

All other adjectives make no change for the past, but take *ho* for the future.

Tabular view of the Tenses of Adjectives.

PRESENT.	PAST.	FUTURE.
Adj. in *ma-* uncontracted.		
madìtra (dìtra).	nadìtra ..	.. hadìtra
Adj. in *ma-* contracted.		
{ maòzatra (òzatra). ..	maòzatra ..	.. hò maòzatra.
{ maìnty (ìnty).	maìnty ..	.. ,, maìnty.
{ màɪina (àrɪna)	màrɪna ..	.. ,, màrina.
{ mèrɪka (èrɪka)	merɪka ..	.. ,, mèrìka.

---

* *Màlahèlo*, although an adjective in *ma-* contracted, is an exception to this rule, because its past is *naḍahèlo*, and its future *haḍahèlo*. Again, in some parts of Madagascar, contracted adjectives in *ma-* make their past in *na-*, and their future in *ha-*.

On looking at these five adjectives it will be noticed that the first of them alone has the accent on the *second* syllable; hence we may deduce the following *Rule*, to help us to know the class to which any adjective beginning with *m-* may belong :—

If the accent is on the second syllable, it belongs to the first class, and begins with *ma-* uncontracted.

If the accent is on the first syllable, *ma-* either has its *a* suppressed (as in *màrina*), or its *a* forms a diphthong with the *i* or *o* of the root-word of the adjective (as in *maìnty*).

Imperative and Optative Moods of Adjectives.

Any adjective can be made imperative or optative by following the rules given for active verbs or those for root-passives; and either the meaning of the adjective, or else the context, will determine whether a command or a wish is intended to be expressed. As, *mazòto*, ' diligent ' ; *màzotòa*, ' be diligent ' : *faingana*, ' quick ' ; *faingàna*, ' be quick.'

Construction of Adjectives.

The following adjectives, and some others, have a quasi-transitive sense, and govern a direct accusative as their complement; as, *fèno àzy nỳ tràno*, ' the house is full of them '. In English we require a preposition in such cases, in Malagasy no preposition.

adàla, 'foolish about'.

akaìky, 'near to'.

antònona, 'fit for', 'suited to'.

ampy, 'enough for'.

bètsaka, 'having *much* of', 'abounding in'.

bè, 'having *many* of', 'abounding in'.

dìboka, } 'full of'.
fèno,

gàga, 'surprised at'.

hènika, } 'full of'.
hìboka,

hìboka (only another form of *dìboka*).

mànina, 'longing after'.

mànitra, 'perfumed with'.

maìmbo, 'smelling offensively of'.

màlahèlo, 'grieved about', 'sorrowing for'.

màmo, 'intoxicated with'.

mèndrika, 'suitable for', 'worthy of'.

sàhy, 'without fear of'.

sàsatra, 'tired of'.

tàhaka, 'like', 'similar to'.

vòky, 'satisfied with'.

vìtsy, 'having few of'.

Adjectives can be followed by passive or relative verbs, with a gerundial force; as, *sàrotra atào*, 'difficult to be done'.

PRONOUNS.
THE PERSONAL PRONOUNS.

OF Personal Pronouns there are two forms, separate and inseparable (or suffixed), as shown in the following table:

Singular Number.

	Separate forms.		Inseparable forms.	
PERSON.	NOM. CASE	ACC AND POSSESS. CASES.	FULL FORM.	CONTR. FORM.
First . .	{ *izàho* } { *aho* }	*àhy.*	*-ko*	*-o.*
Second . .	*hianào*	*anào.*	*-nào*	*-ào.*
Third . .	*izy*	*àzy.*	*-ny*	*-n', -y.*

Plural Number.

First, inclus.	*isìka*	*antsìka.*	*-ntsìka*	*-tsìka.*
„ exclus.	*izahày*	*anày.*	*-này*	*-ày.*
Second . .	*hianarèo*	*ànarèo.*	*-narèo*	*-arèo.*
Third . .	*ìzy*	*àzy.*	*-ny*	*-n', -y.*

Izàho is more emphatic than *àho*, and is generally used when the predicate follows, while *àho* usually follows its predicate. There are some exceptions to this rule, especially the verb *hòy* ('say, says, said'), which usually takes *izàho* 'say I.'

Isìka includes both the speaker and the person spoken to, while *izahày* excludes the person addressed; or, *isìka,* 'we,' (and you), *izahày,* 'we,' (but not you).

The separate forms for the possessive case are used in two ways :—

(1) as predicates ; as, *àhy nỳ vòla,* 'the money is mine'.

(2) for any case, with the article prefixed (the noun being understood) ; as, *ènto nỳ ando,* 'being thine' (lit. the of thee).

The inseparable or suffixed forms may denote—

(1) A possessive case ; as, *nỳ vòlako,* 'my money'.

(2) An ablative case, showing the agent of a passive or a relative verb ; as, *vòasàsako,* 'washed by me'. They are less often used with adjectives in this instrumental sense ; as, *fìry nỳ òlona izày èfa hèndrinào?* 'How many are the people who have become wise through you'?

(3) An indirect objective case, after verbs, adjectives, prepositions, &c. In these cases the suffixed pronoun is

attached to the preposition *àmy*; as, *misèho àmiko*, ' to appear to me '.

(4) Rarely a dative case; as, *màminày*, ' sweet to us '.

As there is no reflexive pronoun in Malagasy, *tèna* (body) is used for *self*; as, *namòno tèna ìzy*, ' he killed himself'.

The Rule for attaching the suffix pronouns to any word is as follows:—(1) For words *not* ending in *-na*, *-ka*, or *-tra;* attach the full form of the suffixed pronoun, without contraction. (2) For words ending in *-na*, *-ka*, or *-tra;* if the accent is on the antepenult, take one or other of the contracted forms of the suffixed pronouns, and either throw away or shorten their last syllable. If the accent is on the penult, either the full or the contracted forms may be used; as, *tràtro* and *tràtrako*, ' my chest ';—except in the case of passive and relative verbs and relative nouns in *-ana*, when only the contracted forms of these pronouns may be used; as, *sasàna*, ' washed ', *sasàko*, ' washed by me '.

Examples of the modes of attachment of suffixed Pronouns.

1. To words *not* ending in *-na*, *-ka*, or *-tra*.

	NOUN.	VERB.	PREPOSITION.
	Vòla, money.	Àzo, got.	Àmy, to, at, &c.
Sing.	vòlako, my money.	àzoko, got by me.	àmiko, to me.
	vòlanào, thy money.	àzonào, ,, ,, thee.	àminào, to thee.
	vòlany, his (or her) money.	àzony, ,, ,, him, (her, or it).	àminy, to him (her, or it).
Plur.	vòlanày, our money.	àzonày, ,, ,, us.	àminày, to us.
	vòlantsìka, our money.	àzontsìka ,, ,, us.	àmintsìka, to us.
	vòlanarèo, your money.	àzonarèo, ,, ,, you.	àminarèo, to you.
	vòlany, their money.	àzony, ,, ,, them.	àminy, to them.

2. To words ending in *-na*, *-ka*, or *-tra*. (N.B.—Only nouns are here given as examples, but verbs are treated in exactly the same way.)

	Hàrona, a basket.	Sàtroka, a hat *or*, hats.	Hèvitra, a thought.
Sing.	hàroko, my basket.	sàtroko, my hat.	hèvitro, my thought.
	hàronào, thy basket.	sàtrokào, thy hat.	hèvitrào, thy thought.
	hàrony, his (or her) basket.	sàtrony, his (or her) hat.	hèviny, his (or her) thought.
Plur.	hàronày, our basket.	sàtrokày, our hats.	hèvitrày, our thought.
	hàrontsìka, our basket.	sàtrotsìka, our hats.	hèvitsìka, our thought.
	hàronarèo, your basket.	sàtrokarèo, your hats	hòvitrarèo, your thought.
	hàrony, their basket.	sàtrony, their hats.	hèviny, their thought.

DEMONSTRATIVE PRONOUNS.

These are very numerous, the choice of one rather than another being regulated by the distance, real or imaginary, of the object pointed out. By the insertion of *re*, they become plural; while by inserting *za* another class of these pronouns is formed, expressing the *unseen, remembered,* or *conceived,* as opposed to what is seen and actually pointed out.

Comparative Table of the chief Demonstrative Pronouns and analogous Adverbs of Place.

DEMONSTRATIVE PRONOUNS.

(Object seen.)				(Object unseen.)
Singular.		*Plural.*		*Singular or Plural.*
Itỳ,	this.	irèty,	these.	izàty.
Itò (*obsolete*),	,,	trèto,	,,	izàto.
Ĭo,	that.	irèo,	those.	izào.
Ĭtsy,	,,	irètsy,	,,	izàtsy.
Ĭny,	,,	irèny,	,,	izàny.
Iròa,	,,	irèròa,	,,	izaròa.
Irỳ,	,,	irèˌy,	,,	izarỳ.

ADVERBS OF PLACE.

(*Object seen.*)		(*Object unseen.*)	
Etỳ,	here.	*atỳ,*	here.
Eto,	,,	*àto,*	,,
Eo,	there.	*ào,*	there.
Etsỳ,	,,	*atsỳ,*	,.
Eny,	,,	*àny,*	,,
Eròa,	,,	*aròa,*	,,
Erỳ,	,,	*arỳ,*	,,

All demonstrative pronouns are used *both before and after* the word or phrase they qualify; as, *io hàzo io*, 'that tree'. This use of them is very convenient, especially with a long phrase, as all the connected words are thereby bound together.

INTERROGATIVE PRONOUNS.

These, which are few in number, are as follows :—

iza, zòvy 'who,' 'which'? *inona,* 'what'? *àn'iza, an-jòvy,* 'whose'? *àn'inona* (used of places only), 'where', 'what'?

The indefinite interrogatives are made by doubling these, and inserting *nà* between; as, *nà iza nà iza,* 'whosoever'.

THE RELATIVE PRONOUN.

There is only one relative pronoun, *izày,* which cannot be declined, and is used for any case of either number.

COMPARATIVE TABLE OF THE NUMERALS.

	CARDINALS. Answering to, *Fìry?* How many?	ORDINALS. Answering to, *Fàha-fìry?* Which (in order)?	FRACTIONALS. Answering to *Ampahafì-rìny?* What part (of it)?	MULTIPLICATIVES. Answering to, *Im-pìry?* How often?	TIMES OF DOING. Answering to, *Fà-nimpìriny?* What time of doing it?
		fàhiraìka, vòalòhany, &c.	... ...	indràv	... ...
1	ìsa, ìráy, ìraìka		ampaharòany	indròa	fànindròa.
2	ròa		àmpahatèlony	intèlo	fànintèlo.
3	tèlo		àmpahèfany	inèfatra	&c. &c.
4	èfatra		àmpahadìminy, &c.	indìmy	
5	dìmy			inènina	
6	ènina			impìto	
7	fìto			imbàlo	
8	vàlo			intsìvy	
9	sìvy			impòlo	
10	fòlo				
11	{ ìraìka àmby nỳ fòlo } (or, ìraìkambinifòlo)			indràikambinifòlo	
12	ròambinifòlo			indròambinifòlo	
20	ròapòlo			indròapòlo	
21	ìraìkambiròapòlo			indràikambiròapòlo	
30	tèlopòlo			intèlopòlo	
40	èfapòlo			inèfapòlo	
50	dìmampòlo			indìmampòlo	
60	ènimpòlo			inènimpòlo	
70	fìtopòlo			impìtopòlo	
80	vàlopòlo			imbàlopòlo	
90	sìvifòlo			intsìvifòlo	
100	zàto			injàto	
500	dìmanjàto			indàmanjàto	
1000	arìvo			arìvo (*nà* ìnarìvo)	
10,000	ìrày alìna				
100,000	ìrày bètsy				
1,000,000	tàpitrìsa(contr. from *ta-pìtra ìsa*, 'ended (the) numbers'.)				

ORDINALS.
Vòalòhany (from *lòha*, 'head') is the usual word for 'first'. The remainder of the Ordinals are merely the Cardinals with *fàha-* prefixed to them, as in the case of *fàhiraìka.*

FRACTIONALS.
The Fractionals are made from the Cardinals by prefixing *àmpaha-*, and then affixing *-ny.*
Or from the Ordinals by prefixing *am-*, changing *f* into *p*, and then affixing *-ny.*
They are generally followed by a suffixed pronoun or a possessive case: and the numerator of a fraction is expressed, as in English, by a Cardinal; as, *ròa àmpahatèlony*, 'two-thirds of it'.

TIMES OF DOING.
These are made by prefixing *fàn-* to the Multiplicatives, and are seldom used in the higher numbers. They are treated as nouns, take the suffix pronoun *-ny* (in which respect they resemble the Fractionals), and may be followed by a possessive case.

N.B.—The Multiplicatives are made from the Cardinals by prefixing *in-*, and making euphonic consonantal changes only in the following few cases :—*nf* into *mp* (*impìto, impìtopòlo, impòlo*) ; *nv* into *mb* (*imbàlo, imbàlopòlo*) ; *ns* into *nts* (*intsìvy, intsìvifòlo*) ; *nz* into *nj* (*injàto*).

`*Isa* is used in counting (as *ìsa, ròa,* &c.—hence the verb *manìsa,* ' to count') ; *irày,* as a numeral adjective (as, *tràno irày,* ' one house ') ; and *iraìka,* in compound numbers (as *iraìkàmbinifòlo*) only in the Hova dialect, but as equivalent to, and instead of, *ìsa* and *irày,* in several of the other dialects of Madagascar.

N.B.—In counting in Malagasy the units come first, then the tens, &c. : *roàmbinifòlo* (*ròa àmby nỳ fòlo*), ' twelve ' (literally, *two an addition to the ten*).

Indrày alone means *again;* but when used as meaning *once,* the verb *mandèha* (to go) or the verb *màka* (to fetch) must be added; as, *tsỹ àzo hànina indrày mandèha* (or *indrày màka izy*), ' it cannot be eaten (at) once ', or ' *at one go* '.

The Ordinals are often used as Fractionals (as, *fahènimbàry,* the sixth part of the rice-measure called *vàry irày*). And they are used of measurements ; as, *fàhafiry mòa nỳ trànonào ?—Fàhadìmy.* " How many (fathoms in length) is your house ?—Five ".

Distributives are made by doubling the Cardinals and prefixing *tsi-* ; as, *tsiràirày,* ' one by one '; *tsiròaròa,* ' two by two '. Some of the numerals have verbal forms in *mi-* or *man-,* as follows :—

Mifìry, to be divided into how many ? *miròa,* to be divided into two ; *mitèlo,* to be divided into three, &c.

Firìna? (passive participle of *mifìry*)—divided into how many? *telòina*, divided into three; *efàrina*, divided into four, &c. They also have imperative moods :—*telòy*, divide it into three; *efàro*, divide it into four, &c.

Mànindròa (*manào indròa*), to do (a thing) twice.

Mànintèlo, to do (a thing) thrice.

Indràosına, 'being done twice'; *intelòina*, 'being done thrice'. These are sometimes used as the passive participles of the corresponding verbs, *mànindròa, mànintèlo,* &c.

Number of days is expressed by turning the cardinals into abstract nouns in *ha—ana*; as, *hàfirìana?* 'how many days'? *indrò-àndro,* (*indròa àndro*), 'two days'; *hàtelòana,* 'three days'; *hefàrana,* 'four days', &c.

N.B.—The only known exception to this rule is in the use of *indrò-àndro,* instead of *haròana,* for 'two days'.

Another thing to be remembered is that, while an adjective generally follows its noun (as, *tràno tsàra,* 'a good house'), the numeral (*i.e.* the cardinal) is often placed *before* a noun; as, *ròa làhy,* 'two men'.

THE ARTICLE.

The Definite Article.—There is only one definite article, *nỳ,* which is used before common nouns, and has the same defining power as our English article *the.* Its special uses are as follows.

a (when used) :—

1. Like the Greek article, it is much used to turn other parts of speech into nouns; as, *nỳ manòratra,* 'the art of writing', or 'the people who write'.

2. It is used generically, with reference to the whole of a class; as, *nỳ vòrona*, ' birds ' (or, *the* birds). This is the only sense in which *nỳ* can be used with proper names ; as, *nỳ Màlagàsy*, ' Malagasy ' (*as a nation*).

3. It is used in general comparisons after words implying likeness (as *tòy, tàhaka, &c.*) ; as, *tòy nỳ vòrona*, ' like birds '.

4. It is used before a noun when made definite by a suffixed pronoun ; as, *nỳ sàtroko*, ' the hat of me ', *i.e.* my hat.

5. It is used with abstract nouns; as, *nỳ màrina*, ' truth '.

6. With the words *anànkirày* (certain), *sàsany* (some), *rehètra* (all), and *màro* (many), the Malagasy often use the article where the English dispense with it ; as,

> *nỳ lèhilàhy anànkirày*, 'a certain man '.
> *nỳ òlona sàsany*, ' some people '.
> *nỳ òlona rehètra*, ' all people' (*or*, all *the* people).
> *nỳ òlona màro*, ' many people '.

b (when omitted) :—

1. Before nouns in apposition ; as, *Heròdra mpanjàka*, ' Herod the king ', (*or*, King Herod).

2. Before nouns in the vocative case ; as, *Rainày izày àny an-dànitra*, ' Our father who (art) in heaven' !

3. Before predicates ; as, *sàtroko ìo*, ' that is my hat '.

4. Before accusatives when they are adverbial, instrumental, or limiting.

5. After *nò* in some idiomatic phrases, where *nò* seems equivalent to *nỳ* or *izày*; as, *hòy nò navàliny àzy*, or *hòy nỳ navàliny àzy*.

The Indefinite Article.—The Malagasy language has no indefinite article, but the place of it is supplied in one or other of these four ways :—

1. By omitting *nỳ* ; as, *nahìta òmby àho,* ' I saw an ox', (*or,* oxen) ; (2) by the use of *anànkiràg* and *sàsany* in the half-definite sense of *some, certain* ; (3) by using the relative pronoun *izày,* in an indefinite sense, as, *ìza nò hatòky izày adàla ?* ' who would trust a fool' (*or,* one who is a fool) ? (4) by using the verb *mìsy ;* as, *mìsy òlona namàngy àzy,* ' a person (*or,* some persons) visited him '; *misìa mànkatỳ nỳ ankìzi-làhy,* ' let a servant (*or* one, *or* some, of the servants) come here'.

There are also in Malagasy the following common personal prefixes, *i, ri, ra, rày, ilày (ilèy, ilèhy),* and *andrìana.* Of these, *i* and *ra,* though generally prefixed to proper nouns, are sometimes prefixed to common nouns used as names of persons ; as, *ivàdinào,* ' your wife'; *ralèhilàhy,* ' the (*or,* that) man '.

The Emphatic or Discriminative Particle ' nò.'

' *Nò* ' is a particle which is both emphatic and exclusive, and *not* a substitute or equivalent for the English copula ' is'. As the Rev. W. E. Cousins says :—" It serves to make an emphatic assertion, and at the same time implies the exclusion or discrimination of some object or objects to which the predicate used in that assertion does not apply ; this discriminated object often being stated in the following clause, as in the proverb, ' *Nỳ kitòza nò tsàra ràha mihàntona ; fà nỳ tèny tsỳ tsàra mihàntona* '. ' It is *kitòza* (sun-dried meat) that is good when hung; but words are not good (when) hung'; *i.e.* they are better spoken ".

The reasons for believing that *nò* may have been originally an article (if not identical with *nỳ*) are as follows :—

(1) *Nò* is nearly identical in form with *nỳ*.

(2) It makes the use of *nỳ* unnecessary; as, *ìza nò tsàra* (not, *ìza nò nỳ tsàra*)? ' which is the good one '?

(3) In some idiomatic phrases it seems to have the force of *nỳ*, or of the relative pronoun *izày*.

Synopsis of the various uses of ' NÒ.'

A.   To emphasize or discriminate.

    (1) A subject—

       in assertive sentences; as, *ìzy nò hanào izàny*, ' it is he who shall do that '.

       in interrogative sentences; as, *aìza nò alèhanào,* ' where is it that you are going '?

       N.B.—When the answer to a question would be a subject, *nò* should be used; as, *ìza nò ìzy?* ' Which is it ' ?—the answer being, 'This is it'. But where *nò* is not used, the answer would be a predicate; as, *ìza ìzy ?* or, *ìza mòa ìzy ?* ' Who is he '?—the answer would be very different, ' He is my brother', &c.

       in imperative sentences; as, *nỳ tsàra nò hàno,* ' the good are those which should be eaten ' (*i.e.* eat the good).

       in hortative sentences; as, *aza nỳ ràtsy nò hànina,* ' let not the bad ones be those which are eaten '.

(2) An adjunct; as, *omàly nò nanàovany izàny*, 'it was yesterday that they did (*or*, made) that'.

(3) A statement for which a reason is to be given; as, *nỹ hàndrina nò tsỹ manìry vòlo, nỹ hènatra*, 'it is the forehead which is not covered with hair, shame (causes that)'; *i.e.*, shame is the reason why the forehead is not covered with hair. In such cases, *hò* is often added; as, *nỹ akòho nò hò lèhìbè, nỹ vòlony*, 'their feathers make the fowls appear large'.

B Non-emphatic uses of 'NÒ'.

(1) As a declarative conjunction, 'in that', 'because'; as, *nanào sòa hìanào nò nìàntra àzy*, 'you did a good deed in that (*or*, because) you pitied him'.

(2) As a sign of the past tense of passive verbs in -*ana* and -*ina*.

(3) As a shortened form of *nòny*. This is found in "*Harè-màhasòa*", p. 146. *Nòny tsy*, 'but for'.

(4) As a shortened form of *nòho* in a comparison (rarely so used).

N.B.—Of 'NÒ', the Rev. W. E. Cousins says:—"The correct or incorrect use of the particle '*nò*' is no unfair criterion of the skill a European has attained in speaking Malagasy".

ADVERBS.

In the Malagasy language adverbs, especially those of place and time, are numerous.

A. But adverbs of *quality* or *manner* are few, their place being supplied—

1. by adjectives; as, *mihìra tsàra,* 'to sing well'. A more common and very useful idiom, is the reversal of this phrase, the adjective still keeping its adjectival force, while the verb is exchanged for a relative noun in the 'limiting accusative' case; as, *tsàra-fihìra,* 'good as regards the manner of singing'.

2. by prepositional phrases or compound prepositions. These are formed by joining *an-* as a prefix to root-nouns, as *an-dràriny,* 'justly'; to abstract nouns, as *àn-kafetsèna* (from *fètsy*), 'cunningly'; to relative nouns, as *àm-pifehèzana* (from *fèhy*), 'with authority, authoritatively'; to verbal nouns in *-ana,* as *àn-tsivalànana* (from *vàlana*), 'crossways'; to active verbs in the future tense, as *àn-kamàndrika* (from *fàndrika*), 'with a view to entrap', 'deceitfully'.

3. by verbs; as, *apètraka mìtsivàlana,* 'placed crossways'.

B. The Adverbs of negative, affirmation, or doubt, are the following :—

èny, yes.	*angàha, angàmba,* perhaps.
tsìa, no.	*tòkony hò,* probably.
tsỳ, not.	*sèndra,* perchance.
àza, let not (the sign	*tàhiny,* perchance.
of prohibition).	

Of the two last words, *tàhiny* is used of suppositions, *sèndra* not of suppositions. Thus, *sèndra nahìta àzy ìzy,* 'he happened to meet them'; *ràha tàhiny mahìta àzy ìzy,* 'if he should happen to meet them'.

C. The interrogative adverbs are the following :—

1. Of place :—

aìza, (present), *taìza* (past), where?
hò aìza (future), whither? going where?
àvy taìza (*lit.* came from where?), whence? from what place?

2. Of time :—

ovìana (past) *ràhovìana* (future), when?
[contracted from *ràha, ovìana*].

3. Of manner, &c. :—

ahòana, how? (used also as an interjection, How. . . . !)
manào (past, *nanào*; future, *hanào*) *ahòana,* in what manner, of what kind or quality?
[*literally,* doing what? *or,* acting how?]

atào (past, *natào*; future, *hatào*) *ahòana,* how?
(implying difficulty or impossibility).
[*literally,* done how?]

atào can take as its agent either a suffix pronoun
(as *hatàoko ahòana,* how can I do it?) or a
noun (as, *hatàon' nỹ òlona ahòana nò fandòsi-
tra,* 'how shall the people escape'? (*literally,*
what shall the people do as regards a way of
escape?) This last idiom is a common use
of the modal noun.

D. Adverbs of place are very numerous. The following
list shows fourteen of them, which are closely connected with the demonstrative pronouns both in
form and in meaning:—

The chief adverbs of place are the following:

etỹ, èto, here; *èo, ètsy, èny, eròa, erỹ,* there;
atỹ, àto, here; *ào, àtsy, àny, aròa, arỹ,* there.

These different forms cannot be interchanged at pleasure,
because the choice of one form rather than another depends
upon the distance of the place spoken of.

The forms beginning with *a* belong rather to the vague
and unseen, while those with *e* to what is seen, and clearly
pointed out; as, *atỹ an-tàny,* here on earth; *etỹ an-tànako,*
'here in my hand'; *aò am-bàta,* in a box'; *èo imàsonào,*
'before your eyes'.

Repetition of adverbs of place sometimes occurs (as, *àny
an-èfitra àny,* ' there in the desert'); but it is not compulsory,
as in the case of demonstrative pronouns.

Tenses of Adverbs—The only two kinds of adverbs which

have tenses are those of (1) time, and (2) interrogation : and of these, *t* is the sign of the past tense, and *hò* of the future; thus, *atỹ*, am here; *tatỹ*, was here; *hò atỹ*, will be here ;—*aìza*, where is ? *taìza*, where was ? *hò aìza*, where will be ?

Adverbial verbs are made from adverbs by putting the active prefix *mank-* before them; as, *mànkatỹ*, to come here; *mankàny*, to go there. Of these verbs, only *mankàny* has an imperative mood (*mànkanèsa*) or a relative voice (*ànkanèsana*), These are made to serve with all the other adverbs of place ; as, *mànkanèsa atỹ hìanào*, ' come here'; *nahòana nò tsỹ nànkanèsanào tàny ?* ' why did you not go there'?

With *àvy* (coming) put before them, they imply ' motion from', and are equivalent to *hence, thence*; as, *àvy èo ìzy*, ' he is coming thence, he is coming hither'.

Adverbs of place are made indefinite in meaning by being repeated with *hò* inserted; as, *àtohòàto* (or, *àto hò àto*), hereabouts ; *tèohòèo*, thereabouts. They are also often used to express *relations of time* (as, *tèo*, recently, lately), especially when used indefinitely (as, *tàtohòàto*, or *tàto hò àto*, lately).

E.   The chief abverbs of time are the following :—

> *Anìo*, to-day (*future*).
> *Àndro àny*, to-day (*past*).
> *Omàly*, yesterday.
> *Ampìtso,*
> *Ràhampìtso,* } to-morrow.
> *Àndrotrìny àndrotrizaỹ*, at that day (*past*).

Rehèfa, rehèfèfa, presently.

Ràha àfaka àtsy hò àtsy kokòa, after a time,
    (*i.e.* some days).

Ràhatrizaỳ, hereafter (*indefinite future*).

Faĥiny, formerly.

Fàhizàny, fàhizaỳ, at that time,—(*faha-* is so used
    with many words to express past time).

Hàtrizaỳ, since the time of.

Hàtrizaìhàtrizaỳ, from of old, from eternity (*in-
    definite past*).

Ankèhitrìny, ankèhitrìo, ⎫
Izào, àmin' izào, ⎬ now, at the present time.

Vào faìngana (or *haìngana*), quite recently.

Mandrìtra nỳ àndro, ⎫
Tontòlo àndro, ⎬ all day long.

Màndrakarìva (*màndraka,* until; *harìva,* even-
    ing), continually

Matètika, often.

Indraìndraỳ [i.e. *indràỳ,* once *repeated*], sometimes.

Isan-àndro, daily, every day, ⎫ *sany* is so
                                 ⎬ used with
Isam-bòlana, monthly, every month. ⎭ many words.

Tsỳ—intsòny, no longer,—not any more.

Àmin' izaỳ (present), ⎫
Tàmin' izaỳ (past), ⎬ thereupon, upon that.

Miàrakàminizaỳ (miàraka àmin' izaỳ) at that mo-
    ment, immediately (*present*).

    niàraka tàmin' izaỳ, at that moment, immediately,
    (*past*).

Sahàdy, already, so early.

Ràhatèo, already, beforehand.

F. The chief adverbs of manner and degree are the following :—

Fàtratra, earnestly.

Tsimòramòra, easily.

Tsikèlikèly, little by little.

Tsipòtipòtika, piecemeal, in small quantities, bit by bit.

Lòatra, too, exceedingly.

Kòa, too, also.

Kòsa, on the contrary, on the other hand.

Àza,
Àvy, } even.

Àvy, apiece, each, individually (as, *nomèna sikàjy àvy ìzy,* 'they were given sixpence each').

Saìky, or *saìka,*
Vaìky, or *vaìka,* } almost, all but (used of something nearly, but not quite, effected).

Sàmy,
Àvokòa, } respectively, individually, wholly. *Sàmy* precedes, and *àvokòa* follows, the qualified word; as, *sàmy màrina* (or, *màrina àvokòa*) *ìzy rehètra,* 'they are all (individually) true'.

Hakìtro, to the heels. The prefix *ha-* (short for *hàtra,* 'up to') is so used with the name of almost any part of the body.

PREPOSITIONS.

There are only a few prepositions in the Malagasy language, their place being supplied by a large number of prepositional phrases or compound prepositions: these are formed by prefixing *a-*, *am-*, *an-*, or *i-* to nouns.

PREPOSITION.	MEANING.	GOVERNMENT.
Àmy . . .	to, for, from, in, by, with, at *or* on (of time), &c.	The meaning of *àmy* is so variable, and it has to serve for so many of our English prepositions, that it practically has no special meaning of its own, but merely points out the indirect object or the adjunct to a verb.
Àny . . .	belonging to.	Most of the prepositions, whether simple or compound, are followed by the suffix pronouns; as, *àmiko, an-ilako.*
Akaìky . .	near to.	
Àfa-tsỳ (àfa-ka, tsỳ) .	except.	*Hàtra* is (1) generally joined with *àmy*; as, *hatràmy nỳ andrèfana kà hatràmy nỳ àtsinànona*, from east to west; or (2) with adverbs of place: ae; *hatrèto*, thus far, hitherto; or
Ambàraka	until.	(3) is merely followed by a noun with *nỳ* or *izaỳ* before it; as, *hàtry nỳ omàly*, since yesterday; *hàtr' izaỳ naìnako*, since my birth.
Màndraka		
Àraka . .	according to, after. (This is the root of the verb *ma-nàraka*, 'to follow.')	*Ambàraka* and *màndraka* are generally contracted and joined with habitual modal nouns, or with adjectives or phrases preceded by *fàha-*; as, *ambàra-* (or *màndra-*) *pirèriko* (root *vèrina*), until my return; *màndra-pàhafàtiny*, until his death. They are rarely followed by a relative; as, *màndra-panaò-vanào àzy*, until your doing it.
Hàtra . .	from, to (towards, up to, as far as).	*Akaìky* takes either a suffixed pronoun or the separate form in the accusative case; as, *akaìky anào* (or *akaìkindo*), near you.
Hò, hò àny .	for, to.	
Nòhò . .	on account of, because.	*Nòho* and *àfa-tsy* govern only a nominative case.
Tandrìfy .	opposite to.	*Hò* takes after it the pronoun *àzy*; as, *hò àzy*, for him, *or*, to be his. Otherwise it requires *àny*; as, *hò àny nỳ tènany*, for himself, *Hò àzy*, also means 'of its own accord'; as, *maniry hò àzy nỳ hàzo*, 'the tree grows of its own accord'; *misèho hò àzy*, 'visible of itself'.

The following are the chief prepositional phrases or compound prepositions made by prefixing *a-*, *am-*, *an-*, or *i-* to nouns :—

(*a-*)

Àfovòana (*fò* and *vòa?* or, *fò* reduplicated?), in the heart of, in the midst of.

Alòha (*lòha*), ahead, before.

Àòrìana, behind.

Amòrona (*mòrona*), on the edge of, on the brink (*or*, margin) of.

Atsìmo, south of.

Àtsinànana (*tsìnana ?*), east of.

Avàratra (*vàratra ?*), north of.

(*am-*)

Ambàny (*vàny?*), beneath, below, under.

Ambòny (*vòny ?*), above, upon.

Ambòdy (*vòdy*), at the rump (*or*, tail) of, at the bottom of.

Ambàdika (*vàdika*), on the other side of (*i.e.* as of a thing turned upside down).

Àmpovòany (*fò* and *vòa?* or, *fò* reduplicated ?), in the middle of.

Ampìta (*ìta*), on the other side of, across (a river).

(*an-*)

Ànatrèhana (*àtrika*), in the presence of.

Anàty (*àty*), inside of, within, among.

Andàfy (*làfy*), }
Andàny (*làny*), } on the other side of.

An-dòha (*loha*), on the head of, on, at the head of.

Andrèfana, west of.

Anèlanèlana (*èlanèlana,* from *èla*), in the intervals
    between, between.
Anìla (*ìla*), at the side of, beside.
Ankìla (*hìla*), on the side of.
Ankòatra (*hòatra*), beyond, further than.
Ankavìa (*havìa*), at the left hand of.
Ankavànana (*havànana,* from *hàvana*), at the right
    hand of.
Antènatèna (*tèna*), in the body (*or,* substance) of.
Antàmpona (*tàmpona*), on the top (*or,* summit) of.

(*i-*)

Ifòtotra (*fòtotra*), at the root of.
Imàso (*màso*), in the eyes (*or,* sight) of.
Ivèla, (*vèla*) outside of.
Ivòho (*vòho*), at the back of, behind.

The want of prepositions is also supplied in the following
ways :—

1. By certain verbs, some implying motion to or from
(as *àvy, miàla,* &c.), others not implying any
motion (as *mànodìdina*).

2. By certain active verbs, which contain a prepositional force and govern a direct accusative, where
in English they would need a preposition; as,
mandaìnya àzy, 'to tell a lie *to* him'; *milàza àzy,*
'to tell *about* him,' (but *milàza amìny,* 'to tell *to*
him').

3. The relative voice of a verb often contains a pre-

positional force ; as, *nitondràny ràno àho*, ' I was the person (in respect) to whom he brought water'.

4. Many Malagasy verbs govern two accusatives, which in English would require a preposition before one of them ; as, *manòsotra sòlika àzy,* ' to smear it *with* oil'.

5. "*By*" before the agent of a passive or relative verb, and "*Of*" before a possessive case.—For the different ways of expressing these two prepositions, see "*Indications of Cases*".

CONJUNCTIONS.

The chief conjunctions, divided into classes, are as follows :—

1. Copulative : *àry, sỳ, àmana, àmin',* and; *sàdy, kòa,* also ; *sàdy—nò,* both—and; *dìa,* even; *mhàmy (mbà, àmy),* together with, including ; *ambàny,* and, including.

2. Disjunctive : *nà,* or ; *nà—nà,* whether—or, either—or; *sà, fà,* or ? *Àry* is used at the beginning of sentences, or for the sake of variety in enumerations with *sỳ*. *Àmana* couples nouns which usually go in pairs ; as, *rày àman-drèny,* 'father and mother '; *vòlana àman-kìntana,* 'moon and stars'; *sàdy* adds a supplementary adjective, verb, or even sentence containing an additional statement. *Sà* and *fà*

are used in asking alternative questions only; as, *handéha và izy, sà* (or, *fà*) *tsìa?* 'will they go, or not'?

3. Adversative: *fà*, but; *nèfa, kandrèfa, anèfa, ka-nèfa*, yet; *kànjo*, however, but, nevertheless; *sàingy* (or, *sàngy*), but (*only sometimes*); *kànjo* implies the reverse of one's expectation; *saìngy* sometimes means *but*; as, *saiky nàhavìta izàny izy, saìngy tsỹ mbòla vìta*, 'he was merely able to finish that, but it is not yet done'.

4. Conditional: *ràha, nòny* (with present or future), if; *nòny tsỹ*, had it not been for, but for, (*lite-rally*, 'if not', like the Latin *nisi.*)

5. Causal: *fà*, for, because (*reason*); *nà dìa—àza*, although (*concession*); *satrìa*, because (*cause*); *saìngy*, since, seeing that.

6. Declarative: *fà, nò*, that.

  Fà is used after verbs of *telling, believing, hoping, &c.*, to introduce the noun-sentence or statement, like our English conjunction *that.*

  Nò is used to express the *reason*, in the following way: *gàga àho nò tsỹ tònga ìzy*, 'I am surprised that he has not come'.

7. Inferential: *dìa, àry*, then, therefore. In this sense *àry* is never placed at the beginning of a sentence. Thus, *andèha àry isìka*, 'let us there-fore go'; but *àry andèha isìka*, 'and we go'.

8. Final (result or consequence), *kà, kòa,* and so, so as; *dìa,* then ; *sào, andrào,* lest ; *kà* sometimes 'yet', 'and yet' (*adversative*) ; as, *malàza hò làhy, kà tsỳ màndry an-èfitra,* 'famed as a (brave) man, yet not lying (*i. e.* afraid to lie) in the desert'.

9. Temporal : *ràha, rehèfa, fòny, nòny,* when ; *dìeny,* whilst, while ; *dìa,* then (of time, signifying *progression* of events). *Rehèfa* (*ràha èfa*) means *when* in the sense of *after;* as, *rehèfa vìta izàny,* 'when that was finished'. *Fòny* refers to the past; as, *fòny tsỳ mbòla àry nỳ tàny,* 'when the earth was not yet created'. *Nòny* implies a *succession of events.* _Dìeny_ implies something passing away ; as, *dìeny mbòla tanòra hìanào,* 'while you are still young'.

There are *three peculiarities* noticeable with regard to Malagasy conjunctions : viz.—

1. They are often in couples ; as, *àry dìa* ; *fà satrìa.* 2. The same word often has to serve for several conjunctions ; as, *fà,* for, but, that ; *dìa,* even, therefore, then (of time). 3. They generally do *not* couple the same cases of pronouns ; as, *mitèny àminào sỳ izahaỳ izy,* 'he speaks to you and us (*lit.* we)'.

INTERJECTIONS.

TABLE OF THE CHIEF INTERJECTIONS.

EMOTION EXPRESSED.	INTERJECTIONS.	MEANING.
Surprise . .	*endrày, endrè. ddrè, òdrè, (pronounced* oh-dray) *hày, hànky*	ah! oh!
Denial .	*isy* (pron. *ishy*), *eìsy, àoè, sànatrìa* (forbid that) . .	
Desire . .	*anìe, ènga kà, èndra, ànga .* .	may-! oh that-! would that-!
Exclamation . or calling .	*è, ò (pronounced* oh!), *rỳ, rày, rèy*	eh! ho! ha!
Sorrow . .	*indrìsy*	alas!
Regret . .	*inày, injày*	oh that-! would that-!

Note. — With regard to the interjection *sànatrìa* forbid that— !), perhaps it had the following mode of origin :—

'*Sanàtry*' is the name of a plant used medicinally by the Malagasy ; it is also the name given to an earthen pot when it has been daubed with streaks of coloured earth or paint in accordance with the directions of the 'diviner' or 'incantation-worker'. When so prepared, the pot is carried to the place where the disease to be removed is said by the 'diviner' to have had its origin ; the pot is believed to attract the disease to itself, and is consequently left there, the person who leaves it exclaiming '*Sànatrìa*,' May it (*i.e.*, the disease) be *sanàtry !*

In this custom of the Malagasy (whatever its origin) there is the same idea of *vicarious suffering* which is so familiar to readers of the Bible, in connection with the scape-goat, *&c.* of the Mosaic Dispensation.

General Rules for the Arrangement of Words in a Sentence.

1. As regards the predicate, its usual place is at the beginning of a simple sentence, *before* the subject. But it may follow the subject, (*a*) indicated only by the sense; (*b*) indicated more closely by *dìa* before it; or (*c*) indicated by *nò* before it, when it applies exclusively to the subject.

2. As regards the object of an active verb, it immediately follows its verb; as, *nanànatra àzy màfy àho*, 'I reproved him sharply'. Unless (as is the case sometimes) an adverb closely connected with the verb intervene; as, *àza mamàly sàrotra àzy hianào*, ' do not answer him roughly'.

3. With a passive verb, the adverb and the object (if there be one), together with all connected words unless too long, come near the verb, the subject following last, at the end of the sentence; as, *natòlotro àzy omàly nỳ vòla*, 'I gave them the money yesterday', *or*, the money was given to them by me yesterday; *nanàriko màfy tèo imàsondraìny ìzy miràhalàhy*, I reproved the brothers (*or*, the brothers were reproved by me) sharply in the presence of their father'.

N.B.—When desired, the subject can be put into a more prominent place, in accordance with exceptions (*a*), (*b*), and (*c*) to Rule 1. above.

4. A qualifying adjective follows its noun; as, *lèhilàhy tsàra*, ' a good man'.

5. A possessive case follows its noun (whether *nỳ* precedes it or not). See *Rules for Indications of Case*. The exception to Rules (4) and (5) is when a word closely connected with the qualified noun intervenes; as, *nỳ tànana ànkavànan-dRalàmbo,* 'the right hand of Ralàmbo'; *nỳ vahòa-dRànavàlona rehètra,* 'all the subjects of Rànavàlona'.

6. In the case of a passive or a relative verb and its agent, the agent *always* comes next to its verb; as, *nòvonòin' nỳ jiolàhy izy,* 'he was killed by the highwaymen.'

Even in the case of compound verbs (as, *mamìndra-fò,* from *indra* and *fò*), when the passive or the relative construction is used, the agent, and all words closely connected with it, must come next to the verb, the noun (in this case, *fò*) being separated from its verb; as, (Active) *namindra-fò tàminào nỳ iòmpon-tròsa,* 'the creditor showed mercy to you'. (Relative) *nàmindràn' nỳ tòmpon-tròsa fò hianào,* 'you were shown mercy by the creditor'.

SHORT SPECIMEN OF ANALYSIS.

Kà òhàbòlana kèly nò hatàoko hò èntiko handà nỳ hanàovanào àhy andriambarènty.

Translation.—And so I will make a little parable (*lit.* a little parable shall be made by me), to be used by me in refusing (*lit.* to refuse) your making me a judge.

Grammatical Notes.

Kà, final conjunction, 'and so'.

Òhabòlana, compound noun, from *òhatra,* 'measure', 'figure', and *vòlana,* 'word', meaning a figure of speech, parable, proverb. It is a contraction for *òhatra-vòlana, -na* being rejected and *v* changed into *b*; here it is the nominative case to *hatào*. The root *vòlana* (a *word*) is used by the Hovas only in the phrase *tsỳ mitèny tsỳ mivòlana*, ' to be silent', 'speechless'; but one or two of the other tribes still use *mivòlana* as synonymous with *mitèny*.

Òha-tèny is used as a synonym of *òhabòlana*.

Kèly, adjective, qualifying *òhabòlana*. It means *little;* its past tense is the same as the present, but its future is *hò kèly*.

Nò, discriminative particle. Its force here is, "I will answer you, not by a simple denial, but by making a parable".

Hatàoko, passive verb in *a-* (future tense), from root *tào*, which is seen in the noun *tào-zàvatra*, 'manufactures'; *-ko* is the suffixed pronoun, first person singular, denoting the agent of the passive verb *hatào*.

Hò èntiko, passive verb in *-ina*, root unknown; a verbal noun in *-ana* (*èntana*, luggage, a load) also exists. *Èntina* makes past *nèntina*, like passives in *-ina*; but future, *hò èntina*, like root-passives. *Hò èntina* is here dependent upon *hatào*, one future passive following another. *Èntina* literally ' borne, carried'; but often translated by ' *used*', as in *ènti-manào*, ' used in making'.

Handà, active verb in *man-*, from root *là*, *l* being changed into *d* for the sake of euphony (future tense); it means *to deny, refuse,* and is here used as an infinitive dependent on *hò èntiko*, a future active following a future passive.

Nỳ, definite article, here used to turn the phrase *nỳ hanàovanào àhy andriambarènty* into a noun.

E

Hanàovanào, relative verb from active verb *manào,* root *tào;* here used of the act, taken in connection with all its circumstances; *-nào,* suffixed pronoun, second person singular, showing the agent of the relative verb *hanàovana.*

Ahy, separate form of personal pronoun, first person singular, objective case.

Andrìambavènty, compound noun, composed of the noun *andrìana,* 'a noble', and the adjective *vavènty,* 'substantial, large'. It means 'a judge': its root is *vènty,* 'substance', the prefix *va-* being either a substitute for the usual adjectival prefix *ma-* (*mavènty* is used among some of the tribes other than the Hova), or a monosyllabic prefix. Both *àhy* and *andrìambavènty* are accusative cases governed by the relative verb *hanàovana.* The relative follows the government of the active construction, which would be *manào àhy andrìambavènty.*

ENGLISH	I HOVA	II ANTANKARANA	III BARA	IV BETSILEO	V BETSIMISARAKA	VI BEZANOZANO	VII SAKALAVA	VIII SIHANAKA	IX TAIMORO	X TAISAKA
PERSONAL PRONOUNS:										
I	izaho, aho			izaho, aho	izaho, aho	aho, anaho	aho mbe	izaho aho		
Thou	hianao			hañao	añao	anao	hanko mbe	hianao		
He, she, it, they	izy		{ i (pronounced as the first o is even) }	neika iby	izy	izy	izy mbe	izy		
We (exclusive of person spoken to)	izahay		ahay	anay	izehay	zahay	izahay mbe	izahay		
We (inclusive of person spoken to)	isika			isika	antsika	sika	isika-mbe	isika		
You	hanareo			hañareo	hanareo	añareo	hianareo-mbe	hianareo		
CONJUNCTIONS:										
When if	raha				là		laha	antsimba		
Even	dia				dia		dia, lia	dia		
PREPOSITIONS:										
Above	ambany		ambony	ambony	añambo		aniaky	ambony		
Below	ambany		ambany	ambany	ambony		anketraka	ambany		
NOUNS:										
Father	ray				ray	ray, baba				
Papa	dada, kaky	ada	baba	aoa	baba	dada, dadhy	dada, baba	dadáy	iba	
Mother	reny	nendry	Rndry	endry	niny	reny	neny	reny		
Mamma	neny	nendry	Tndry	endry	niny	niny	neny, nanja			
Tobacco plant	{ paraky (fr. Arabic?) }		lobaka	paraky	tambako	tambako	lobaka	tambako	tabaka	
Indian corn (maize)	katsaka			tsakotsako	tsikitsaky		tsakotsako	tsakotsako		
Sweet potato	vaamanga		bele	{ ovim anga, vilazo }	manga	tsimon_a	manga, belosa	vaamanga	{ bokala, vorand o, bobokala }	somanga
Rice	vary			vary	vary	vary	va y	vary		
MONTHS — 1st	Alahamady		Hatsia (ka)	Hatsia	Hatsia	Aoha		Hatsia		
2nd	Adaoro		Volasira	Volasira	Vàlasira	Volasira		Volasira		
3d	Adizaona		Zaray	Volapasoa	Valampasa	Foza		?		
4th	Asorotany		Maka	Volamaka	Asara	Maka		Volamaka		
5th	Alahasaty		Saliabla	Hlahla	Tsiahla	Tsoha		Volampadina		
6th	Asombola		hakamasay	hakamasaly	Sakamasaay	Sakamasaly		Sakamasay		
7th	Adimizana		Volambita	Volambta	Volambita	Volambita		Volambita		
8th	Alakarabo		Sakavò	Asara	Sakave	Ts makamaka		Sahare		
9th	Alakaosy		Saramantay	Asaramanara	Saramantaña	Saramantsina		Saramantay		
10th	Adijady		Satramantsa	Asaramantsa	Sa-amàntra	Satamantra		Asaraba		
11th	Adalo		Mianjeloka	Asotrusonjona	Asotry	Asotry		Asotry		
12th	Alohotsy		Vatravatra	Vatravatra	Vatravatra	Vatravatra		Vatravatra		

The twelve Malagasy months do not correspond with our months, but occasionally differing their place in the Malagasy year being kept shorter than ours.

The above columns of words are extracted from 'A Comparative Vocabulary of the chief Dialects of Malagasy,' (in manuscript), by the Author. They are enough to show that a being due to causes acting over a limited region, while strong foreign influence (limited, however, to one tribe) is seen in the case of the Hova names for the months.

The names of the tribes are given at the top of each column, the Hova words being put first, as this is the best known dialect. Notice that n has two distinct sounds in the b are here represented respectively by n and ñ.

A

CATALOGUE OF IMPORTANT WORKS,

PUBLISHED BY

TRÜBNER & CO.

57 AND 59 LUDGATE HILL.

ABEL —LINGUISTIC ESSAYS. By Carl Abel CONTENTS: Language as the Expression of National Modes of Thought—The Conception of Love in some Ancient and Modern Languages—The English Verbs of Command—The Discrimination of Synonyms—Philological Methods—The Connection between Dictionary and Grammar—The Possibility of a Common Literary Language for the Slav Nations—Coptic Intensification—The Origin of Language—The Order and Position of Words in the Latin Sentence. Post 8vo, pp. xii. and 282, cloth. 1882. 9s.

ABEL.—SLAVIC AND LATIN. Ilchester Lectures on Comparative Lexicography. Delivered at the Taylor Institution, Oxford. By Carl Abel, Ph.D. Post 8vo, pp. vi -124, cloth. 1883. 5s.

ABRAHAM'S.—A MANUAL OF SCRIPTURE HISTORY FOR USE IN JEWISH SCHOOLS AND FAMILIES. By L B. Abrahams, B.A., Principal Assistant Master, Jews' Free School With Map and Appendices. Third Edition Crown 8vo, pp viii. and 152, cloth. 1883. 1s. 6d.

AGASSIZ — AN ESSAY ON CLASSIFICATION. By Louis Agassiz. 8vo, pp. vii. and 381, cloth 1859. 12s.

AHLWARDT.—THE DIVANS OF THE SIX ANCIENT ARABIC POETS, ENNĀBIGA, 'ANTARA, THARAFA, ZUHAIR, 'ALQAMA, and IMRUULQUAIS; chiefly according to the MSS. of Paris, Gotha, and Leyden, and the Collection of their Fragments, with a List of the various Readings of the Text Edited by W Ahlwardt, Professor of Oriental Languages at the University of Greifswald. Demy 8vo, pp. xxx. and 340, sewed. 1870 12s.

AHN.—PRACTICAL GRAMMAR OF THE GERMAN LANGUAGE. By Dr. F. Ahn. A New Edition. By Dr. Dawson Turner, and Prof. F. L Weinmann. Crown 8vo, pp. cxii. and 430, cloth. 1878. 3s. 6d.

AHN —NEW, PRACTICAL, AND EASY METHOD OF LEARNING THE GERMAN LANGUAGE. By Dr. F. Ahn First and Second Course. Bound in 1 vol. 12mo, pp. 86 and 120, cloth. 1866. 3s.

AHN.—KEY to Ditto. 12mo, pp 40, sewed. 8d.

AHN.—MANUAL OF GERMAN AND ENGLISH CONVERSATIONS, or Vade Mecum for English Travellers. 12mo, pp. x. and 137, cloth. 1875 1s 6d.

AHN.—GERMAN COMMERCIAL LETTER WRITER, with Explanatory Introductions in English, and an Index of Words in French and English. By Dr. F. Ahn. 12mo, pp. 248, cloth. 1861. 4s. 6d.

A

AHN.—New, Practical, and Easy Method of Learning the French Language. By Dr F. Ahn. First Course and Second Course 12mo, cloth. Each 1s. 6d The Two Courses in 1 vol. 12mo, pp. 114 and 170, cloth. 1865. 3s.

AHN.—New, Practical, and Easy Method of Learning the French Language. Third Course, containing a French Reader, with Notes and Vocabulary. By H W. Ehrbch. 12mo, pp. viii. and 125, cloth. 1866. 1s. 6d

AHN.—Manual of French and English Conversations, for the use of Schools and Travellers. By Dr. F Ahn. 12mo, pp. viii. and 200, cloth. 1862. 2s 6d.

AHN.—French Commercial Letter Writer By Dr. F. Ahn Second Edition. 12mo, pp. 228, cloth 1866. 4s. 6d.

AHN.—New, Practical, and Easy Method of Learning the Italian Language. By Dr. F. Ahn First and Second Course. 12mo, pp 198, cloth. 1872 3s. 6d.

AHN.—Key to Ditto. 12mo, pp. 22, sewed. 1865 1s

AHN.—New, Practical, and Easy Method of Learning the Dutch Language, being a complete Grammar, with Selections. By Dr. F. Ahn 12mo, pp. viii. and 166, cloth 1862. 3s 6d.

AHN.—Ahn's Course Latin Grammar for Beginners. By W. Ihne, Ph D. 12mo, pp. vi. and 184, cloth. 1864 3s.

ALABASTER.—The Wheel of the Law : Buddhism illustrated from Siamese Sources by the Modern Buddhist, a Life of Buddha, and an Account of the Phra Bat. By Henry Alabaster, Esq , Interpreter of Her Majesty's Consulate-General in Siam, Member of the Royal Asiatic Society. Demy 8vo, pp. lviii. and 324, cloth. 1871. 14s

ALLEN —The Colour Sense. See English and Foreign Philosophical Library, Vol. X.

ALLIBONE.—A Critical Dictionary of English Literature and British and American Authors (Living and Deceased). From the Earliest Accounts to the latter half of the 19th century. Containing over 46,000 Articles (Authors), with 40 Indexes of subjects. By S. Austin Allibone In 3 vols. royal 8vo, cloth. £5, 8s.

ALTHAUS.—The Spas of Europe. By Julius Althaus, M.D. 8vo, pp. 516, cloth. 1862 7s 6d.

AMATEUR Mechanic's Workshop (The). A Treatise containing Plain and Concise Directions for the Manipulation of Wood and Metals ; including Casting, Forging, Brazing, Soldering, and Carpentry. By the Author of "The Lathe and its Uses." Sixth Edition. Demy 8vo, pp. vi. and 148, with Two Full-Page Illustrations, on toned paper and numerous Woodcuts, cloth. 1880. 6s.

AMATEUR MECHANICAL SOCIETY.—Journal of the Amateur Mechanical Society. 8vo. Vol. i. pp 344 cloth. 1871-72. 12s. Vol ii. pp. vi. and 290, cloth. 1873-77. 12s. Vol iii pp. iv and 246, cloth. 1878-79. 12s. 6d.

AMERICAN Almanac and Treasury of Facts, Statistical, Financial, and Political. Edited by Ainsworth R. Spofford, Librarian of Congress. Crown 8vo, cloth. 1878, 1879, 1880, 1881, 1882, 1883. 7s. 6d. each.

AMERY.—Notes on Forestry. By C. F. Amery, Deputy Conservator N. W. Provinces, India. Crown 8vo, pp. viii. and 120, cloth 1875. 5s.

AMBERLEY.—An Analysis of Religious Belief. By Viscount Amberley. 2 vols. demy 8vo, pp. xvi and 496 and 512, cloth. 1876. 30s .

AMONGST MACHINES A Description of Various Mechanical Appliances used in the Manufacture of Wood, Metal, and other Substances. A Book for Boys, copiously Illustrated. By the Author of "The Young Mechanic." Second Edition Imperial 16mo, pp. viii. and 336, cloth. 1878. 7s. 6d.

ANDERSON.—Practical Mercantile Correspondence. A Collection of Modern Letters of Business, with Notes, Critical and Explanatory, and an Appendix, containing a Dictionary of Commercial Technicalities, pro forma Invoices, Account Sales, Bills of Lading, and Bills of Exchange; also an Explanation of the German Chain Rule. 24th Edition, revised and enlarged. By William Anderson. 12mo, pp. 288, cloth. 5s.

ANDERSON and TUGMAN.—Mercantile Correspondence, containing a Collection of Commercial Letters in Portuguese and English, with their translation on opposite pages, for the use of Business Men and of Students in either of the Languages, treating in modern style of the system of Business in the principal Commercial Cities of the World. Accompanied by pro forma Accounts, Sales, Invoices, Bills of Lading, Drafts, &c. With an Introduction and copious Notes. By William Anderson and James E Tugman 12mo, pp. xi. and 193, cloth. 1867. 6s.

APEL—Prose Specimens for Translation into German, with copious Vocabularies and Explanations. By H. Apel. 12mo, pp. viii. and 246, cloth. 1862. 4s. 6d.

APPLETON (Dr)—Life and Literary Relics. See English and Foreign Philosophical Library, Vol. XIII.

ARAGO—Les Aristocraties. A Comedy in Verse By Etienne Arago. Edited, with English Notes and Notice on Etienne Arago, by the Rev. E. P. H. Brette, B.D., Head Master of the French School, Christ's Hospital, Examiner in the University of London. Fcap. 8vo., pp. 244, cloth. 1868. 4s

ARMITAGE—Lectures on Painting : Delivered to the Students of the Royal Academy. By Edward Armitage, R.A. Crown 8vo, pp. 256, with 29 Illustrations, cloth. 1883. 7s. 6d.

ARNOLD.—Pearls of the Faith ; or, Islam's Rosary : being the Ninety-nine beautiful names of Allah. With Comments in Verse from various Oriental sources as made by an Indian Mussulman. By Edwin Arnold, M A., C S.I., &c. Second Edition. Crown 8vo, pp xvi. and 320, cloth 1883. 7s. 6d.

ARNOLD.—The Light of Asia ; or, The Great Renunciation (Mahâbhinishkramana) Being the Life and Teaching of Gautama, Prince of India, and Founder of Buddhism (as told in verse by an Indian Buddhist). By Edwin Arnold, M.A., C.S.1, &c. Tenth Edition. Cr. 8vo, pp. xiii. and 238, limp parchment. 1883. 2s. 6d.

ARNOLD.—The Iliad and Odyssey of India. By Edwin Arnold, M.A., F R.G.S , &c., &c. Fcap. 8vo, pp. 24, sewed. - 1s.

ARNOLD—A Simple Transliteral Grammar of the Turkish Language. Compiled from Various Sources. With Dialogues and Vocabulary. By Edwin Arnold, M A , C S I., F.R.G.S. Post 8vo, pp. 80, cloth. 1877. 2s. 6d.

ARNOLD.—Indian Poetry. See Trubner's Oriental Series.

ARTOM.—Sermons. By the Rev. B. Artom, Chief Rabbi of the Spanish and Portuguese Congregations of England. First Series. Second Edition. Crown 8vo, pp. viii. and 314, cloth. 1876. 6s.

ASHER.—On the Study of Modern Languages in general, and of the English Language in particular. An Essay. By David Asher, Ph.D. 12mo, pp. viii. and 80, cloth. 1859. 2s.

ASIATIC SOCIETY OF BENGAL. List of Publications on application.

ASIATIC SOCIETY.—Journal of the Royal Asiatic Society of Great Britain and Ireland, from the Commencement to 1863. First Series, complete in 20 Vols. 8vo, with many Plates. £10, or in parts from 4s. to 6s. each

ASIATIC SOCIETY.—Journal of the Royal Asiatic Society of Great Britain and Ireland. New Series. 8vo. Stitched in wrapper. 1864-82.

Vol I , 2 Parts, pp iv and 490, 16s —Vol II , 2 Parts, pp. 522, 16s.—Vol III., 2 Parts, pp 516, with Photograph, 22s —Vol. IV, 2 Parts, pp 521, 16s —Vol V . 2 Parts, pp. 463, with 10 full-page and folding Plates, 18s —Vol VI , Part 1, pp 212, with 2 Plates and a Map, 8s.— Vol. VI. Part 2, pp 272, with Plate and Map, 8s —Vol VII , Part 1, pp 194, with a Plate, 8s —Vol VII , Part 2, pp 204, with 7 Plates and a Map, 8s.—Vol VIII , Part 1, pp 156, with 3 Plates and a Plan, 8s —Vol VIII , Part 2, pp 152, 8s —Vol IX., Part 1, pp 154, with a Plate, 8s —Vol. IX., Part 2, pp 292, with 3 Plates, 10s 6d —Vol X , Part 1, pp. 156, with 2 Plates and a Map, 8s —Vol X , Part 2, pp 146, 6s —Vol X , Part 3, pp 204, 8s —Vol XI., Part 1, pp 128, 5s —Vol XI , Part 2, pp 158, with 2 Plates, 7s. 6d —Vol XI , Part 3, pp 250, 8s —Vol XII , Part 1, pp 152, 5s —Vol XII , Part 2, pp 182, with 2 Plates and Map,6s — Vol XII , Part 3, pp 100, 4s.—Vol XII , Part 4, pp x , 152 , cxx , 16, 8s —Vol XIII , Part 1, pp 120, 6s —Vol XIII , Part 2, pp 170, with a Map, 8s —Vol XIII , Part 3, pp 178, with a Table, 7s 6d.—Vol XIII., Part 4, pp 282, with a Plate and Table, 10s 6d —Vol XIV , Part 1, pp. 124, with a Table and 2 Plates, 5s —Vol XIV , Part 2, pp 164, with 1 Table, 7s 6d —Vol. XIV., Part 3, pp 206, with 6 Plates, 8s —Vol XIV , Part 4, pp 492, with 1 Plate, 14s —Vol. XV., Part 1, pp 136, 6s , Part 2, pp 158, with 3 Tables, 5s , Part III , pp 192, 6s

ASPLET.—The Complete French Course. Part II. Containing all the Rules of French Syntax, &c , &c. By Georges C. Asplet, French Master, Fiome. Fcap 8vo, pp. xx. and 276, cloth. 1880 2s. 6d.

ASTON.—A Short Grammar of the Japanese Spoken Language. By W. G. Aston, M.A. Third Edition. Crown 8vo, pp. 96, cloth. 1873 12s.

ASTON.—A Grammar of the Japanese Written Language. By W. G. Aston, M.A., Assistant Japanese Secretary H.B M.'s Legation, Yedo, Japan. Second Edition. 8vo, pp. 306, cloth. 1877. 28s.

ASTONISHED AT AMERICA. Being Cursory Deductions, &c , &c. By Zigzag. Fcap 8vo, pp. xvi.-108, boards. 1880. 1s.

AUCTORES SANSCRITI.

Vol. I. The Jaiminiya-Nyaya-Mala-Vistara. Edited for the Sanskrit Text Society, under the supervision of Theodor Goldstucker. Large 4to, pp. 582, cloth. £3, 13s. 6d.

Vol. II. The Institutes of Gautama. Edited, with an Index of Words, by A. F. Stenzler, Ph.D., Prof of Oriental Languages in the University of Breslau. 8vo, pp iv. and 78, cloth 1876 4s 6d. Stitched, 3s 6d

Vol III. Vaitana Sutra : The Ritual of the Atharva Veda. Edited, with Critical Notes and Indices, by Dr. R. Garbe. 8vo, pp. viii and 120, sewed. 1878. 5s

Vols. IV. and V.—Vardhamana's Ganaratnamahodadhi, with the Author's Commentary. Edited, with Critical Notes and Indices, by Julius Eggeling, Ph.D. 8vo. Part I., pp. xii and 240, wrapper. 1879. 6s Part II., pp. 240, wrapper. 1881. 6s.

AUGIER.—Diane. A Drama in Verse By Émile Augier Edited with English Notes and Notice on Augier. By Theodore Karcher, LL.B , of the Royal Military Academy and the University of London. 12mo, pp. xiii and 146, cloth. 1867. 2s. 6d.

AUSTIN.—A Practical Treatise on the Preparation, Combination, and Application of Calcareous and Hydraulic Limes and Cements. To which is added many useful Recipes for various Scientific, Mercantile, and Domestic Purposes. By James G. Austin, Architect. 12mo, pp. 192, cloth. 1862. 5s.

AXON—The Mechanic's Friend. A collection of Receipts and Practical Suggestions relating to Aquaria, Bronzing, Cements, Drawing, Dyes, Electricity, Gilding, Glass-working, &c. Numerous Woodcuts. Edited by W. E. A. Axon, M.R.S.L , F.S.S. Crown 8vo, pp. xii. and 339, cloth. 1875 4s. 6d.

BABA.—An Elementary Grammar of the Japanese Language, with easy progressive Exercises. By Tatui Baba. Crown 8vo, pp. xiv. and 92, cloth. 1873. 5s.

BACON.—THE LIFE AND TIMES OF FRANCIS BACON. Extracted from the Edition of his Occasional Writings by James Spedding. 2 vols. post 8vo, pp. xx., 710, and xiv., 708, cloth. 1878. 21s.

BADEN-POWELL —PROTECTION AND BAD TIMES, with Special Reference to the Political Economy of English Colonisation. By George Baden-Powell, M.A., F.R.A.S , F.S.S , Author of "New Homes for the Old Country," &c., &c. 8vo, pp. xii.-376, cloth. 1879. 6s. 6d.

BADER.—THE NATURAL AND MORBID CHANGES OF THE HUMAN EYE, AND THEIR TREATMENT. By C Bader. Medium 8vo, pp viii. and 506, cloth. 1868. 16s.

BADER.—PLATES ILLUSTRATING THE NATURAL AND MORBID CHANGES OF THE HUMAN EYE. By C. Bader. Six chromo-lithographic Plates, each containing the figures of six Eyes, and four lithographed Plates, with figures of Instruments With an Explanatory Text of 32 pages. Medium 8vo, in a portfolio. 21s. Price for Text and Atlas taken together, £1, 12s.

BADLEY.—INDIAN MISSIONARY RECORD AND MEMORIAL VOLUME. By the Rev. B. H. Badley, of the American Methodist Mission. 8vo, pp. xii. and 280, cloth. 1876 10s. 6d

BALFOUR —WAIFS AND STRAYS FROM THE FAR EAST ; being a Series of Disconnected Essays on Matters relating to China By Frederick Henry Balfour. 1 vol. demy 8vo, pp. 224, cloth. 1876. 10s 6d.

BALFOUR.—THE DIVINE CLASSIC OF NAN-HUA ; being the Works of Chuang Tsze, Taoist Philosopher. With an Excursus, and Copious Annotations in English and Chinese. By F. H Balfour, F R G S , Author of "Waifs and Strays from the Far East," &c. Demy 8vo, pp. xlviii. and 426, cloth. 1881. 14s.

BALL.—THE DIAMONDS, COAL, AND GOLD OF INDIA ; their Mode of Occurrence and Distribution. By V. Ball, M A., F G S , of the Geological Survey of India. Fcap. 8vo, pp. viii. and 136, cloth. 1881. 5s.

BALL.—A MANUAL OF THE GEOLOGY OF INDIA. Part III. Economic Geology. By V. Ball, M.A , F.G S. Royal 8vo, pp. xx. and 640, with 6 Maps and 10 Plates, cloth. 1881. 10s (For Parts I and II see MEDLICOTT.)

BALLAD SOCIETY—Subscriptions, small paper, one guinea ; large paper, two guineas per annum. List of publications on application.

BALLANTYNE.—ELEMENTS OF HINDI AND BRAJ BHAKHA GRAMMAR. Compiled for the use of the East India College at Haileybury. By James R. Ballantyne. Second Edition. Crown 8vo, pp. 38, cloth. 1868. 5s.

BALLANTYNE —FIRST LESSONS IN SANSKRIT GRAMMAR ; together with an Introduction to the Hitopadeśa. New Edition. By James R. Ballantyne, LL.D., Librarian of the India Office. 8vo, pp. viii and 110, cloth. 1873. 3s. 6d.

BARANOWSKI.—VADE MECUM DE LA LANGUE FRANÇAISE, rédigé d'après les Dictionnaires classiques avec les Exemples de Bonnes Locutions que donne l'Académie Française, on qu'on trouve dans les ouvrages des plus célèbres auteurs. Par J. J. Baranowski, avec l'approbation de M. E Littré, Sénateur, &c. 32mo, pp. 224. 1879. Cloth, 2s. 6d. ; morocco, 3s. 6d. ; morocco tuck, 4s.

BARENTS' RELICS.—Recovered in the summer of 1876 by Charles L. W. Gardiner, Esq., and presented to the Dutch Government. Described and explained by J. K J. de Jonge, Deputy Royal Architect at the Hague. Published by command of His Excellency, W. F. Van F.R.P Taelman Kip, Minister of Marine Translated, with a Preface, by S R. Van Campen. With a Map, Illustrations, and a fac-simile of the Scroll. 8vo, pp. 70, cloth. 1877. 5s.

BARRIÈRE and CAPENDU.—LES FAUX BONSHOMMES, a Comedy. By Théodore Barrière and Ernest Capendu. Edited, with English Notes and Notice on Barrière, by Professor Ch. Cassal, LL.D., of University College, London. 12mo, pp. xvi. and 304, cloth. 1868. 4s.

BARTH.—The Religions of India. See Trubner's Oriental Series.

BARTLETT.—Dictionary of Americanisms. A Glossary of Words and Phrases colloquially used in the United States By John Russell Bartlett. Fourth Edition, considerably enlarged and improved. 8vo, pp. xlvi. and 814, cloth. 1877. 20s.

BATTYE.—What is Vital Force? or, a Short and Comprehensive Sketch, including Vital Physics, Animal Morphology, and Epidemics, to which is added an Appendix upon Geology, Is the Dentrital Theory of Geology Tenable? By Richard Fawcett Battye. 8vo, pp iv and 336, cloth. 1877. 7s. 6d

BAZLEY.—Notes on the Epicyclodial Cutting Frame of Messrs. Holtzapffel & Co. With special reference to its Compensation Adjustment, and with numerous Illustrations of its Capabilities. By Thomas Sebastian Bazley, M A. 8vo pp. vi and 192 cloth. Illustrated. 1872. 10s. 6d.

BAZLEY.—The Stars in Their Courses A Twofold Series of Maps, with a Catalogue, showing how to identify, at any time of the year, all stars down to the 5 6 magnitude, inclusive of Heis, which are clearly visible in English latitudes. By T. S Bazley, M.A., Author of "Notes on the Epicycloidal Cutting Frame." Atlas folio, pp. 46 and 24, Folding Plates, cloth. 1878. 15s.

BEAL.—Travels of Fah-Hian and Sung-Yun, Buddhist Pilgrims, from China to India (400 A.D and 518 A.D) Translated from the Chinese By Samuel Beal, B.A., Trin. Coll., Cam., &c Crown 8vo, pp lxxiii and 210, with a coloured Map, cloth, ornamental 1869 10s. 6d

BEAL.—A Catena of Buddhist Scriptures from the Chinese. By S. Beal, B.A , Trinity College, Cambridge; a Chaplain in Her Majesty's Fleet, &c 8vo, pp xiv. and 436, cloth. 1871. 15s.

BEAL—The Romantic Legend of Sakya Buddha. From the Chinese-Sanskrit. By the Rev. Samuel Beal. Crown 8vo . pp. 408, cloth. 1875. 12s.

BEAL.—Dhammapada See Trubner's Oriental Series

BEAL—Buddhist Literature in China : Abstract of Four Lectures, Delivered by Samuel Beal, B A , Professor of Chinese at University College, London Demy 8vo, pp. xx. and 186, cloth. 1882. 10s. 6d.

BEAMES.—Outlines of Indian Philology. With a Map showing the Distribution of Indian Languages By John Beames, M R.A S , Bengal Civil Service, Member of the Asiatic Society of Bengal, the Philological Society of London, and the Société Asiatique of Paris Second enlarged and revised Edition. Crown 8vo. pp. viii. and 96, cloth. 1868. 5s

BEAMES.—A Comparative Grammar of the Modern Aryan Languages of India, to wit, Hindi, Panjabi, Sindhi, Gujarati, Marathi, Oriya. and Bengali. By John Beames, Bengal Civil Service, M R.A S , &c , &c. Demy 8vo Vol. I. On Sounds. Pp. xvi. and 360, cloth. 1872. 16s.—Vol II. The Noun and the Pronoun. Pp. xii. and 348, cloth. 1875. 16s —Vol III. The Verb Pp. xii. and 316, cloth. 1879. 16s.

BELLEW.—From the Indus to the Tigris. A Narrative of a Journey through the Countries of Balochistan, Afghanistan, Khorassan, and Iran in 1872; together with a complete Synoptical Grammar and Vocabulary of the Brahoe Language, and a Record of the Meteorological Observations and Altitudes on the March from the Indus to the Tigris. By Henry Walter Bellew, C S.I., Surgeon, Bengal Staff Corps. Demy 8vo, pp viii. and 496, cloth. 1874. 14s.

BELLEW.—Kashmir and Kashghar . a Narrative of the Journey of the Embassy to Kashghar in 1873-74. By H. W. Bellew, C S.I. Demy 8vo, pp. xxxii and 420, cloth. 1875. 16s.

BELLEW.—THE RACES OF AFGHANISTAN Being a Brief Account of the Principal Nations Inhabiting that Country. By Surgeon-Major H. W Bellew, C.S.I ; late on Special Political Duty at Kabul. 8vo, pp. 124, cloth. 1880. 7s. 6d.

BELLOWS.—ENGLISH OUTLINE VOCABULARY for the use of Students of the Chinese, Japanese, and other Languages. Arranged by John Bellows. With Notes on the Writing of Chinese with Roman Letters, by Professor Summers, King's College, London. Crown 8vo, pp. vi. and 368, cloth. 1867. 6s.

BELLOWS.—OUTLINE DICTIONARY FOR THE USE OF MISSIONARIES, EXPLORERS, AND STUDENTS OF LANGUAGE. By Max Muller, M A , Taylorian Professor in the University of Oxford. With an Introduction on the proper use of the ordinary English Alphabet in transcribing Foreign Languages. The Vocabulary compiled by John Bellows. Crown 8vo, pp. xxxi. and 368, limp morocco. 1867. 7s 6d.

BELLOWS.—TOUS LES VERBES. Conjugations of all the Verbs in the French and English Languages. By John Bellows. Revised by Professor Beljame, B A., LL.B., of the University of Paris, and Official Interpreter to the Imperial Court, and George B. Strickland, late Assistant French Master, Royal Naval School, London. Also a New Table of Equivalent Values of French and English Money, Weights, and Measures. 32mo, 76 Tables, sewed. 1867. 1s.

BELLOWS—FRENCH AND ENGLISH DICTIONARY FOR THE POCKET. By John Bellows. Containing the French-English and English-French divisions on the same page ; conjugating all the verbs ; distinguishing the genders by different types, giving numerous aids to pronunciation ; indicating the *liaison* or *non-liaison* of terminal consonants, and translating units of weight, measure, and value, by a series of tables differing entirely from any hitherto published. The new edition, which is but six ounces in weight, has been remodelled, and contains many thousands of additional words and renderings. Miniature maps of France, the British Isles, Paris, and London, are added to the Geographical Section. Second Edition. 32mo, pp. 608, roan tuck, or persian without tuck. 1877. 10s. 6d. ; morocco tuck, 12s. 6d.

BENEDIX.—DER VETTER. Comedy in Three Acts. By Roderich Benedix. With Grammatical and Explanatory Notes by F. Weinmann, German Master at the Royal Institution School, Liverpool, and G. Zimmermann, Teacher of Modern Languages. 12mo, pp. 128, cloth. 1863. 2s. 6d.

BENFEY.—A PRACTICAL GRAMMAR OF THE SANSKRIT LANGUAGE, for the use of Early Students. By Theodor Benfey, Professor of Sanskrit in the University of Gottingen. Second, revised, and enlarged Edition. Royal 8vo, pp. viii. and 296, cloth. 1868. 10s. 6d

BENTHAM.—THEORY OF LEGISLATION. By Jeremy Bentham. Translated from the French of Etienne Dumont by R. Hildreth. Fourth Edition. Post 8vo, pp. xv. and 472, cloth. 1882 7s. 6d.

BETTS.—*See* VALDES.

BEVERIDGE—THE DISTRICT OF BAKARGANJ. Its History and Statistics. By H. Beveridge, B C S., Magistrate and Collector of Bakarganj. 8vo, pp. xx. and 460, cloth. 1876. 21s.

BICKNELL.—*See* HAFIZ.

BIERBAUM.—HISTORY OF THE ENGLISH LANGUAGE AND LITERATURE.—By F. J. Bierbaum, Ph D. Crown 8vo, pp. viii. and 270, cloth 1883 3s

BIGANDET.—THE LIFE OF GAUDAMA See Trubner's Oriental Series.

BIRCH—FASTI MONASTICI AEVI SAXONICI , or, An Alphabetical List of the Heads of Religious Houses in England previous to the Norman Conquest, to which is prefixed a Chronological Catalogue of Contemporary Foundations. By Walter de Gray Birch. 8vo, pp. vii. and 114, cloth. 1873. 5s.

BIRD.—PHYSIOLOGICAL ESSAYS. Drink Craving, Differences in Men, Idiosyncrasy, and the Origin of Disease. By Robert Bird, M.D. demy 8vo, pp 246, cloth. 1870. 7s. 6d.

BLACK—YOUNG JAPAN, YOKOHAMA AND YEDO. A Narrative of the Settlement and the City, from the Signing of the Treaties in 1858 to the Close of the Year 1879; with a Glance at the Progress of Japan during a Period of Twenty-one Years. By John R. Black, formerly Editor of the "Japan Herald" and the "Japan Gazette." Editor of the "Far East." 2 vols. demy 8vo, pp. xviii. and 418, xiv. and 522, cloth. 1881. £2, 2s.

BLADES.—SHAKSPERE AND TYPOGRAPHY. Being an Attempt to show Shakspere's Personal Connection with, and Technical Knowledge of, the Art of Printing; also Remarks upon some common Typographical Errors, with especial reference to the Text of Shakspere By William Blades. 8vo, pp. viii and 78, with an Illustration, cloth. 1872. 3s.

BLADES.—THE BIOGRAPHY AND TYPOGRAPHY OF WILLIAM CAXTON, England's First Printer. By William Blades. Founded to a great extent upon the Author's "Life and Typography of William Caxton" Brought up to the Present Date, and including all Discoveries since made. Elegantly and appropriately printed in demy 8vo, on hand-made paper, imitation old bevelled binding. 1877. £1, 1s. Cheap Edition. Crown 8vo, cloth. 1881. 5s.

BLADES—THE ENEMIES OF BOOKS. By William Blades, Typograph. Crown 8vo, pp. xvi and 112, parchment wrapper. 1880 5s

BLAKEY.—MEMOIRS OF DR. ROBERT BLAKEY, Professor of Logic and Metaphysics, Queen's College, Belfast, Author of "Historical Sketch of Moral Science," &c., &c. Edited by the Rev. Henry Miller, of St. Andrews (Presbyterian Church of England), Hammersmith. Crown 8vo, pp. xii. and 252, cloth. 1879. 5s.

BLEEK.—REYNARD THE FOX IN SOUTH AFRICA; or, Hottentot Fables and Tales, chiefly Translated from Original Manuscripts in the Library of His Excellency Sir George Grey, K.C.B. By W H. I. Bleek, Ph.D. Post 8vo, pp. xxvi. and 94, cloth. 1864. 3s 6d.

BLEEK—A BRIEF ACCOUNT OF BUSHMAN FOLK LORE, and other Texts. By W. H. I. Bleek. Ph.D. Folio, pp. 21, paper. 2s. 6d.

BOEHMER—SPANISH REFORMERS OF TWO CENTURIES, from 1520, their Lives and Writings. Described by E Boehmer, D.D., Ph D. Vol. 1. royal 8vo, pp. 232, cloth. 1874 12s 6d Roxburghe, 15s.

BOEHMER—*See* VALDES, and SPANISH REFORMERS

BOJESEN.—A GUIDE TO THE DANISH LANGUAGE. Designed for English Students. By Mrs. Maria Bojesen. 12mo, pp. 250, cloth. 1863. 5s

BOLIA—THE GERMAN CALIGRAPHIST: Copies for German Handwriting By C. Bolia Oblong 4to, sewed. 1s

BOOLE.—MESSAGE OF PSYCHIC SCIENCE TO MOTHERS AND NURSES. By Mary Boole. Crown 8vo, pp. xiv and 266, cloth. 1883 5s

BOY ENGINEERS.—See under LUKIN.

BOYD—NÁGÁNANDA; or, the Joy of the Snake World A Buddhist Drama in Five Acts. Translated into English Prose, with Explanatory Notes, from the Sanskrit of Sá-Harsha-Deva By Palmer Boyd, B A., Sanskrit Scholar of Trinity College, Cambridge With an Introduction by Professor Cowell. Crown 8vo, pp. xvi. and 100, cloth. 1872. 4s. 6d.

BRAMSEN—JAPANESE CHRONOLOGICAL TABLES, showing the Date, according to the Julian or Gregorian Calendar, of the First Day of each Japanese Month. From Tai-Kwa, 1st year, to Mei-ji, 6th year (645 A D. to 1873 A D) With an Introductory Essay on "Japanese Chronology and Calendars. By W. Bramsen. Oblong fcap. 4to, pp. 50-84, cloth. 1880. 14s.

BRAMSEN —THE COINS OF JAPAN. By W. Bramsen. Part 1 The Copper, Lead, and Iron Coins issued by the Central Government. 4to, pp. 10, with Plates of 74 Coins, boards. 1880. 5s.

BRAMSEN.—JAPANESE WEIGHTS, with their Equivalents in French and English Weights. Compiled by W. Bramsen. Fcap folio sheet. 1877 1s.

BRAMSEN —JAPANESE LINEAL MEASURES, with their Equivalents in French and English Measures. Compiled by W. Bramsen. Fcap folio sheet. 1877. 1s.

BRENTANO.—ON THE HISTORY AND DEVELOPMENT OF GILDS, AND THE ORIGIN OF TRADE-UNIONS. By Lujo Brentano, of Aschaffenburg, Bavaria, Doctor Juris Utriusque et Philosophiæ 1. The Origin of Gilds 2 Religious (or Social) Gilds. 3. Town-Gilds or Gild-Merchants. 4. Craft-Gilds. 5. Trade-Unions. 8vo, pp. xvi. and 136, cloth. 1870. 3s 6d.

BRETSCHNEIDER —EARLY EUROPEAN RESEARCHES INTO THE FLORA OF CHINA. By E. Bretschneider, M D., Physician of the Russian Legation at Peking Demy 8vo, pp. iv. and 194, sewed. 1881. 7s. 6d.

BRETSCHNEIDER —BOTANICON SINICUM Notes on Chinese Botany, from Native and Western Sources. By E. Bretschneider, M.D. Crown 8vo, pp. 228, wrapper. 1882. 10s. 6d.

BRETTE —FRENCH EXAMINATION PAPERS SET AT THE UNIVERSITY OF LONDON FROM 1839 TO 1871. Arranged and edited by the Rev. P. H. Ernest Brette, B.D. Crown 8vo, pp. viii. and 278, cloth. 3s. 6d.; interleaved, 4s. 6d.

BRITISH MUSEUM.—LIST OF PUBLICATIONS OF THE TRUSTEES OF THE BRITISH MUSEUM, on application.

BROWN.—THE DERVISHES ; OR, ORIENTAL SPIRITUALISM. By John P. Brown, Secretary and Dragoman of the Legation of the United States of America at Constantinople. Crown 8vo, pp. viii. and 416, cloth, with 24 Illustrations. 1868. 14s.

BROWN.—SANSKRIT PROSODY AND NUMERICAL SYMBOLS EXPLAINED. By Charles Philip Brown, M R A S , Author of a Telugu Dictionary, Grammar, &c , Professor of Telugu in the University of London. 8vo, pp. viii. and 56, cloth. 1869. 3s. 6d.

BROWNE.—HOW TO USE THE OPHTHALMOSCOPE ; being Elementary Instruction in Ophthalmoscopy. Arranged for the use of Students. By Edgar A. Browne, Surgeon to the Liverpool Eye and Ear Infirmary, &c. Second Edition Crown 8vo, pp. xi. and 108, with 35 Figures, cloth 1883. 3s. 6d.

BROWNE —A BÁNGÁLI PRIMER, in Roman Character. By J. F. Browne, B.C.S. Crown 8vo, pp. 32, cloth. 1881. 2s.

BROWNE.—A HINDI PRIMER IN ROMAN CHARACTER. By J F Browne, B.C.S. Crown 8vo, pp. 36, cloth. 1882. 2s 6d.

BROWNE.—AN URIYÁ PRIMER IN ROMAN CHARACTER. By J. F. Browne, B.C.S. Crown 8vo, pp. 32, cloth 1882. 2s. 6d.

BROWNING SOCIETY'S PAPERS.—Demy 8vo, wrappers. 1881-84. Part I., pp. 116. 10s. Bibliography of Robert Browning from 1833-81. Part II., pp. 142. 10s. Part III., pp. 168. 10s.

BROWNING'S POEMS, ILLUSTRATIONS TO. 4to, boards. Parts I. and II. 10s. each.

BRUNNOW.—*See* SCHEFFEL.

BRUNTON.—MAP OF JAPAN. See under JAPAN.

BUDGE—ARCHAIC CLASSICS   Assyrian Texts; being Extracts from the Annals of Shalmaneser II., Sennacherib, and Assur-Bani-Pal   With Philological Notes. By Ernest A. Budge, B.A., M.R A.S., Assyrian Exhibitioner, Christ's College, Cambridge. Small 4to, pp. viii. and 44, cloth.   1880.   7s 6d.

BUDGE.—HISTORY OF ESARHADDON.   See Trubner's Oriental Series.

BUNYAN.—SCENES FROM THE PILGRIM'S PROGRESS.   By. R. B. Rutter   4to, pp. 142, boards, leather back.   1882.   5s.

BURGESS :—
ARCHÆOLOGICAL SURVEY OF WESTERN INDIA :—
REPORT OF THE FIRST SEASON'S OPERATIONS IN THE BELGÂM AND KALADI DISTRICTS.   January to May 1874.   By James Burgess, F.R G S.   With 56 Photographs and Lithographic Plates.   Royal 4to, pp viii. and 45; half bound.   1875   £2, 2s.
REPORT ON THE ANTIQUITIES OF KÂTHIÂWÂD AND KACHH, being the result of the Second Season's Operations of the Archæological Survey of Western India, 1874–75.   By James Burgess, F R.G S   Royal 4to, pp. x. and 242, with 74 Plates; half bound.   1876.   £3, 3s
REPORT ON THE ANTIQUITIES IN THE BIDAR AND AURANGABAD DISTRICTS, in the Territories of His Highness the Nizam of Haiderabad, being the result of the Third Season's Operations of the Archæological Survey of Western India, 1875–76.   By James Burgess, F R G S , M.R.A.S., Archæological Surveyor and Reporter to Government, Western India   Royal 4to, pp. viii. and 138, with 63 Photographic Plates ; half bound.   1878.   £2, 2s.
REPORT ON THE BUDDHIST CAVE TEMPLES AND THEIR INSCRIPTIONS; containing Views, Plans, Sections, and Elevation of Façades of Cave Temples , Drawings of Architectural and Mythological Sculptures , Facsimiles of Inscriptions, &c. ; with Descriptive and Explanatory Text, and Translations of Inscriptions, &c., &c.   By James Burgess, LL D., F.R G S , &c.   Royal 4to, pp. x. and 140, with 86 Plates and Woodcuts , half-bound.
REPORT ON ELURA CAVE TEMPLES, AND THE BRAHMANICAL AND JAINA CAVES IN WESTERN INDIA   By James Burgess, LL D , F.R.G S , &c.   Royal 4to, pp. viii. and 90, with 66 Plates and Woodcuts ; half-bound   } 2 Vols. 1883. £6, 6s.

BURMA.—THE BRITISH BURMA GAZETTEER   Compiled by Major H. R Spearman, under the direction of the Government of India.   2 vols. 8vo, pp 764 and 878, with 11 Photographs, cloth.   1880   £2, 10s.

BURNE—SHROPSHIRE FOLK-LORE   A Sheaf of Gleanings   Edited by Charlotte S. Burne, from the Collections of Georgina F Jackson.   Part I.   Demy 8vo, pp. xvi –176, wrapper   1883.   7s. 6d.

BURNELL.—ELEMENTS OF SOUTH INDIAN PALÆOGRAPHY, from the Fourth to the Seventeenth Century A D , being an Introduction to the Study of South Indian Inscriptions and MSS.   By A. C. Burnell.   Second enlarged and improved Edition.   4to, pp. xiv. and 148, Map and 35 Plates, cloth.   1878.   £2, 12s 6d.

BURNELL.—A CLASSIFIED INDEX TO THE SANSKRIT MSS IN THE PALACE AT TANJORE.   Prepared for the Madras Government.   By A. C. Burnell, Ph D., &c , &c.   4to, stiff wrapper   Part I , pp. iv.–80, Vedic and Technical Literature   Part II., pp iv.–80, Philosophy and Law.   Part III , Drama, Epics, Puranas, and Zantras ; Indices.   1879.   10s. each.

BURNEY.—THE BOYS' MANUAL OF SEAMANSHIP AND GUNNERY, compiled for the use of the Training-Ships of the Royal Navy.   By Commander C. Burney, R.N., F R G S , Superintendent of Greenwich Hospital School.   Seventh Edition.   Approved by the Lords Commissioners of the Admiralty to be used in the Training-Ships of the Royal Navy.   Crown 8vo, pp xii and 352, with numerous Illustrations, cloth.   1879.   6s.

BURNEY --THE YOUNG SEAMAN'S MANUAL AND RIGGER'S GUIDE. By Commander C. Burney, R.N., F.R.G.S. Sixth Edition. Revised and corrected. Approved by the Lords Commissioners of the Admiralty. Crown 8vo pp. xxxviii and 592, cloth. With 200 Illustrations and 16 Sheets of Signals. 1878. 7s. 6d.

BURTON.—CAPTAIN RICHARD F. BURTON'S HANDBOOK FOR OVERLAND EXPEDITIONS; being an English Edition of the "Prairie Traveller," a Handbook for Overland Expeditions. With Illustrations and Itineraries of the Principal Routes between the Mississippi and the Pacific, and a Map. By Captain Randolph B. Marcy (now General and Chief of the Staff, Army of the Potomac). Edited, with Notes, by Captain Richard F. Burton. Crown 8vo, pp. 270, numerous Woodcuts, Itineraries, and Map, cloth. 1863. 6s. 6d

BUTLER.—THE SPANISH TEACHER AND COLLOQUIAL PHRASE-BOOK. An easy and agreeable method of acquiring a Speaking Knowledge of the Spanish Language. By Francis Butler Fcap 8vo, pp. xviii. and 240, half-roan. 2s 6d.

BUTLER.—HUNGARIAN POEMS AND FABLES FOR ENGLISH READERS. Selected and Translated by E. D. Butler, of the British Museum ; with Illustrations by A. G. Butler. Foolscap, pp. vi. and 88, limp cloth. 1877. 2s.

BUTLER.—THE LEGEND OF THE WONDROUS HUNT. By John Arany. With a few Miscellaneous Pieces and Folk-Songs. Translated from the Magyar by E. D. Butler, F.R.G.S. Crown 8vo, pp. viii. and 70. Limp cloth. 2s. 6d.

CAITHNESS.—SERIOUS LETTERS TO SERIOUS FRIENDS By the Countess of Caithness, Authoress of "Old Truths in a New Light " Crown 8vo, pp. viii and 352, cloth. 1877. 7s. 6d.

CAITHNESS.—LECTURES ON POPULAR AND SCIENTIFIC SUBJECTS. By the Earl of Caithness, F.R.S. Delivered at various times and places Second enlarged Edition. Crown 8vo, pp. 174, cloth 1879. 2s 6d.

CALCUTTA REVIEW.—SELECTIONS FROM Nos. I.-XVII. 5s. each.

CALDER —THE COMING ERA. By Alexander Calder, Officer of the Legion of Honour, and Author of "The Man of the Future " 8vo, pp. 422, cloth. 1879. 10s. 6d.

CALDWELL.—A COMPARATIVE GRAMMAR OF THE DRAVIDIAN OR SOUTH INDIAN FAMILY OF LANGUAGES. By the Rev. R. Caldwell, LL.D. A second, corrected, and enlarged Edition. Demy 8vo, pp. 804, cloth. 1875. 28s.

CALENDARS OF STATE PAPERS. List on application.

CALL.—REVERBERATIONS. Revised. With a chapter from My Autobiography. By W. M. W. Call, M A., Cambridge, Author of "Lyra Hellenica" and "Golden Histories " Crown 8vo, pp. viii. and 200, cloth. 1875. 4s. 6d.

CALLAWAY.—NURSERY TALES, TRADITIONS, AND HISTORIES OF THE ZULUS. In their own words, with a Translation into English, and Notes. By the Rev. Canon Callaway, M.D. Vol. I, 8vo, pp. xiv and 378, cloth. 1868. 16s.

CALLAWAY.—THE RELIGIOUS SYSTEM OF THE AMAZULU.

Part I.—Unkulunkulu ; or, The Tradition of Creation as existing among the Amazulu and other Tribes of South Africa, in their own words, with a Translation into English, and Notes. By the Rev. Canon Callaway, M.D. 8vo, pp. 128, sewed. 1868. 4s.

Part II.—Amatongo ; or, Ancestor-Worship as existing among the Amazulu, in their own words, with a Translation into English, and Notes. By the Rev. Canon Callawsy, M D 8vo, pp. 127, sewed. 1869. 4s.

Part III —Izinyanga Zokubula , or, Divination, as existing among the Amazulu, in their own words, with a Translation into English, and Notes. By the Rev. Canon Callaway, M D. 8vo, pp. 150, sewed. 1870 4s

Part IV.—On Medical Magic and Witchcraft. 8vo, pp. 40, sewed, 1s. 6d.

CAMERINI.—L'Eco Italiano, a Practical Guide to Italian Conversation. By E. Camerini. With a Vocabulary. 12mo, pp. 98, cloth. 1860. 4s. 6d.

CAMPBELL.—The Gospel of the World's Divine Order. By Douglas Campbell. New Edition. Revised Crown 8vo, pp. viii. and 364, cloth. 1877. 4s. 6d.

CANDID Examination of Theism. By Physicus. Post 8vo, pp. xviii. and 198, cloth. 1878. 7s. 6d.

CANTICUM CANTICORUM, reproduced in facsimile, from the Scriverius copy in the British Museum. With an Historical and Bibliographical Introduction by I. Ph. Berjean. Folio, pp. 36, with 16 Tables of Illustrations, vellum. 1860. £2, 2s.

CAREY.—The Past, the Present, and the Future By H. C. Carey. Second Edition. 8vo, pp 474, cloth. 1856. 10s. 6d.

CARLETTI—History of the Conquest of Tunis. Translated by J. T. Carletti. Crown 8vo, pp 40, cloth. 1883. 2s. 6d

CARNEGY.— Notes on the Land Tenures and Revenue Assessments of Upper India. By P. Carnegy. Crown 8vo, pp. viii. and 136, and forms, cloth. 1874. 6s.

CATHERINE II., Memoirs of the Empress. Written by herself. With a Preface by A. Herzen. Trans. from the French. 12mo, pp. xvi. and 352, hds. 1859. 7s. 6d.

CATLIN—O-Kee-Pa. A Religious Ceremony; and other Customs of the Mandans. By George Catlin. With 13 coloured Illustrations. Small 4to, pp. vi. and 52, cloth. 1867. 14s.

CATLIN—The Lifted and Subsided Rocks of America, with their Influence on the Oceanic, Atmospheric, and Land Currents, and the Distribution of Races. By George Catlin. With 2 Maps. Cr. 8vo, pp. xii. and 238, cloth. 1870. 6s. 6d.

CATLIN.—Shut your Mouth and Save your Life. By George Catlin, Author of "Notes of Travels amongst the North American Indians," &c, &c. With 29 Illustrations from Drawings by the Author. Eighth Edition, considerably enlarged. Crown 8vo, pp. 106, cloth. 1882. 2s. 6d

CAXTON—The Biography and Typography of. See Blades.

CAXTON CELEBRATION, 1877.—Catalogue of the Loan Collection of Antiquities, Curiosities, and Appliances Connected with the Art of Printing. Edited by G. Bullen, F.S.A. Post 8vo, pp xx. and 472, cloth, 3s. 6d.

CAZELLES—Outline of the Evolution-Philosophy. By Dr. W. E. Cazelles. Translated from the French by the Rev. O. B. Frothingham. Crown 8vo, pp. 156, cloth. 1875. 3s 6d.

CESNOLA.—Salaminia (Cyprus) The History, Treasures, and Antiquities of Salamis in the Island of Cyprus. By A Palma di Cesnola, F S A., &c. With an Introduction by S Birch, Esq, D C.L., LL.D., Keeper of the Egyptian and Oriental Antiquities in the British Museum. Royal 8vo, pp. xlviii. and 325, with upwards of 700 Illustrations and Map of Ancient Cyprus, cloth. 1882. 31s. 6d.

CHALMERS.—The Speculations on Metaphysics, Polity, and Morality of "The Old Philosopher," Lau-tsze. Translated from the Chinese, with an Introduction by John Chalmers, M.A. Fcap 8vo, pp. xx and 62, cloth. 1868. 4s. 6d.

CHALMERS.—Structure of Chinese Characters, under 300 Primary Forms; after the Shwoh-wan, 100 A D, and the Phonetic Shwoh-wan, 1833. By J. Chalmers, M.A, LL D, A B. Demy 8vo, pp x. and 200, with two plates, limp cloth. 1882 12s 6d.

CHAMBERLAIN.—The Classical Poetry of the Japanese. By Basil Hall Chamberlain, Author of "Yeigo Henkaku, Ichiran." Post 8vo, pp xii. and 228, cloth. 1880 7s 6d.

CHAPMAN.—CHLOROFORM AND OTHER ANÆSTHETICS · Their History and Use during Childbirth. By John Chapman, M D. 8vo, pp. 51, sewed   1859.   1s.

CHAPMAN.—DIARRHŒA AND CHOLERA : Their Nature, Origin, and Treatment through the Agency of the Nervous System.   By John Chapman, M.D., M.R.C.P., M.R.C.S.   8vo, pp. xix. and 248, cloth.   7s. 6d.

CHAPMAN.—MEDICAL CHARITY : its Abuses, and how to Remedy them   By John Chapman, M D. 8vo, pp. viii. and 108, cloth.   1874   2s. 6d.

CHAPMAN.—SEA-SICKNESS, AND HOW TO PREVENT IT. An Explanation of its Nature and Successful Treatment, through the Agency of the Nervous System, by means of the Spinal Ice Bag ; with an Introduction on the General Principles of Neuro-Therapeutics. By John Chapman, M D., M R C P., M R C.S.   Second Edition. 8vo, pp. viii. and 112, cloth.   1868. 3s

CHAPTERS ON CHRISTIAN CATHOLICITY. By a Clergyman. 8vo, pp. 282, cloth. 1878. 5s.

CHARNOCK —A GLOSSARY OF THE ESSEX DIALECT   By Richard Stephen Charnock, Ph.D., F.S.A. Fcap., pp. xii. and 64, cloth. 1880. 3s. 6d.

CHARNOCK.—PRŒNOMINA ; or, The Etymology of the Principal Christian Names of Great Britain and Ireland. By R S Charnock, Ph.D., F S.A   Crown 8vo, pp. xvi. and 128, cloth. 1882. 6s.

CHATTOPADHYAYA —THE YÁTRÁS ; or, The Popular Dramas of Bengal. By N. Chattopadhyaya. Post 8vo, pp. 50, wrapper. 1882. 2s.

CHAUCER SOCIETY.—Subscription, two guineas per annum. List of Publications on application.

CHILDERS.—A PALI-ENGLISH DICTIONARY, with Sanskrit Equivalents, and with numerous Quotations, Extracts, and References.   Compiled by Robert Cæsar Childers, late of the Ceylon Civil Service. Imperial 8vo, double columns, pp. 648, cloth. 1875. £3, 3s.

CHILDERS.—THE MAHAPARINIBBANASUTTA OF THE SUTTA PITAKA. The Pali Text. Edited by the late Professor R. C. Childers. 8vo, pp. 72, limp cloth. 1878. 5s.

CHINTAMON —A COMMENTARY ON THE TEXT OF THE BHAGAVAD-GITÁ ; or, the Discourse between Khrishna and Arjuna of Divine Matters. A Sanskrit Philosophical Poem. With a few Introductory Papers. By Hurrychund Chintamon, Political Agent to H. H. the Guicowar Mulhai Rao Maharajah of Baroda. Post 8vo, pp. 118, cloth. 1874. 6s.

CHRONICLES AND MEMORIALS OF GREAT BRITAIN AND IRELAND DURING THE MIDDLE AGES. List on application.

CLARK —MEGHADUTA, THE CLOUD MESSENGER   Poem of Kalidasa. Translated by the late Rev. T. Clark, M.A. Fcap. 8vo, pp. 64, wrapper. 1882. 1s.

CLARK.—A FORECAST OF THE RELIGION OF THE FUTURE. Being Short Essays on some important Questions in Religious Philosophy   By W. W. Clark. Post 8vo, pp. xii. and 238, cloth.   1879. 3s. 6d.

CLARKE —THE EARLY HISTORY OF THE MEDITERRANEAN POPULATIONS, &c., in their Migrations and Settlements. Illustrated from Autonomous Coins, Gems, Inscriptions, &c. By Hyde Clarke. 8vo, pp. 80, cloth. 1882. 5s.

CLAUSEWITZ.—ON WAR   By General Carl von Clausewitz. Translated by Colonel J. J. Graham, from the third German Edition. Three volumes complete in one. Fcap 4to, double columns, pp. xx. and 564, with Portrait of the author, cloth. 1873. £1, 1s.

CLEMENT AND HUTTON.—Artists of the Nineteenth Century and their Works A Handbook containing Two Thousand and Fifty Biographical Sketches. By Clara Erskine Clement and Lawrence Hutton. 2 vols. crown 8vo, pp. lxxxvii. 386 and 44, and lvii. 374 and 44, cloth. 1879. 21s.

COLEBROOKE.—The Life and Miscellaneous Essays of Henry Thomas Colebrooke. The Biography by his Son, Sir T. E. Colebrooke, Bart., M P. 3 vols. Vol. I The Life   Demy 8vo, pp xii. and 492, with Portrait and Map, cloth. 1873. 14s.   Vols. II. and III. The Essays. A new Edition, with Notes by E. B. Cowell, Professor of Sanskrit in the University of Cambridge. Demy 8vo, pp. xvi. and 544, and x. and 520, cloth. 1873. 28s.

COLENSO.—Natal Sermons A Series of Discourses Preached in the Cathedral Church of St Peter's, Maritzburg   By the Right Rev. John William Colenso, D.D., Bishop of Natal   8vo, pp. viii. and 373, cloth. 1866. 7s. 6d.   The Second Series. Crown 8vo, cloth. 1868. 5s.

COLLINS —A Grammar and Lexicon of the Hebrew Language, Entitled Sefer Hassoham By Rabbi Moseh Ben Yitshak, of England. Edited from a MS. in the Bodleian Library of Oxford, and collated with a MS. in the Imperial Library of St Petersburg, with Additions and Corrections, by G. W. Collins, M.A. Demy 4to, pp. viii. and 20, wrapper. 1882. 3s.

COLYMBIA.—Crown 8vo, pp. 260, cloth. 1873. 5s.
"The book is amusing as well as clever "—*Athenæum*   "Many exceedingly humorous passages "—*Public Opinion.*   "Deserves to be read "—*Scotsman*   "Neatly done "—*Graphic* "Very amusing "—*Examiner*

COMTE —A General View of Positivism. By Auguste Comte. Translated by Dr. J. H. Bridges. 12mo, pp xi. and 426, cloth. 1865. 8s. 6d.

COMTE —The Catechism of Positive Religion : Translated from the French of Auguste Comte By Richard Congreve. 18mo, pp. 428, cloth. 1858. 6s 6d.

COMTE —The Eight Circulars of Auguste Comte Translated from the French, under the auspices of R Congreve. Fcap 8vo, pp. iv. and, 90 cloth. 1882. 1s. 6d.

COMTE —Preliminary Discourse on the Positive Spirit Prefixed to the "Traité Philosophique d'Astronomie Populaire." By M Auguste Comte Translated by W. M. W. Call, M.A , Camb. Crown 8vo, pp ¶154, cloth. 1883. 2s. 6d.

COMTE.—The Positive Philosophy of Auguste Comte. Translated and condensed by Harriet Martineau. 2 vols. Second Edition   8vo, cloth. Vol. I., pp. xxiv. and 400 ; Vol II., pp xiv. and 468. 1875. 25s.

CONGREVE —The Roman Empire of the West. Four Lectures delivered at the Philosophical Institution, Edinburgh, February 1855, by Richard Congreve, M.A 8vo, pp 176, cloth. 1855. 4s.

CONGREVE.—Elizabeth of England. Two Lectures delivered at the Philosophical Institution, Edinburgh, January 1862 By Richard Congreve. 18mo, pp. 114, sewed 1862 2s. 6d.

CONTOPOULOS.—A Lexicon of Modern Greek-English and English Modern Greek. By N. Contopoulos. Part I. Modern Greek-English. Part II. English Modern Greek. 8vo, pp. 460 and 582, cloth. 1877. 27s.

CONWAY.—The Sacred Anthology · A Book of Ethnical Scriptures. Collected and Edited by Moncure D. Conway. Fifth Edition. Demy 8vo, pp. viii. and 480, cloth. 1876. 12s.

CONWAY.—IDOLS AND IDEALS With an Essay on Christianity. By Moncure D. Conway, M.A., Author of "The Eastern Pilgrimage," &c. Crown 8vo, pp. 352, cloth. 1877. 5s.

CONWAY.—EMERSON AT HOME AND ABROAD. See English and Foreign Philosophical Library.

CONWAY.—TRAVELS IN SOUTH KENSINGTON. By M D. Conway Illustrated. 8vo, pp. 234, cloth. 1882. 12s.
, CONTENTS —The South Kensington Museum—Decorative Art and Architecture in England —Bedford Park.

COOMARA SWAMY.—THE DATHAVANSA ; or, The History of the Tooth Relic of Gotama Buddha, in Pali verse. Edited, with an English Translation, by Mutu Coomara Swamy, F.R.A.S. Demy 8vo, pp. 174, cloth. 1874. 10s. 6d. English Translation. With Notes. pp. 100. 6s.

COOMARA SWAMY.—SUTTA NIPATA , or, Dialogues and Discourses of Gotama Buddha (2500 years old). Translated from the original Pali. With Notes and Introduction. By Mutu Coomara Swamy, F.R.A.S. Crown 8vo, pp. xxxvi. and 160, cloth. 1874. 6s.

CORNELIA. A Novel. Post 8vo, pp. 250, boards. 1863. 1s. 6d.

COTTA.—GEOLOGY AND HISTORY. A popular Exposition of all that is known of the Earth and its Inhabitants in Pre-historic Times. By Bernhard Von Cotta, Professor of Geology at the Academy of Mining, Freiberg, in Saxony. 12mo, pp. iv. and 84, cloth. 1865. 2s.

COUSIN.—THE PHILOSOPHY OF KANT. Lectures by Victor Cousin. Translated from the French. To which is added a Biographical and Critical Sketch of Kant's Life and Writings. By A. G. Henderson Large post 8vo, pp. xciv. and 194, cloth. 1864. 6s.

COUSIN.—ELEMENTS OF PSYCHOLOGY . included in a Critical Examination of Locke's Essay on the Human Understanding, and in additional pieces. Translated from the French of Victor Cousin, with an Introduction and Notes. By Caleb S. Henry, D.D. Fourth improved Edition, revised according to the Author's last corrections. Crown 8vo, pp. 568, cloth. 1871. 8s.

COWELL.—PRAKRITA-PRAKASA ; or, The Prakrit Grammar of Vararuchi, with the Commentary (Manorama) of Bhamaha ; the first complete Edition of the Original Text, with various Readings from a collection of Six MSS. in the Bodleian Library at Oxford, and the Libraries of the Royal Asiatic Society and the East India House ; with Copious Notes, an English Translation, and Index of Prakrit Words, to which is prefixed an Easy Introduction to Prakrit Grammar. By Edward Byles Cowell, of Magdalen Hall, Oxford, Professor of Sanskrit at Cambridge. New Edition, with New Preface, Additions, and Corrections. Second Issue. 8vo, pp. xxxi and 204, cloth. 1868. 14s.

COWELL.—A SHORT INTRODUCTION TO THE ORDINARY PRAKRIT OF THE SANSKRIT DRAMAS. With a List of Common Irregular Prakrit Words. By E B. Cowell, Professor of Sanskrit in the University of Cambridge, and Hon. LL.D. of the University of Edinburgh. Crown 8vo, pp. 40, limp cloth. 1875. 3s 6d.

COWELL.—THE SARVADARSANA SAMGRAHA. See Trübner's Oriental Series.

COWLEY.—POEMS. By Percy Tunnicliff Cowley. Demy 8vo, pp. 104, cloth. 1881. 5s.

CRAIG—THE IRISH LAND LABOUR QUESTION, Illustrated in the History of Ralahine and Co-operative Farming. By E T. Craig. Crown 8vo, pp. xii. and 202, cloth. 1882. 2s. 6d. Wrappers, 2s.

CRANBROOK.—CREDIBILIA , or, Discourses on Questions of Christian Faith. By the Rev. James Cranbrook, Edinburgh. Reissue. Post 8vo, pp iv. and 190, cloth. 1868. 3s. 6d.

CRANBROOK.—THE FOUNDERS OF CHRISTIANITY; or, Discourses upon the Origin of the Christian Religion. By the Rev. James Cranbrook, Edinburgh. Post 8vo, pp xii. and 324. 1868. 6s.

CRAVEN.—THE POPULAR DICTIONARY IN ENGLISH AND HINDUSTANI, AND HINDU-STANI AND ENGLISH. With a Number of Useful Tables Compiled by the Rev. T. Craven, M.A. 18mo, pp. 430, cloth. 1881. 3s. 6d.

CRAWFORD.—RECOLLECTIONS OF TRAVEL IN NEW ZEALAND AND AUSTRALIA. By James Coutts Crawford, F.G S , Resident Magistrate, Wellington, &c , &c With Maps and Illustrations. 8vo, pp. xvi. and 468, cloth. 1880. 18s.

CROSLAND.—APPARITIONS ; An Essay explanatory of Old Facts and a New Theory. To which are added Sketches and Adventures By Newton Crosland. Crown 8vo, pp viii. and 166, cloth. 1873. 2s. 6d.

CROSLAND —PITH : ESSAYS AND SKETCHES GRAVE AND GAY, with some Verses - and Illustrations. By Newton Crosland. Crown 8vo, pp. 310, cloth. 1881 5s.

CROSS.—HESPERIDES. The Occupations, Relaxations, and Aspirations of a Life. By Launcelot Cross, Author of "Characteristics of Leigh Hunt," "Brandon Tower," "Business," &c. Demy 8vo, pp. iv.–486, cloth. 1883. 10s. 6d.

CUBAS.—THE REPUBLIC OF MEXICO IN 1876. A Political and Ethnographical Division of the Population, Character, Habits, Costumes, and Vocations of its Inhabitants Written in Spanish by A G Cubas. Translated into English by G E Henderson. Illustrated with Plates of the Principal Types of the Ethnographic Families, and several Specimens of Popular Music. 8vo, pp. 130, cloth. 1881. 5s.

CUMMINS —A GRAMMAR OF THE OLD FRIESIC LANGUAGE. By A. H. Cummins, A M. Crown 8vo, pp. x. and 76, cloth. 1881. 3s 6d.

CUNNINGHAM —THE ANCIENT GEOGRAPHY OF INDIA. I. The Buddhist Period, including the Campaigns of Alexander and the Travels of Hwen-Thsang. By Alexander Cunningham, Major-General, Royal Engineers (Bengal Retired). With 13 Maps 8vo, pp xx and 590, cloth. 1870. £1, 8s.

CUNNINGHAM.—THE STUPA OF BHARHUT. A Buddhist Monument ornamented with numerous Sculptures illustrative of Buddhist Legend and History in the Third Century B.C By Alexander Cunningham, C S I., C I E , Maj -Gen., R.E. (B.R), Dir.-Gen. Archæol Survey of India. Royal 8vo, pp. viii. and 144, with 57 Plates, cloth. 1879. £3, 3s.

CUNNINGHAM.—ARCHÆOLOGICAL SURVEY OF INDIA. Reports from 1862-80. By A. Cunningham, C S I , C I E , Major-General, R E. (Bengal Retired), Director-General, Archæological Survey of India. With numerous Plates, cloth, Vols I - XII. 10s. each. (Except Vols. VII., VIII., and IX., and also Vols XIII., XIV., and XV., which are 12s. each)

CUSHMAN.—CHARLOTTE CUSHMAN · Her Letters and Memories of her Life. Edited by her friend, Emma Stebbins. Square 8vo, pp. viii. and 308, cloth. With Portrait and Illustrations. 1879 12s. 6d.

CUST.—LANGUAGES OF THE EAST INDIES. See Truhner's Oriental Series.

CUST.—LINGUISTIC AND ORIENTAL ESSAYS See Trubner's Oriental Series.

CUST.—PICTURES OF INDIAN LIFE, Sketched with the Pen from 1852 to 1881. By R. N. Cust, late I C S., Hon Sec. Royal Asiatic Society. Crown 8vo, pp. x. and 346, cloth. With Maps. 1881. 7s 6d.

DANA.—A TEXT-BOOK OF GEOLOGY, designed for Schools and Academies. By James D. Dana, LL.D., Professor of Geology, &c., at Yale College. Illustrated. Crown 8vo, pp. vi. and 354, cloth. 1876. 10s.

DANA.—MANUAL OF GEOLOGY, treating of the Principles of the Science, with special Reference to American Geological History ; for the use of Colleges, Academies, and Schools of Science. By James D Dana, LL.D. Illustrated by a Chart of the World, and over One Thousand Figures. 8vo, pp. xvi. and 800, and Chart, cl 21s.

DANA.—THE GEOLOGICAL STORY BRIEFLY TOLD. An Introduction to Geology for the General Reader and for Beginners in the Science. By J. D. Dana, LL.D. Illustrated. 12mo, pp. xii. and 264, cloth. 7s. 6d.

DANA.—A SYSTEM OF MINERALOGY. Descriptive Mineralogy. comprising the most Recent Discoveries. By J. D. Dana, aided by G. J. Brush. Fifth Edition, re-written and enlarged, and illustrated with upwards of 600 Woodcuts, with two Appendixes and Corrections. Royal 8vo, pp. xlviii. and 892, cloth. £2, 2s.

DANA.—A TEXT BOOK OF MINERALOGY. With an Extended Treatise on Crystallo-graphy and Physical Mineralogy. By E. S Dana, on the Plan and with the Co-operation of Professor J D. Dana Third Edition, revised. Over 800 Wood-cuts and 1 Coloured Plate. 8vo, pp. viii. and 486, cloth. 1879. 18s.

DANA.—MANUAL OF MINERALOGY AND LITHOLOGY , Containing the Elements of the Science of Minerals and Rocks, for the Use of the Practical Mineralogist and Geologist, and for Instruction in Schools and Colleges. By J. D. Dana. Fourth Edition, rearranged and rewritten. Illustrated by numerous Woodcuts Crown 8vo, pp. viii. and 474, cloth. 1882. 7s. 6d.

DATES AND DATA RELATING TO RELIGIOUS ANTHROPOLOGY AND BIBLICAL ARCHÆ-OLOGY. (Primæval Period.) 8vo, pp. viii. and 106, cloth. 1876 5s.

DAUDET.—LETTERS FROM MY MILL. From the French of Alphonse Daudet, by Mary Corey. Fcap. 8vo, pp. 160. 1880. Cloth, 3s.; boards, 2s

DAVIDS—BUDDHIST BIRTH STORIES. See Trübner's Oriental Series.

DAVIES.—HINDU PHILOSOPHY. 2 vols See Trübner's Oriental Series.

DAVIS—NARRATIVE OF THE NORTH POLAR EXPEDITION, U.S. SHIP *Polaris*, Cap-tain Charles Francis Hall Commanding Edited under the direction of the Hon. G M. Robeson, Secretary of the Navy, by Rear-Admiral C H Davis, U.S N Third Edition. With numerous Steel and Wood Engravings, Photolithographs, and Maps. 4to, pp. 696, cloth. 1881. £1, 8s

DAY.—THE PREHISTORIC USE OF IRON AND STEEL ; with Observations on certain matter ancillary thereto By St John V Day, C.E , F.R.S.E , &c. 8vo, pp. xxiv. and 278, cloth. 1877. 12s.

DE FLANDRE.—MONOGRAMS OF THREE OR MORE LETTERS, DESIGNED AND DRAWN ON STONE. By C De Flandre, F.S A. Scot., Edinburgh. With Indices, showing the place and style or period of every Monogram, and of each individual Letter. 4to, 42 Plates, cloth. 1880. Large paper, £7, 7s. , small paper, £3, 3s

DELBRUCK.—INTRODUCTION TO THE STUDY OF LANGUAGE: A Critical Survey of the History and Methods of Comparative Philology of the Indo-European Languages. By B. Delbrück. Authorised Translation, with a Preface by the Author 8vo, pp. 156, cloth 1882. 5s. Sewed, 4s.

DELEPIERRE.—HISTOIRE LITTÉRAIRE DES FOUS. Par Octave Delepierre. Crown 8vo, pp. 184, cloth. 1860. 5s.

DELEPIERRE.—MACARONEANA ANDRA ; overum Nouveaux Mélanges de Littérature Macaronique. Par Octave Delepierre. Small 4to, pp. 180, printed by Whitting-ham, and handsomely bound in the Roxburghe style. 1862. 10s. 6d.

DELEPIERRE.—ANALYSE DES TRAVAUX DE LA SOCIETE DES PHILOBIBLON DE LON-DRES. Par Octave Delepierre. Small 4to, pp viii. and 134, bound in the Rox-burghe style. 1862 10s 6d.

B

DELEPIERRE.—Revue Analytique des Ouvrages Écrits en Centons, depuis les Temps Anciens, jusqu'au xixième Siècle. Par un Bibliophile Belge. Small 4to, pp. 508, stiff covers. 1868 £1, 10s

DELEPIERRE—Tableau de la Littérature du Centon, chez les Anciens et chez les Modernes. Par Octave Delepierre. 2 vols, small 4to, pp. 324 and 318. Paper cover. 1875 £1, 1s.

DELEPIERRE—L'Enfer : Essai Philosophique et Historique sur les Légendes de la Vie Future. Par Octave Delepierre. Crown 8vo, pp. 160, paper wrapper. 1876 6s Only 250 copies printed

DENNYS—A Handbook of the Canton Vernacular of the Chinese Language. Being a Series of Introductory Lessons for Domestic and Business Purposes. By N. B. Dennys, M R A.S., &c. Royal 8vo, pp. iv. and 228, cloth 1874 30s.

DENNYS—A Handbook of Malay Colloquial, as spoken in Singapore, being a Series of Introductory Lessons for Domestic and Business Purposes. By N. B. Dennys, Ph D , F.R G S., M R.A.S. Impl 8vo, pp. vi. and 204, cloth. 1878. 21s.

DENNYS - The Folk-Lore of China, and its Affinities with that of the Aryan and Semitic Races. By N. B. Dennys, Ph D., F.R G.S., M.R.A.S. 8vo, pp 166, cloth. 1876. 10s 6d

DE VALDES—See Valdes.

DE VERE.—Studies in English ; or, Glimpses of the Inner Life of our Language. By M Schele de Vere, LL.D. 8vo, pp. vi. and 365, cloth 1867. 10s 6d.

DE VERE -Americanisms : The English of the New World. By M. Schele de Vere, LL.D. 8vo, pp. 685, cloth 1872 20s.

DE VINNE—The Invention of Printing. A Collection of Texts and Opinions. Description of Early Prints and Playing Cards, the Block-Books of the Fifteenth Century, the Legend of Lourens Janszoon Coster of Haarlem, and the Works of John Gutenberg and his Associates Illustrated with Fac-similes of Early Types and Woodcuts. By Theo L. De Vinne Second Edition In royal 8vo, elegantly printed, and bound in cloth, with embossed portraits, and a multitude of Fac-similes and Illustrations. 1877. £1, 1s.

DEWEY.—Classification and Subject Index for cataloguing and arranging the books and pamphlets of a Library. By Melvil Dewey. 8vo, pp 42, boards. 1876. 5s.

DICKSON.—Who was Scotland's First Printer ? Ane Compendious and breue Tractate, in Commendation of Andrew Myllar. Compylit be Robert Dickson, F.S.A. Scot. Fcap. 8vo, pp 24, parchment wrapper. 1881. 1s.

DOBSON—Monograph of the Asiatic Chiroptera, and Catalogue of the Species of Bats in the Collection of the Indian Museum, Calcutta. By G. E. Dobson, M.A., M.B., F.L.S., &c. 8vo, pp. viii and 228, cloth. 1876. 12s.

D'ORSEY.—A Practical Grammar of Portuguese and English, exhibiting in a Series of Exercises, in Double Translation, the Idiomatic Structure of both Languages, as now written and spoken. Adapted to Ollendorff's System by the Rev. Alexander J. D. D'Orsey, of Corpus Christi College, Cambridge, and Lecturer on Public Reading and Speaking at King's College, London. Third Edition. 12mo, pp. viii. and 298, cloth. 1868. 7s

D'ORSEY.—Colloquial Portuguese ; or, Words and Phrases of Every-day Life. Compiled from Dictation and Conversation. For the Use of English Tourists in Portugal, Brazil, Madeira, &c By the Rev A. J D D'Orsey. Third Edition, enlarged. 12mo, pp. viii. and 126, cloth. 1868. 3s. 6d.

DOUGLAS —CHINESE-ENGLISH DICTIONARY OF THE VERNACULAR OR SPOKEN LAN-GUAGE OF AMOY, with the principal variations of the Chang-Chew and Chin-Chew Dialects. By the Rev. Carstairs Douglas, M A., LL D , Glasg., Missionary of the Presbyterian Church in England. High quarto, double columns, pp 632, cloth. 1873 £3, 3s.

DOUGLAS.—CHINESE LANGUAGE AND LITERATURE Two Lectures delivered at the Royal Institution, by R. K. Douglas, of the British Museum, and Professor of Chinese at King's College. Crown 8vo, pp 118, cloth. 1875. 5s.

DOUGLAS —THE LIFE OF JENGHIZ KHAN. Translated from the Chinese. With an Introduction. By Robert K. Douglas, of the British Museum, and Professor of Chinese at King's College Crown 8vo, pp xxxvi and 106, cloth. 1877. 5s

DOUSE.—GRIMM'S LAW. A Study ; or, Hints towards an Explanation of the so-called "Lautverschiebung ;" to which are added some Remarks on the Primitive Indo-European K, and several Appendices By T. Le Marchant Douse. 8vo, pp. xvi. and 232, cloth 1876. 10s. 6d

DOWSON —DICTIONARY OF HINDU MYTHOLOGY, &c. See Trubner's Oriental Series.

DOWSON.—A GRAMMAR OF THE URDŪ OR HINDŪSTĀNĪ LANGUAGE. By John Dowson, M R A S., Professor of Hindūstānī, Staff College, Sandhurst. Crown 8vo, pp. xvi. and 264, with 8 Plates, cloth. 1872. 10s. 6d

DOWSON.—A HINDŪSTĀNĪ EXERCISE BOOK ; containing a Series of Passages and Extracts adapted for Translation into Hindūstānī. By John Dowson, M. R A S., Professor of Hindūstānī, Staff College, Sandhurst. Crown 8vo, pp. 100, limp cloth. 1872. 2s. 6d.

DUNCAN —GEOGRAPHY OF INDIA, comprising a Descriptive Outline of all India, and a Detailed Geographical, Commercial, Social, and Political Account of each of its Provinces. With Historical Notes By George Duncan. Tenth Edition (Revised and Corrected to date from the latest Official Information). 18mo, pp. viii. and 182, limp cloth 1880. 1s. 6d.

DUSAR.—A GRAMMAR OF THE GERMAN LANGUAGE, with Exercises. By P Friedrich Dusar, First German Master in the Military Department of Cheltenham College. Second Edition. Crown 8vo, pp viii. and 208, cloth. 1879. 4s. 6d.

EARLY ENGLISH TEXT SOCIETY —Subscription, one guinea per annum. *Extra Series.* Subscriptions—Small paper, one guinea, large paper, two guineas, per annum. List of publications on application.

EASTWICK.—KHIRAD AFROZ (the Illuminator of the Understanding). By Maulaví Hafizu'd-dín A New Edition of the Hindūstānī Text, carefully revised with Notes, Critical and Explanatory By Edward B Eastwick, F.R.S , F.S.A., M R A.S , Professor of Hindūstānī at Haileybury College. Imperial 8vo, pp. xiv. and 319, cloth. Reissue, 1867. 18s.

EASTWICK.—THE GULISTAN. See Trubner's Oriental Series.

EBERS.—THE EMPEROR A Romance By Georg Ebers. Translated from the German by Clara Bell. In two volumes, 16mo, pp iv. 319 and 322, cloth 1881 7s. 6d.

EBERS —A QUESTION : The Idyl of a Picture by his friend, Alma Tadema Related by Georg Ebers. From the German, by Mary J SAFFORD 16mo, pp. 125, with Frontispiece, cloth. 1881. 4s

ECHO (DEUTSCHES). THE GERMAN ECHO. A Faithful Mirror of German Conver-sation. By Ludwig Wolfram. With a Vocabulary. By Henry P Skelton. Post 8vo, pp. 130 and 70, cloth. 1863. 3s.

ECHO FRANÇAIS. A Practical Guide to Conversation.   By Fr. de la Fruston. With a complete Vocabulary   By Anthony Maw Border.   Post 8vo, pp. 120 and 72, cloth.   1860.   3s.

ECO ITALIANO (L'). A Practical Guide to Italian Conversation   By Eugene Camerini.   With a complete Vocabulary.   By Henry P. Skelton.   Post 8vo, pp. vi., 128, and 98, cloth   1860   4s. 6d.

ECO DE MADRID.   The Echo of Madrid   A Practical Guide to Spanish Conversation.   By J. E. Hartzenbusch and Henry Lemming.   With a complete Vocabulary, containing copious Explanatory Remarks.   By Henry Lemming. Post 8vo, pp. xii , 144, and 83, cloth   1860.   5s

EDDA SÆMUNDAR HINNS FRODA.   The Edda of Sæmund the Learned.   Translated from the Old Norse, by Benjamin Thorpe   Complete in 1 vol. fcap. 8vo, pp. viii. and 152, and pp viii. and 170, cloth   1866.   7s 6d

EDKINS.—China's Place in Philology.   An attempt to show that the Languages of Europe and Asia have a common origin   By the Rev. Joseph Edkins.   Crown 8vo, pp. xxiii. and 403, cloth   1871   10s 6d

EDKINS—Introduction to the Study of the Chinese Characters.   By J. Edkins, D D , Peking, China   Royal 8vo, pp. 340, paper boards.   1876.   18s.

EDKINS—Religion in China.   See English and Foreign Philosophical Library, Vol XIII.

EDKINS.—Chinese Buddhism   See Trubner's Oriental Series

EDWARDS—Memoirs of Libraries, together with a Practical Handbook of Library Economy.   By Edward Edwards.   Numerous Illustrations   2 vols royal 8vo, cloth. Vol I. pp. xxviii. and 841 ; Vol. ii pp. xxxvi. and 1104.   1859   £2, 8s.
    Ditto, large paper, imperial 8vo, cloth.   £4, 4s

EDWARDS—Chapters of the Biographical History of the French Academy. 1629–1863   With an Appendix relating to the Unpublished Chronicle "Liber de Hyda."   By Edward Edwards   8vo, pp. 180, cloth   1864.   6s
    Ditto, large paper, royal 8vo.   10s 6d.

EDWARDS.—Libraries and Founders of Libraries.   By Edward Edwards   8vo. pp. xix. and 506, cloth.   1865.   18s.
    Ditto, large paper, imperial 8vo, cloth.   £1, 10s.

EDWARDS.—Free Town Libraries, their Formation, Management, and History in Britain, France, Germany, and America.   Together with Brief Notices of Book Collectors, and of the respective Places of Deposit of their Surviving Collections By Edward Edwards   8vo, pp. xvi. and 634, cloth   1869.   21s

EDWARDS.—Lives of the Founders of the British Museum, with Notices of its Chief Augmentors and other Benefactors.   1570–1870.   By Edward Edwards. With Illustrations and Plans.   2 vols 8vo, pp. xii. and 780, cloth.   1870   30s

EDWARDES.—See English and Foreign Philosophical Library, Vol XVII.

EGER AND GRIME—An Early English Romance.   Edited from Bishop Percy's Folio Manuscripts, about 1650 A.D   By John W. Hales, M A., Fellow and late Assistant Tutor of Christ's College, Cambridge, and Frederick J Furnivall, M A., of Trinity Hall, Cambridge   4to, large paper, half bound, Roxburghe style, pp. 64   1867.   10s. 6d.

EGGELING.—See Auctores Sanskriti, Vols. IV. and V.

EGYPTIAN GENERAL STAFF PUBLICATIONS —
    Provinces of the Equator · Summary of Letters and Reports of the Governor-General.   Part 1.   1874.   Royal 8vo, pp. viii. and 90, stitched, with Map. 1877.   5s

EGYPTIAN GENERAL STAFF PUBLICATIONS—*cont,nued*.

GENERAL REPORT ON THE PROVINCE OF KORDOFAN. Submitted to General C. P. Stone, Chief of the General Staff Egyptian Army. By Major H G Prout, Corps of Engineers, Commanding Expedition of Reconnaissance. Made at El-Obeiyad (Kordofan), March 12th, 1876. Royal 8vo, pp. 232, stitched, with 6 Maps. 1877. 10s. 6d

REPORT ON THE SEIZURE BY THE ABYSSINIANS of the Geological and Mineralogical Reconnaissance Expedition attached to the General Staff of the Egyptian Army. By L. H. Mitchell, Chief of the Expedition. Containing an Account of the subsequent Treatment of the Prisoners and Final Release of the Commander Royal 8vo, pp. xii and 126, stitched, with a Map 1878. 7s. 6d.

EGYPTIAN CALENDAR for the year 1295 A.H. (1878 A.D.) : Corresponding with the years 1594, 1595 of the Koptic Era 8vo, pp 98, sewed 1878. 2s 6d.

EHRLICH.—FRENCH READER : With Notes and Vocabulary. By H. W. Ehrlich. 12mo, pp. viii and 125, limp cloth 1877 1s 6d.

EITEL.—BUDDHISM : Its Historical, Theoretical, and Popular Aspects. In Three Lectures. By E. J. Eitel, M.A., Ph.D. Second Edition. Demy 8vo, pp. 130. 1873. 5s.

EITEL.—FENG-SHUI ; or, The Rudiments of Natural Science in China. By E. J. Eitel, M A , Ph.D. Royal 8vo, pp. vi. and 84, sewed. 1873. 6s.

EITEL—HANDBOOK FOR THE STUDENT OF CHINESE BUDDHISM. By the Rev. E. J. Eitel, of the London Missionary Society Crown 8vo, pp. viii and 224, cloth. 1870 18s.

ELLIOT.—MEMOIRS ON THE HISTORY, FOLK-LORE, AND DISTRIBUTION OF THE RACES OF THE NORTH-WESTERN PROVINCES OF INDIA By the late Sir Henry M. Elliot, K C.B. Edited, revised, and rearranged by John Beames, M.R.A.S , &c., &c. In 2 vols. demy 8vo, pp xx., 370, and 396, with 3 large coloured folding Maps, cloth. 1869. £1, 16s.

ELLIOT.—THE HISTORY OF INDIA, as told by its own Historians. The Muhammadan Period. Edited from the Posthumous Papers of the late Sir H. M. Elliot, K.C.B., East India Company's Bengal Civil Service Revised and continued by Professor John Dowson, M.R.A.S., Staff College, Sandhurst. 8vo. Vol. I. o.p.—Vol. II., pp. x. and 580, cloth. 18s—Vol III , pp. xii. and 627, cloth. 24s.—Vol IV., pp xii. and 564, cloth. 1872. 21s.—Vol. V., pp. x. and 576, cloth. 1873. 21s.—Vol. VI , pp. viii. 574, cloth. 21s.—Vol. VII., pp. viii.-574. 1877. 21s. Vol. VIII , pp xxxii.-444. With Biographical, Geographical, and General Index. 1877. 24s

ELLIS—ETRUSCAN NUMERALS. By Robert Ellis, B.D , late Fellow of St. John's College, Cambridge. 8vo, pp. 52, sewed. 1876. 2s. 6d.

ENGLISH DIALECT SOCIETY.—Subscription, 10s. 6d. per annum. List of publications on application.

ENGLISH AND FOREIGN PHILOSOPHICAL LIBRARY (THE).
Post 8vo, cloth, uniformly bound.

I to III.—A HISTORY OF MATERIALISM, and Criticism of its present Importance. By Professor F A. Lange. Authorised Translation from the German by Ernest C. Thomas In three volumes. Vol. I. Second Edition. pp. 350. 1878. 10s. 6d.—Vol II , pp. viii and 398. 1880. 10s 6d —Vol. III , pp. viii and 376. 1881. 10s. 6d.

IV.—NATURAL LAW : an Essay in Ethics. By Edith Simcox Second Edition Pp. 366. 1878 10s. 6d.

V and VI.—THE CREED OF CHRISTENDOM , its Foundations contrasted with Superstructure. By W. R. Greg. Eighth Edition, with a New Introduction. In two volumes, pp. 280 and 290. 1883. 15s.

ENGLISH AND FOREIGN PHILOSOPHICAL LIBRARY—*continued.*

VII.—OUTLINES OF THE HISTORY OF RELIGION TO THE SPREAD OF THE UNIVERSAL RELIGIONS. By Prof. C. P. Tiele. Translated from the Dutch by J Estlin Carpenter, M.A., with the author's assistance. Second Edition. Pp xx. and 250 1880. 7s. 6d.

VIII —RELIGION IN CHINA; containing a brief Account of the Three Religions of the Chinese; with Observations on the Prospects of Christian Conversion amongst that People By Joseph Edkins, D.D., Peking. Second Edition. Pp. xvi. and 260 1878. 7s 6d.

IX.—A CANDID EXAMINATION OF THEISM. By Physicus. Pp. 216. 1878. 7s. 6d.

X.—THE COLOUR-SENSE, its Origin and Development, an Essay in Comparative Psychology By Grant Allen, B A, author of "Physiological Æsthetics." Pp xii. and 282. 1879. 10s. 6d

XI —THE PHILOSOPHY OF MUSIC; being the substance of a Course of Lectures delivered at the Royal Institution of Great Britain in February and March 1877. By William Pole, F.R S., F.R S.E., Mus Doc., Oxon. Pp 336 1879 10s 6d.

XII.—CONTRIBUTIONS TO THE HISTORY OF THE DEVELOPMENT OF THE HUMAN RACE: Lectures and Dissertations, by Lazarus Geiger Translated from the Second German Edition, by David Asher, Ph.D. Pp. x. and 156. 1880. 6s.

XIII.—DR APPLETON : his Life and Literary Relics. By J H. Appleton, M.A., and A. H Sayce, M A Pp. 350 1881. 10s 6d

XIV —EDGAR QUINET: His Early Life and Writings. By Richard Heath. With Portraits, Illustrations, and an Autograph Letter. Pp. xxiii. and 370. 1881. 12s. 6d.

XV.—THE ESSENCE OF CHRISTIANITY By Ludwig Feuerbach. Translated from the Second German Edition by Marian Evans, translator of Strauss's "Life of Jesus" Second English Edition. Pp xx. and 340. 1881. 7s 6d

XVI.—AUGUSTE COMTE AND POSITIVISM. By the late John Stuart Mill, M.P. Third Edition Pp 200 1882. 3s 6d.

XVII.—ESSAYS AND DIALOGUES OF GIACOMO LEOPARDI. Translated by Charles Edwardes. With Biographical Sketch Pp. xliv and 216. 1882. 7s. 6d.

XVIII —RELIGION AND PHILOSOPHY IN GERMANY : A Fragment. By Heinrich Heine. Translated by J Snodgrass. Pp. xii. and 178, cloth. 1882 6s

XIX.—EMERSON AT HOME AND ABROAD By M. D Conway. Pp. viii. and 310 With Portrait 1883. 10s. 6d.

XX.—ENIGMAS OF LIFE. By W. R. Greg. Fifteenth Edition, with a Postscript CONTENTS Realisable Ideals—Malthus Notwithstanding—Non-Survival of the Fittest—Limits and Directions of Human Development—The Significance of Life—De Profundis—Elsewhere—Appendix. Pp xx. and 314, cloth. 1883 10s. 6d.

XXI.—ETHIC DEMONSTRATED IN GEOMETRICAL ORDER AND DIVIDED INTO FIVE PARTS, which treat (1) Of God, (2) Of the Nature and Origin of the Mind, (3) Of the Origin and Nature of the Affects, (4) Of Human Bondage, or of the Strength of the Affects, (5) Of the Power of the Intellect, or of Human Liberty By Benedict de Spinoza Translated from the Latin by William Hale White. Pp. 328. 1883 10s 6d.

Extra Series.

I. and II.—LESSING . His Life and Writings By James Sime, M A Second Edition 2 vols, pp xxii. and 328, and xvi. and 358, with portraits. 1879 21s.

ENGLISH AND FOREIGN PHILOSOPHICAL LIBRARY—*continued.*

III.—AN ACCOUNT OF THE POLYNESIAN RACE. its Origin and Migrations, and the Ancient History of the Hawaiian People to the Times of Kamehameha I. By Abraham Fornander, Circuit Judge of the Island of Maui, H I   Vol I., pp. xvi. and 248   1877.   7s 6d

IV. and V.—ORIENTAL RELIGIONS, and their Relation to Universal Religion—India. By Samuel Johnson. In 2 vols., pp viii and 408; viii. and 402   1879.   21s.

VI.—AN ACCOUNT OF THE POLYNESIAN RACE: its Origin and Migration, and the Ancient History of the Hawaiian People to the Times of Kamehameha I. By Abraham Fornander, Circuit Judge of the Island of Maui, H.I. Vol II., pp. viii. and 400, cloth. 1880.   10s. 6d.

ETHERINGTON.—THE STUDENT'S GRAMMAR OF THE HINDÍ LANGUAGE   By the Rev. W. Etherington, Missionary, Benares.   Second Edition.   Crown 8vo, pp. xiv., 255, and xiii., cloth.   1873.   12s.

EYTON —DOMESDAY STUDIES   AN ANALYSIS AND DIGEST OF THE STAFFORDSHIRE SURVEY.   Treating of the Method of Domesday in its Relation to Staffordshire, &c., with Tables, Notes, &c.   By the Rev. Robert W Eyton, late Rector of Ryton, Salop.   4to, pp vii and 135, cloth.   1881.   £1, 1s.

FABER.—THE MIND OF MENCIUS.   See Trubner's Oriental Series.

FALKE.—ART IN THE HOUSE.   Historical, Critical, and Æsthetical Studies on the Decoration and Furnishing of the Dwelling.   By Jacob von Falke, Vice-Director of the Austrian Museum of Art and Industry at Vienna.   Translated from the German   Edited, with Notes, by Charles C. Perkins, M.A   Royal 8vo, pp xxx. 356, cloth.   With Coloured Frontispiece, 60 Plates, and over 150 Illustrations in the Text.   1878.   £3.

FARLEY.—EGYPT, CYPRUS, AND ASIATIC TURKEY.   By J. Lewis Farley, author of "The Resources of Turkey," &c.   8vo, pp. xvi. and 270, cloth gilt.   1878.   10s. 6d.

FEATHERMAN.—THE SOCIAL HISTORY OF THE RACES OF MANKIND.   Vol V. THE ARAMÆANS.   By A. Featherman.   Demy 8vo, pp. xvii. and 664, cloth.   1881.   £1, 1s.

FENTON.—EARLY HEBREW LIFE: a Study in Sociology.   By John Fenton.   8vo, pp. xxiv. and 102, cloth.   1880   5s

FERGUSON AND BURGESS —THE CAVE TEMPLES OF INDIA   By James Ferguson, D C.L., F.R.S., and James Burgess, F.R.G.S.   Impl 8vo, pp xx and 536, with 98 Plates, half bound.   1880.   £2, 2s.

FERGUSSON.—CHINESE RESEARCHES.   First Part.   Chinese Chronology and Cycles.   By Thomas Fergusson, Member of the North China Branch of the Royal Asiatic Society.   Crown 8vo, pp. viii. and 274, sewed.   1881.   10s. 6d.

FEUERBACH.—THE ESSENCE OF CHRISTIANITY.   By Ludwig Feuerbach.   Translated from the Second German Edition by Marian Evans, translator of Strauss's "Life of Jesus."   Second English Edition.   Post 8vo, pp. xx. and 340, cloth.   1881.   7s. 6d.

FICHTE.—J. G. FICHTE'S POPULAR WORKS : The Nature of the Scholar—The Vocation of Man—The Doctrine of Religion   With a Memoir by William Smith, LL D.   Demy 8vo, pp. viii and 564, cloth.   1873.   15s.

FICHTE.—THE CHARACTERISTICS OF THE PRESENT AGE.   By Johann Gottlieb Fichte.   Translated from the German by William Smith.   Post 8vo, pp. xi. and 271, cloth.   1847.   6s.

FICHTE.—MEMOIR OF JOHANN GOTTLIEB FICHTE.   By William Smith.   Second Edition.   Post 8vo, pp. 168, cloth.   1848.   4s.

FICHTE —ON THE NATURE OF THE SCHOLAR, AND ITS MANIFESTATIONS. By Johann Gottlieb Fichte Translated from the German by William Smith. Second Edition Post 8vo, pp. vii. and 131, cloth. 1848. 3s.

FICHTE —THE SCIENCE OF KNOWLEDGE. By J G. Fichte. Translated from the German by A. E. Kroeger. Crown 8vo, pp 378, cloth 1868 10s

FICHTE.—THE SCIENCE OF RIGHTS. By J G Fichte Translated from the German by A. E. Kroeger. Crown 8vo, pp. 506, cloth. 1869. 10s.

FICHTE —NEW EXPOSITION OF THE SCIENCE OF KNOWLEDGE By J. G Fichte. Translated from the German by A. E. Kroeger 8vo, pp vi and 182, cloth. 1869. 6s.

FIELD.—OUTLINES OF AN INTERNATIONAL CODE By David Dudley Field Second Edition. Royal 8vo, pp iii and 712, sheep. 1876. £2, 2s

FIGANIERE —ELVA : A STORY OF THE DARK AGES By Viscount de Figanière, G.C. St Anne, &c. Crown 8vo, pp viii and 194, cloth. 1878. 5s.

FISCHEL.—SPECIMENS OF MODERN GERMAN PROSE AND POETRY, with Notes, Grammatical, Historical, and Idiomatical To which is added a Short Sketch of the History of German Literature. By Dr M. M. Fischel, formerly of Queen's College, Harley Street, and late German Master to the Stockwell Grammar School Crown 8vo, pp. viii. and 280, cloth. 1880. 4s

FISKE.—THE UNSEEN WORLD, and other Essays. By John Fiske, M.A., LL B. Crown 8vo, pp 350. 1876. 10s.

FISKE.—MYTHS AND MYTH-MAKERS, Old Tales and Superstitions, interpreted by Comparative Mythology. By John Fiske, M.A., LL B., Assistant Librarian, and late Lecturer on Philosophy at Harvard University. Crown 8vo, pp. 260, cloth. 1873. 10s. 6d.

FITZGERALD —AUSTRALIAN ORCHIDS By R D Fitzgerald, F.L S Folio —Part I. 7 Plates —Part II. 10 Plates —Part III. 10 Plates.—Part IV. 10 Plates.— Part V. 10 Plates.—Part VI 10 Plates Each Part, Coloured 21s ; Plain, 10s. 6d

FITZGERALD.—AN ESSAY ON THE PHILOSOPHY OF SELF-CONSCIOUSNESS. Comprising an Analysis of Reason and the Rationale of Love By P F. Fitzgerald. Demy 8vo, pp. xvi and 196, cloth. 1882. 5s

FORJETT —EXTERNAL EVIDENCES OF CHRISTIANITY. By E. H. Forjett 8vo, pp. 114, cloth. 1874. 2s 6d

FORNANDER —THE POLYNESIAN RACE. See English and Foreign Philosophical Library, Extra Series, Vols. III. and VI.

FORSTER —POLITICAL PRESENTMENTS —By William Forster, Agent-General for New South Wales. Crown 8vo, pp. 122, cloth 1878. 4s 6d

FOULKES —THE DAYA BHAGA, the Law of Inheritance of the Sarasvati Vilasa. The Original Sanskrit Text, with Translation by the Rev Thos Foulkes, F.L S., M R.A.S , F R G S., Fellow of the University of Madras, &c Demy 8vo, pp. xxvi. and 194–162, cloth. 1881. 10s. 6d.

FOX —MEMORIAL EDITION OF COLLECTED WORKS, by W. J. Fox. 12 vols 8vo, cloth. £3.

FRANKLYN —OUTLINES OF MILITARY LAW, AND THE LAWS OF EVIDENCE. By H. B. Franklyn, LL.B. Crown 16mo, pp viii. and 152, cloth. 1874. 3s. 6d.

FREEMAN.—LECTURES TO AMERICAN AUDIENCES By E. A Freeman, D.C.L., LL.D , Honorary Fellow of Trinity College, Oxford. I The English People in its Three Homes II. The Practical Bearings of General European History. Post 8vo, pp. viii -454, cloth. 1883. 8s. 6d.

FRIEDRICH —PROGRESSIVE GERMAN READER, with Copious Notes to the First Part. By P. Friedrich. Crown 8vo, pp. 166, cloth. 1868. 4s. 6d.

FRIEDRICH —A GRAMMATICAL COURSE OF THE GERMAN LANGUAGE. By P. Friedrich. Second Edition. Crown 8vo, pp viii. and 102, cloth 1877 3s. 6d.

FRIEDRICH.—A GRAMMAR OF THE GERMAN LANGUAGE, WITH EXERCISES. See under DUSAR.

FRIEDERICI —BIBLIOTHECA ORIENTALIS, or a Complete List of Books, Papers, Serials, and Essays, published in England and the Colonies, Germany and France; on the History, Geography, Religions, Antiquities, Literature, and Languages of the East Compiled by Charles Friederici 8vo, boards 1876, pp. 86, 2s 6d. 1877, pp. 100, 3s. 1878, pp. 112, 3s. 6d. 1879, 3s. 1880, 3s

FRŒMBLING.—GRADUATED GERMAN READER. Consisting of a Selection from the most Popular Writers, arranged progressively; with a complete Vocabulary for the first part By Friedrich Otto Frœmbling Eighth Edition. 12mo, pp. viii and 306, cloth. 1883. 3s. 6d.

FRŒMBLING —GRADUATED EXERCISES FOR TRANSLATION INTO GERMAN. Consisting of Extracts from the best English Authors, arranged progressively; with an Appendix, containing Idiomatic Notes By Friedrich Otto Frœmbling, Ph.D., Principal German Master at the City of London School Crown 8vo, pp. xiv. and 322, cloth With Notes, pp. 66. 1867. 4s 6d. Without Notes, 4s.

FROUDE —THE BOOK OF JOB. By J. A Froude, M.A , late Fellow of Exeter College, Oxford. Reprinted from the *Westminster Review.* 8vo, pp 38, cloth. 1s.

FRUSTON.—ECHO FRANÇAIS. A Practical Guide to French Conversation. By F. de la Fruston. With a Vocabulary. 12mo, pp. vi and 192, cloth 3s.

FRYER.—THE KHYENG PEOPLE OF THE SANDOWAY DISTRICT, ARAKAN. By G. E. Fryer, Major, M.S C., Deputy Commissioner, Sandoway. With 2 Plates 8vo, pp. 44, cloth. 1875. 3s 6d

FRYER.—PÁLI STUDIES. No. I Analysis, and Páli Text of the Subodhálankara, or Easy Rhetoric, by Sangharakkhita Thera 8vo, pp. 35, cloth. 1875. 3s. 6d.

FURNIVALL.—EDUCATION IN EARLY ENGLAND. Some Notes used as forewords to a Collection of Treatises on "Manners and Meals in Olden Times,' for the Early English Text Society. By Frederick J. Furnivall, M.A. 8vo, pp. 4 and lxxiv., sewed 1867. 1s.

GALDOS —MARIANELA. By B. Perez Galdos From the Spanish, by Clara Bell. 16mo, pp. 264, cloth. 1883. 4s.

GALDOS.—GLORIA : A Novel. By B. Perez Galdos From the Spanish, by Clara Bell. Two volumes, 16mo, pp vi. and 318, iv. and 362, cloth 1883. 7s. 6d

GALLOWAY.—A TREATISE ON FUEL. Scientific and Practical By Robert Galloway, M R I A., F C S , &c. With Illustrations. Post 8vo, pp. x. and 136, cloth. 1880. 6s.

GALLOWAY —EDUCATION : SCIENTIFIC AND TECHNICAL; or, How the Inductive Sciences are Taught, and How they Ought to be Taught By Robert Galloway, M.R.I.A., F.C S. 8vo, pp. xvi. and 462, cloth. 1881. 10s. 6d.

GAMBLE.—A MANUAL OF INDIAN TIMBERS : An Account of the Structure, Growth, Distribution, and Qualities of Indian Woods. By J. C. Gamble, M A., F.L S 8vo, pp. xxx. and 522, with a Map, cloth. 1881. 10s.

GARBE.—See AUCTORES SANSKRITI, Vol. III.

GARFIELD.—THE LIFE AND PUBLIC SERVICE OF JAMES A. GARFIELD, Twentieth President of the United States. A Biographical Sketch. By Captain F. H. Mason, late of the 42d Regiment, U S.A. With a Preface by Bret Harte. Crown 8vo. pp. vi. and 134, cloth. With Portrait. 1881. 2s. 6d.

GARRETT.—A CLASSICAL DICTIONARY OF INDIA : Illustrative of the Mythology, Philosophy, Literature, Antiquities, Arts, Manners, Customs, &c., of the Hindus. By John Garrett, Director of Public Instruction in Mysore 8vo, pp. x. and 794, cloth. With Supplement, pp. 160. 1871 and 1873. £1, 16s.

GAUTAMA.—The Institutes of. See Auctores Sanskriti, Vol. II.

GAZETTEER of the Central Provinces of India. Edited by Charles Grant, Secretary to the Chief Commissioner of the Central Provinces Second Edition. With a very large folding Map of the Central Provinces of India. Demy 8vo, pp. clvii. and 582, cloth. 1870 £1, 4s.

GEIGER.—A Peep at Mexico ; Narrative of a Journey across the Republic from the Pacific to the Gulf, in December 1873 and January 1874 By J. L. Geiger, F.R.G.S. Demy 8vo, pp. 368, with Maps and 45 Original Photographs. Cloth, 24s.

GEIGER.—Contributions to the History of the Development of the Human Race : Lectures and Dissertations, by Lazarus Geiger Translated from the Second German Edition, by David Asher, Ph.D. Post 8vo, pp x.–156, cloth. 1880. 6s.

GELDART.—Faith and Freedom. Fourteen Sermons. By E M. Geldart, M.A. Crown 8vo, pp vi. and 168, cloth. 1881. 4s. 6d.

GELDART—A Guide to Modern Greek By E. M. Geldart, M.A. Post 8vo, pp. xii and 274, cloth. 1883. 7s. 6d. Key, pp. 28, cloth. 1883. 2s 6d.

GELDART.—Greek Grammar See Trubner's Collection

GEOLOGICAL MAGAZINE (The) . or, Monthly Journal of Geology. With which is incorporated "The Geologist" Edited by Henry Woodward, LL D., F R S., F G S , &c., of the British Museum Assisted by Professor John Morris, M.A., F G.S , &c , and Robert Etheridge, F R S., L. & E , F.G S , &c., of the Museum of Practical Geology. 8vo, cloth. 1866 to 1882. 20s. each.

GHOSE—The Modern History of the Indian Chiefs, Rajas, Zamindars, &c By Loke Nath Ghose. 2 vols. post 8vo, pp. xii and 218, and xviii. and 612, cloth 1883. 21s

GILES.—Chinese Sketches —By Herbert A. Giles, of H.B M.'s China Consular Service. 8vo, pp 204, cloth. 1875. 10s. 6d.

GILES—A Dictionary of Colloquial Idioms in the Mandarin Dialect. By Herbert A. Giles 4to, pp. 65, half bound. 1873 28s.

GILES.—Synoptical Studies in Chinese Character. By Herbert A. Giles 8vo, pp 118, half bound. 1874. 15s.

GILES.—Chinese without a Teacher Being a Collection of Easy and Useful Sentences in the Mandarin Dialect With a Vocabulary. By Herbert A. Giles. 12mo, pp. 60, half bound. 1872 5s.

GILES.—The San Tzu Ching , or, Three Character Classic ; and the Ch'Jen Tsu Wen ; or, Thousand Character Essay Metrically Translated by Herbert A Giles. 12mo, pp. 28, half bound 1873. 2s. 6d.

GLASS.—Advance Thought. By Charles E Glass. Crown 8vo, pp. xxxvi. and 188, cloth. 1876 6s.

GOETHE'S Faust.—See Scoones and Wysard.

GOETHE'S Minor Poems.—See Selss.

GOLDSTÜCKER.—A Dictionary, Sanskrit and English, extended and improved from the Second Edition of the Dictionary of Professor H H. Wilson, with his sanction and concurrence. Together with a Supplement, Grammatical Appendices, and an Index, serving as a Sanskrit-English Vocabulary. By Theodore Goldstucker. Parts I. to VI. 4to, pp. 400. 1856–63. 6s. each.

GOLDSTÜCKER.—See AUCTORES SANSKRITI, Vol. I.

GOOROO SIMPLE. Strange Surprising Adventures of the Venerable G. S and his Five Disciples, Noodle, Doodle, Wiseacre, Zany, and Foozle : adorned with Fifty Illustrations, drawn on wood, by Alfred Crowquill. A companion Volume to "Munchhausen" and "Owlglass," based upon the famous Tamul tale of the Gooroo Paramartan, and exhibiting, in the form of a skilfully-constructed consecutive narrative, some of the finest specimens of Eastern wit and humour. Elegantly printed on tinted paper, in crown 8vo, pp. 223, richly gilt ornamental cover, gilt edges. 1861. 10s 6d.

GORKOM —HANDBOOK OF CINCHONA CULTURE. By K. W. Van Gorkom, formerly Director of the Government Cinchona Plantations in Java Translated by B. D. Jackson, Secretary of the Linnæan Society of London. With a Coloured Illustration. Imperial 8vo, pp. xii. and 292, cloth. 1882. £2.

GOUGH —The SARVA-DARSANA-SAMGRAHA. See Trubner's Oriental Series.

GOUGH.—PHILOSOPHY OF THE UPANISHADS. See Trubner's Oriental Series.

GOVER —THE FOLK-SONGS OF SOUTHERN INDIA. By C E Gover, Madras. Contents : Canarese Songs , Badaga Songs ; Coorg Songs ; Tamil Songs ; The Cural ; Malayalam Songs , Telugu Songs. 8vo, pp xxviii. and 300, cloth. 1872. 10s. 6d.

GRAY —DARWINIANA : Essays and Reviews pertaining to Darwinism By Asa Gray. Crown 8vo, pp. xii. and 396, cloth. 1877. 10s.

GRAY.—NATURAL SCIENCE AND RELIGION : Two Lectures Delivered to the Theological School of Yale College. By Asa Gray. Crown 8vo, pp 112, cloth. 1880 5s.

GREEN.—SHAKESPEARE AND THE EMBLEM-WRITERS . An Exposition of their Similarities of Thought and Expression. Preceded by a View of the Emblem-Book Literature down to A.D. 1616. By Henry Green, M.A. In one volume, pp xvi. 572, profusely illustrated with Woodcuts and Photolith. Plates, elegantly bound in cloth gilt, 1870. Large medium 8vo, £1, 11s. 6d. ; large imperial 8vo. £2, 12s. 6d.

GREEN.—ANDREA ALCIATI, and his Books of Emblems : A Biographical and Bibliographical Study. By Henry Green, M.A. With Ornamental Title, Portraits, and other Illustrations. Dedicated to Sir William Stirling-Maxwell, Bart , Rector of the University of Edinburgh. Only 250 copies printed. Demy 8vo, pp. 360, handsomely bound. 1872. £1, 1s.

GREENE.—A NEW METHOD OF LEARNING TO READ, WRITE, AND SPEAK THE FRENCH LANGUAGE , or, First Lessons in French (Introductory to Ollendorff's Larger Grammar) By G W. Greene, Instructor in Modern Languages in Brown University. Third Edition, enlarged and rewritten. Fcap. 8vo, pp. 248, cloth. 1869. 3s. 6d.

GREENE.—THE HEBREW MIGRATION FROM EGYPT By J. Baker Greene, LL.B., M.B., Trin. Coll., Dub. Second Edition. Demy 8vo, pp. xii. and 440, cloth. 1882. 10s. 6d.

GREG.—TRUTH VERSUS EDIFICATION. By W. R. Greg. Fcap. 8vo, pp. 32, cloth. 1869. 1s.

GREG.—WHY ARE WOMEN REDUNDANT ? By W. R. Greg. Fcap. 8vo, pp. 40, cloth. 1869. 1s.

GREG.—LITERARY AND SOCIAL JUDGMENTS. By W. R. Greg. Fourth Edition, considerably enlarged. 2 vols. crown 8vo, pp. 310 and 288, cloth. 877. 15s.

GREG.—MISTAKEN AIMS AND ATTAINABLE IDEALS OF THE ARTISAN CLASS.   By W.
R. Greg. Crown 8vo, pp. vi and 332, cloth. 1876. 10s. 6d.

GREG —ENIGMAS OF LIFE. By W. R. Greg Fifteenth Edition, with a postscript
Contents : Realisable Ideals. Malthus Notwithstanding.   Non-Survival of the
Fittest. Limits and Directions of Human Development The Significance of Life.
De Profundis. Elsewhere. Appendix. Post 8vo, pp xxii and 314, cloth.
1883. 10s 6d.

GREG —POLITICAL PROBLEMS FOR OUR AGE AND COUNTRY. By W. R. Greg. Con-
tents I. Constitutional and Autocratic Statesmanship II. England's Future
Attitude and Mission. III Disposal of the Criminal Classes. IV Recent
Change in the Character of English Crime V The Intrinsic Vice of Trade-
Unions. VI. Industrial and Co-operative Partnerships VII. The Economic
Problem. VIII. Political Consistency. IX. The Parliamentary Career. X. The
Price we pay for Self-government. XI Vestiyism XII. Direct v Indirect
Taxation XIII. The New Régime, and how to meet it Demy 8vo, pp. 342,
cloth. 1870. 10s. 6d.

GREG.—THE GREAT DUEL · Its true Meaning and Issues   By W R Greg. Crown
8vo, pp. 96, cloth. 1871. 2s. 6d.

GREG.—THE CREED OF CHRISTENDOM   See English and Foreign Philosophical
Library, Vols V. and VI

GREG.—ROCKS AHEAD ; or, The Warnings of Cassandra. By W. R Greg. Second
Edition, with a Reply to Objectors Crown 8vo, pp xliv and 236, cloth 1874
9s.

GREG.—MISCELLANEOUS ESSAYS. By W. R. Greg. Crown 8vo, pp. 260, cloth.
1881. 7s. 6d.
    CONTENTS :—Rocks Ahead and Harbours of Refuge Foreign Policy of Great
    Britain. The Echo of the Antipodes A Grave Perplexity before us Obli-
    gations of the Soil. The Right Use of a Surplus The Great Twin
    Brothers : Louis Napoleon and Benjamin Disraeli Is the Popular Judgment
    in Politics more Just than that of the Higher Orders? Harriet Martineau.
    Verify your Compass. The Prophetic Element in the Gospels. Mr. Frederick
    Harrison on the Future Life. Can Truths be Apprehended which could
    not have been discovered?

GREG.—INTERLEAVES IN THE WORKDAY PROSE OF TWENTY YEARS. By Percy Greg.
Fcap 8vo, pp. 128, cloth. 1875 2s. 6d

GRIFFIN.—THE RAJAS OF THE PUNJAB   Being the History of the Principal States
in the Punjab, and their Political Relations with the British Government. By
Lepel H. Griffin, Bengal Civil Service, Acting Secretary to the Government of the
Punjab, Author of "The Punjab Chiefs," &c.   Second Edition.   Royal 8vo,
pp xvi. and 630, cloth. 1873 £1, 1s.

GRIFFIN —THE WORLD UNDER GLASS   By Frederick Griffin, Author of "The
Destiny of Man," "The Storm King," and other Poems. Fcap 8vo, pp 204,
cloth gilt. 1879. 3s. 6d

GRIFFIN.—THE DESTINY OF MAN, THE STORM KING, and other Poems. By F.
Griffin. Second Edition. Fcap 8vo, pp. vii –104, cloth. 1883 2s 6d.

GRIFFIS —THE MIKADO'S EMPIRE. Book I History of Japan, from 660 B C. to
1872 A D.—Book II. Personal Experiences, Observations, and Studies in Japan,
1870–1874. By W. E Griffis, A.M 8vo, pp. 636, cloth. Illustrated. 1877.
20s.

GRIFFIS.—JAPANESE FAIRY WORLD Stories from the Wonder-Lore of Japan. By
W. E. Griffis. Square 16mo, pp. viii. and 304, with 12 Plates. 1880. 7s. 6d.

GRIFFITH —The Birth of the War God. See Trubner's Oriental Series.

GRIFFITH —Yusuf and Zulaikha. See Trubner's Oriental Series.

GRIFFITH.—Scenes from the Ramayana, Meghaduta, &c. Translated by Ralph T. H. Griffith, M.A , Principal of the Benares College. Second Edition. Crown 8vo, pp. xviii. and 244, cloth. 1870. 6s.

Contents —Preface—Ayodhya—Ravan Doomed—The Birth of Rama—The Heir-Apparent—Manthara's Guile—Dasaratha's Oath—The Step-mother—Mother and Son—The Triumph of Love—Farewell ?—The Hermit's Son—The Trial of Truth—The Forest—The Rape of Sita—Rama's Despair—The Messenger Cloud—Khumhakarna—The Supphant Dove—True Glory—Feed the Poor—The Wise Scholar

GRIFFITH.—The Rámáyan of Válmíki. Translated into English Verse By Ralph T. H. Griffith, M A., Principal of the Benares College. Vol I , containing Books I. and II., demy 8vo, pp. xxxii. and 440, cloth. 1870. —Vol. II , containing Book II., with additional Notes and Index of Names. Demy 8vo, pp. 504, cloth. 1871 —Vol. III., demy 8vo, pp. 390, cloth. 1872. —Vol. IV , demy 8vo, pp. viii. and 432, cloth. 1873. —Vol. V., demy 8vo, pp. viii and 360, cloth. 1875. The complete work, 5 vols. £7, 7s.

GROTE.—Review of the Work of Mr. John Stuart Mill entitled "Examination of Sir William Hamilton's Philosophy." By George Grote, Author of the "History of Ancient Greece," "Plato, and the other Companions of Socrates," &c. 12mo, pp. 112, cloth. 1868. 3s. 6d

GROUT.—Zulu-Land ; or, Life among the Zulu-Kafirs of Natal and Zulu-Land, South Africa By the Rev Lewis Grout. Crown 8vo, pp. 352, cloth. With Map and Illustrations. 7s. 6d.

GROWSE —Mathura · A District Memoir. By F S. Growse, B.C.S , M.A., Oxon, C.I.E., Fellow of the Calcutta University. Second edition, illustrated, revised, and enlarged, 4to, pp. xxiv. and 520, hoards 1880. 42s.

GUBERNATIS —Zoological Mythology ; or, The Legends of Animals. By Angelo de Gubernatis, Professor of Sanskrit and Comparative Literature in the Instituto di Studii Superiori e di Perfezionamento at Florence, &c. 2 vols. 8vo, pp xxvi. and 432, and vii. and 442, cloth. 1872. £1, 8s.

This work is an important contribution to the study of the comparative mythology of the Indo-Germanic nations The author introduces the denizens of the air, earth, and water in the various characters assigned to them in the myths and legends of all civilised nations, and traces the migration of the mythological ideas from the times of the early Aryans to those of the Greeks, Romans, and Teutons

GULSHAN I. RAZ : The Mystic Rose Garden of Sa'd ud din Mahmud Shabis-tari The Persian Text, with an English Translation and Notes, chiefly from the Commentary of Muhammed Bin Yahya Lahiji By E H Whinfield, M.A., Bar-rister-at-Law, late of H M.B C.S. 4to, pp. xvi., 94, 60, cloth. 1880. 10s. 6d.

GUMPACH.—Treaty Rights of the Foreign Merchant, and the Transit System in China. By Johannes von Gumpach. 8vo, pp. xviii. and 421, sewed. 10s. 6d.

HAAS.—Catalogue of Sanskrit and Pali Books in the British Museum. By Dr. Ernst Haas. Printed hy permission of the Trustees of the British Museum. 4to, pp. viii. and 188, paper hoards. 1876. 21s.

HAFIZ OF SHIRAZ.—Selections from his Poems Translated from the Persian by Hermann Bicknell. With Preface by A. S. Bicknell. Demy 4to, pp xx. and 384, printed on fine stout plate-paper, with appropriate Oriental Bordering in gold and colour, and Illustrations by J. R. Herbert, R.A. 1875. £2, 2s.

HAFIZ.—See Truhner's Oriental Series.

HAGEN —NORICA ; or, Tales from the Olden Time. Translated from the German of August Hagen. Fcap. 8vo, pp. xiv. and 374. 1850. 5s.

HAGGARD.—CETTWAYO AND HIS WHITE NEIGHBOURS , or, Remarks on Recent Events in Zululand, Natal, and the Transvaal. By H R Haggard. Crown 8vo, pp. xvi. and 294, cloth. 1882. 10s. 6d.

HAGGARD —See "The Vazir of Lankuran."

HAHN.—TSUNI- || GOAM, the Supreme Being of the Khoi-Khoi. By Theophilus Hahn, Ph D., Custodian of the Grey Collection, Cape Town, &c., &c. Post 8vo, pp. xiv. and 154. 1882. 7s 6d.

HALDEMAN.—PENNSYLVANIA DUTCH A Dialect of South Germany with an Infusion of English. By S. S Haldeman, A.M , Professor of Comparative Philology in the University of Pennsylvania, Philadelphia. 8vo, pp. viii and 70, cloth. 1872. 3s. 6d

HALL —ON ENGLISH ADJECTIVES IN -ABLE, WITH SPECIAL REFERENCE TO RELIABLE. By FitzEdward Hall, C E , M A , Hon D C L. Oxon; formerly Professor of Sanskrit Language and Literature, and of Indian Jurisprudence in King's College, London. Crown 8vo, pp. viii. and 238, cloth. 1877. 7s 6d.

HALL —MODERN ENGLISH. By FitzEdward Hall, M A , Hon. D.C.L Oxon. Crown 8vo, pp. xvi. and 394, cloth. 1873. 10s 6d.

HALL —SUN AND EARTH AS GREAT FORCES IN CHEMISTRY By T. W. Hall, M.D. L R C S.E. Crown 8vo, pp. xii. and 220, cloth. 1874. 3s.

HALL.—THE PEDIGREE OF THE DEVIL. By F T. Hall, F R A S. With Seven Autotype Illustrations from Designs by the Author Demy 8vo, pp. xvi and 256, cloth. 1883 7s. 6d.

HALL —ARCTIC EXPEDITION See NOURSE.

HALLOCK —THE SPORTSMAN'S GAZETTEER AND GENERAL GUIDE. The Game Animals, Birds, and Fishes of North America : their Habits and various methods of Capture, &c , &c With a Directory to the principal Game Resorts of the Country. By Charles Hallock. Fourth Edition. Crown 8vo, cloth. Maps and Portrait. 1878. 15s

HAM --THE MAID OF CORINTH. A Drama in Four Acts. By J. Panton Ham. Crown 8vo, pp 65, sewed 2s 6d.

HARDY.—CHRISTIANITY AND BUDDHISM COMPARED. By the late Rev R Spence Hardy, Hon. Member Royal Asiatic Society 8vo, pp 138, sewed. 1875. 7s. 6d.

HARLEY.—THE SIMPLIFICATION OF ENGLISH SPELLING, specially adapted to the Rising Generation. An Easy Way of Saving Time in Writing, Printing, and Reading By Dr. George Harley, F.R S., F.C.S 8vo pp 128, cloth. 1877. 2s. 6d.

HARRISON —THE MEANING OF HISTORY Two Lectures delivered by Frederic Harrison, M.A. 8vo, pp. 80, sewed. 1862. 1s.

HARRISON —WOMAN'S HANDIWORK IN MODERN HOMES. By Constance Cary Harrison. With numerous Illustrations and Five Coloured Plates, from designs by Samuel Colman, Rosina Emmet, George Gibson, and others. 8vo, pp xii and 242, cloth 1881 10s

HARTING —BRITISH ANIMALS EXTINCT WITHIN HISTORIC TIMES : with some Account of British Wild White Cattle By J. E Harting, F L S., F.Z.S. With Illustrations by Wolf, Whymper, Sherwin, and others. Demy 8vo, pp. 256, cloth. 1881. 14s. A few copies, large paper, 31s. 6d.

HARTZENBUSCH and LEMMING.—Eco de Madrid. A Practical Guide to Spanish Conversation. By J. E. Hartzenbusch and H. Lemming. Second Edition. Post 8vo, pp. 250, cloth. 1870. 5s.

HASE.—Miracle Plays and Sacred Dramas : An Historical Survey. By Dr. Karl Hase. Translated from the German by A. W. Jackson, and Edited by the Rev. W. W. Jackson, Fellow of Exeter College, Oxford. Crown 8vo, pp 288. 1880. 9s.

HAUG —Glossary and Index of the Pahlavi Texts of the Book of Arda Viraf, the Tale of Gosht—J. Fryano, the Hadokht Nask, and to some extracts from the Dinkard and Nirangistan ; prepared from Destur Hoshangji Jamaspji Asa's Glossary to the Arda Viraf Namak, and from the Original Texts, with Notes on Pahlavi Grammar by E. W. West, Ph D. Revised by M Haug, Ph.D , &c. Published by order of the Bombay Government. 8vo, pp viii. and 352, sewed. 1874. 25s.

HAUG — The Sacred Language, &c., of the Parsis. See Trübner's Oriental Series.

HAUPT.—The London Arbitrageur ; or, The English Money Market, in connection with Foreign Bourses A Collection of Notes and Formulæ for the Arbitration of Bills, Stocks, Shares, Bullion, and Coins, with all the Important Foreign Countries. By Ottomar Haupt. Crown 8vo, pp. viii. and 196, cloth. 1870. 7s. 6d.

HAWKEN —Upa-Sastrā : Comments, Linguistic, Doctrinal, on Sacred and Mythic Literature. By J D. Hawken. Crown 8vo, pp. viii. and 288, cloth. 1877. 7s. 6d.

HAZEN.—The School and the Army in Germany and France, with a Diary of Siege Life at Versailles. By Brevet Major-General W. B Hazen, U.S A , Col. 6th Infantry. 8vo, pp. 408, cloth. 1872. 10s 6d.

HEATH.—Edgar Quinet. See English and Foreign Philosophical Library, Vol. XIV.

HEBREW LITERATURE SOCIETY.—Subscription, one guinea per annum. List of publications on application.

HECKER.—The Epidemics of the Middle Ages. Translated by G B. Babington, M D , F R.S. Third Edition, completed by the Author's Treatise on Child-Pilgrimages By J. F C. Hecker. 8vo, pp. 384, cloth 1859. 9s. 6d.
Contents —The Black Death—The Dancing Mania—The Sweating Sickness—Child Pilgrimages

HEDLEY —Masterpieces of German Poetry. Translated in the Measure of the Originals, by F. H. Hedley. With Illustrations by Louis Wanke. Crown 8vo, pp. viii. and 120, cloth. 1876. 6s.

HEINE.—Religion and Philosophy in Germany. See English and Foreign Philosophical Library, Vol. XVIII.

HEINE.—Wit, Wisdom, and Pathos from the Prose of Heinrich Heine. With a few pieces from the "Book of Songs." Selected and Translated by J. Snodgrass. With Portrait. Crown 8vo, pp. xx and 340, cloth. 1879. 7s. 6d.

HEINE.—Pictures of Travel. Translated from the German of Henry Heine, by Charles G. Leland. 7th Revised Edition. Crown 8vo, pp. 472, with Portrait, cloth. 1873. 7s. 6d.

HEINE.—Heine's Book of Songs. Translated by Charles G. Leland. Fcap. 8vo, pp. xiv. and 240, cloth, gilt edges. 1874. 7s. 6d.

HENDRIK.—MEMOIRS OF HANS HENDRIK, THE ARCTIC TRAVELLER; serving under Kane, Hayes, Hall, and Nares, 1853-76. Written by Himself Translated from the Eskimo Language, by Dr Henry Rink Edited by Prof. Dr. G. Stephens, F S.A. Crown 8vo, pp. 100, Map, cloth. 1878. 3s. 6d.

HENNELL —PRESENT RELIGION As a Faith owning Fellowship with Thought. Vol I Part I. By Sara S Hennell Crown 8vo, pp. 570, cloth. 1865. 7s. 6d.

HENNELL.— PRESENT RELIGION : As a Faith owning Fellowship with Thought. Part II. First Division. Intellectual Effect : shown as a Principle of Metaphysical Comparativism By Sara S Hennell. Crown 8vo, pp. 618, cloth. 1873. 7s 6d.

HENNELL.—PRESENT RELIGION, Vol. III. Part II. Second Division. The Effect of Present Religion on its Practical Side. By S. S. Hennell. Crown 8vo, pp. 68, paper covers. 1882 2s

HENNELL --COMPARATIVISM shown as Furnishing a Religious Basis to Morality. (Present Religion. Vol III Part II. Second Division : Practical Effect.) By Sara S Hennell Crown 8vo, pp. 220, stitched in wrapper. 1878. 3s. 6d

HENNELL —THOUGHTS IN AID OF FAITH. Gathered chiefly from recent Works in Theology and Philosophy. By Sara S. Hennell. Post 8vo, pp. 428, cloth 1860. 6s.

HENWOOD —THE METALLIFEROUS DEPOSITS OF CORNWALL AND DEVON ; with Appendices on Subterranean Temperature ; the Electricity of Rocks and Veins, the Quantities of Water in the Cornish Mines ; and Mining Statistics. (Vol. V of the Transactions of the Royal Geographical Society of Cornwall.) By William Jory Henwood, F.R S., F G.S. 8vo, pp x and 515, with 113 Tables, and 12 Plates, half bound. £2, 2s.

HENWOOD —OBSERVATIONS ON METALLIFEROUS DEPOSITS, AND ON SUBTERRANEAN TEMPERATURE. (Vol VIII. of the Transactions of the Royal Geological Society of Cornwall.) By William Jory Henwood, F.R.S , F G S., President of the Royal Institution of Cornwall In 2 Parts. 8vo, pp xxx , vii. and 916 ; with 38 Tables, 31 Engravings on Wood, and 6 Plates. £1, 16s.

HEPBURN —A JAPANESE AND ENGLISH DICTIONARY. With an English and Japanese Index. By J C. Hepburn, M D , LL.D. Second Edition. Imperial 8vo, pp. xxxii., 632, and 201, cloth. £8, 8s.

HEPBURN.—JAPANESE-ENGLISH AND ENGLISH-JAPANESE DICTIONARY. By J C. Hepburn, M D , LL D. Abridged by the Author. Square fcap , pp. vi and 536, cloth 1873. 18s

HERNISZ.—A GUIDE TO CONVERSATION IN THE ENGLISH AND CHINESE LANGUAGES, for the Use of Americans and Chinese in California and elsewhere. By Stanislas Hernisz. Square 8vo, pp 274, sewed. 1855 10s. 6d.

HERSHON —TALMUDIC MISCELLANY. See Trubner's Oriental Series.

HERZEN.— DU DEVELOPPEMENT DES IDÉES REVOLUTIONNAIRES EN RUSSIE. Par Alexander Herzen. 12mo, pp xxiii and 144, sewed 1853 2s. 6d.

HERZEN.—A separate list of A. Herzen's works in Russian may he had on application.

HILL.— THE HISTORY OF THE REFORM MOVEMENT in the Dental Profession in Great Britain during the last twenty years. By Alfred Hill, Licentiate in Dental Surgery, &c. Crown 8vo, pp. xvi. and 400, cloth. 1877. 10s 6d.

HILLEBRAND.—FRANCE AND THE FRENCH IN THE SECOND HALF OF THE NINETEENTH CENTURY. By Karl Hillebrand Translated from the Third German Edition Post 8vo, pp xx. and 262, cloth. 1881. 10s. 6d.

HINDOO MYTHOLOGY POPULARLY TREATED. Being an Epitomised Description of the various Heathen Deities illustrated on the Silver Swami Tea Service presented, as a memento of his visit to India, to H R H the Prince of Wales, K G , G C.S.I., by His Highness the Gaekwar of Baroda. Small 4to, pp. 42, limp cloth. 1875. 3s. 6d.

HITTELL.—THE COMMERCE AND INDUSTRIES OF THE PACIFIC COAST OF NORTH AMERICA. By J. S. Hittell, Author of "The Resources of California." 4to, pp. 820. 1882. £1, 10s.

HODGSON.—ESSAYS ON THE LANGUAGES, LITERATURE, AND RELIGION OF NÉPAL AND TIBET. Together with further Papers on the Geography, Ethnology, and Commerce of those Countries. By B. H. Hodgson, late British Minister at the Court of Nepál. Royal 8vo, cloth, pp. xii. and 276. 1874. 14s.

HODGSON.— ESSAYS ON INDIAN SUBJECTS. See Trubner's Oriental Series.

HODGSON.—THE EDUCATION OF GIRLS ; AND THE EMPLOYMENT OF WOMEN OF THE UPPER CLASSES EDUCATIONALLY CONSIDERED. Two Lectures. By W. B. Hodgson, LL.D. Second Edition. Crown 8vo, pp. xvi. and 114, cloth. 1869. 3s. 6d.

HODGSON.—TURGOT: His Life, Times, and Opinions. Two Lectures. By W. B. Hodgson, LL.D. Crown 8vo, pp. vi. and 83, sewed 1870. 2s.

HOERNLE —A COMPARATIVE GRAMMAR OF THE GAUDIAN LANGUAGES, with Special Reference to the Eastern Hindi. Accompanied by a Language Map, and a Table of Alphabets. By A. F. Rudolf Hoernle Demy 8vo, pp 474, cloth. 1880 18s.

HOLBEIN SOCIETY.—Subscription, one guinea per annum. List of publications on application.

HOLMES-FORBES.—THE SCIENCE OF BEAUTY. An Analytical Inquiry into the Laws of Æsthetics. By Avary W Holmes-Forbes, of Lincoln's Inn, Barrister-at-Law. Post 8vo, cloth, pp vi. and 200. 1881. 5s.

HOLST —THE CONSTITUTIONAL AND POLITICAL HISTORY OF THE UNITED STATES. By Dr. H. von Holst. Translated by J. J. Lalor and A. B. Mason. Royal 8vo Vol I 1750-1833 State Sovereignty and Slavery. Pp xvi and 506. 1876 18s —Vol. II. 1828-1846. Jackson's Administration—Annexation of Texas. Pp. 720. 1879. £1, 2s —Vol. III. 1846-1850. Annexation of Texas—Compromise of 1850. Pp. x and 598. 1881 18s.

HOLYOAKE.—THE ROCHDALE PIONEERS. Thirty-three Years of Co-operation in Rochdale. In two parts. Part I. 1844-1857 ; Part II. 1857-1877. By G. J. Holyoake Crown 8vo, pp. 174, cloth. 1882. 2s 6d.

HOLYOAKE.—THE HISTORY OF CO-OPERATION IN ENGLAND · its Literature and its Advocates. By G J. Holyoake. Vol. I. The Pioneer Period, 1812–44 Crown 8vo, pp. xii. and 420, cloth. 1875. 6s.—Vol. II. The Constructive Period, 1845-78. Crown 8vo, pp. x. and 504, cloth. 1878. 8s.

HOLYOAKE.—THE TRIAL OF THEISM ACCUSED OF OBSTRUCTING SECULAR LIFE. By G. J. Holyoake. Crown 8vo, pp. xvi. and 256, cloth. 1877. 4s.

HOLYOAKE.—REASONING FROM FACTS : A Method of Everyday Logic. By G. J. Holyoake. Fcap., pp. xii. and 94, wrapper. 1877. 1s. 6d.

HOLYOAKE.—SELF-HELP BY THE PEOPLE. Thirty-three Years of Co-operation in Rochdale. In Two Parts. Part I , 1844-1857 , Part II., 1857-1877 By G. J. Holyoake. Ninth Edition. Crown 8vo, pp 174, cloth. 1883. 2s. 6d

HOPKINS.—ELEMENTARY GRAMMAR OF THE TURKISH LANGUAGE. With a few Easy Exercises. By F L. Hopkins, M.A , Fellow and Tutor of Trinity Hall, Cambridge. Crown 8vo, pp. 48, cloth. 1877. 3s 6d.

HORDER.—A SELECTION FROM "THE BOOK OF PRAISE FOR CHILDREN," as Edited by W. Garrett Horder. For the Use of Jewish Children. Fcap. 8vo, pp 80, cloth. 1883. 1s. 6d

HOWELLS —DR BREEN'S PRACTICE : A Novel. By W. D Howells English Copyright Edition. Crown 8vo, pp. 272, cloth. 1882. 6s.

C

HOWSE.—A GRAMMAR OF THE CREE LANGUAGE. With which is combined an Analysis of the Chippeway Dialect. By Joseph Howse, F.R.G.S. 8vo, pp. xx. and 324, cloth. 1865. 7s. 6d.

HULME.—MATHEMATICAL DRAWING INSTRUMENTS, AND HOW TO USE THEM. By F. Edward Hulme, F.L.S., F.S.A., Art-Master of Marlborough College, Author of "Principles of Ornamental Art," "Familiar Wild Flowers," "Suggestions on Floral Design," &c. With Illustrations Second Edition. Imperial 16mo, pp. xvi and 152, cloth. 1881. 3s 6d.

HUMBERT.—ON "TENANT RIGHT." By C. F. Humbert. 8vo, pp. 20, sewed. 1875. 1s.

HUMBOLDT.—THE SPHERE AND DUTIES OF GOVERNMENT Translated from the German of Baron Wilhelm Von Humboldt by Joseph Coulthard, jun. Post 8vo, pp. xv. and 203, cloth. 1854. 5s.

HUMBOLDT.—LETTERS OF WILLIAM VON HUMBOLDT TO A FEMALE FRIEND. A complete Edition Translated from the Second German Edition by Catherine M. A. Couper, with a Biographical Notice of the Writer 2 vols. crown 8vo, pp. xxviii. and 592, cloth. 1867. 10s.

HUNT.—THE RELIGION OF THE HEART. A Manual of Faith and Duty. By Leigh Hunt. Fcap. 8vo, pp xxiv. and 259, cloth. 2s. 6d.

HUNT.—CHEMICAL AND GEOLOGICAL ESSAYS. By Professor T. Sterry Hunt. Second Edition. 8vo, pp. xxii. and 448, cloth. 1879. 12s.

HUNTER.—A COMPARATIVE DICTIONARY OF THE NON-ARYAN LANGUAGES OF INDIA AND HIGH ASIA. With a Dissertation, Political and Linguistic, on the Aboriginal Races. By W. W. Hunter, B.A., M.R.A.S., Hon. Fel. Ethnol. Soc., Author of the "Annals of Rural Bengal," of H M's Civil Service. Being a Lexicon of 144 Languages, illustrating Turanian Speech. Compiled from the Hodgson Lists, Government Archives, and Original MSS., arranged with Prefaces and Indices in English, French, German, Russian, and Latin. Large 4to, toned paper, pp. 230, cloth. 1869. 42s.

HUNTER.—THE INDIAN MUSSULMANS. By W. W. Hunter, B.A., LL D., Director-General of Statistics to the Government of India, &c., Author of the "Annals of Rural Bengal," &c. Third Edition. 8vo, pp. 219, cloth. 1876. 10s. 6d.

HUNTER.—FAMINE ASPECTS OF BENGAL DISTRICTS. A System of Famine Warnings. By W W. Hunter, B.A., LL D. Crown 8vo, pp 216, cloth. 1874. 7s 6d

HUNTER.—A STATISTICAL ACCOUNT OF BENGAL. By W. W. Hunter, B A., LL.D., Director-General of Statistics to the Government of India, &c. In 20 vols. 8vo, half morocco. 1877. £5.

HUNTER.—CATALOGUE OF SANSKRIT MANUSCRIPTS (BUDDHIST). Collected in Nepal by B. H Hodgson, late Resident at the Court of Nepal Compiled from Lists in Calcutta, France, and England, by W. W. Hunter, C.I E., LL.D. 8vo, pp. 28, paper. 1880. 2s.

HUNTER.—THE IMPERIAL GAZETTEER OF INDIA. By W. W. Hunter, C.I E., LL.D., Director-General of Statistics to the Government of India In Nine Volumes 8vo, pp xxxii. and 544, 539, 567, xix. and 716, 509, 513, 555, 537, and xii. and 478, half morocco. With Maps. 1881.

HUNTER.—THE INDIAN EMPIRE: Its History, People, and Products. By W. W. Hunter, C.I.E., LL D. Post 8vo, pp. 568, with Map, cloth. 1882. 16s.

HUNTER.—AN ACCOUNT OF THE BRITISH SETTLEMENT OF ADEN, IN ARABIA. Compiled by Capt. F. M. Hunter, Assistant Political Resident, Aden. 8vo, pp. xii. and 232, half bound. 1877. 7s. 6d.

HUNTER.—A STATISTICAL ACCOUNT OF ASSAM. By W. W. Hunter, B.A., LL.D., C.I.E., Director-General of Statistics to the Government of India, &c. 2 vols. 8vo, pp. 420 and 490, with 2 Maps, ha morocco. 1879. 10s.

HUNTER.—A BRIEF HISTORY OF THE INDIAN PEOPLE. By W. W. Hunter, C.I.E., LL.D. Second Edition. Crown 8vo, pp. 222, cloth. With Map. 1883. 3s. 6d.

HURST —HISTORY OF RATIONALISM: embracing a Survey of the Present State of Protestant Theology. By the Rev. John F. Hurst, A.M. With Appendix of Literature. Revised and enlarged from the Third American Edition. Crown 8vo, pp. xvii. and 525, cloth. 1867. 10s. 6d.

HYETT.—PROMPT REMEDIES FOR ACCIDENTS AND POISONS : Adapted to the use of the Inexperienced till Medical aid arrives. By W. H Hyett, F.R S. A Broadsheet, to hang up in Country Schools or Vestries, Workshops, Offices of Factories, Mines and Docks, on board Yachts, in Railway Stations, remote Shooting Quarters, Highland Manses, and Private Houses, wherever the Doctor lives at a distance. Sold for the benefit of the Gloucester Eye Institution. In sheets, 21½ by 17½ inches, 2s. 6d. ; mounted, 3s. 6d.

HYMANS.—PUPIL *Versus* TEACHER. Letters from a Teacher to a Teacher. Fcap. 8vo, pp. 92, cloth. 1875. 2s.

IHNE.—A LATIN GRAMMAR FOR BEGINNERS. By W. H. Ihne, late Principal of Carlton Terrace School, Liverpool. Crown 8vo, pp vi and 184, cloth. 1864. 3s.

IKHWÁNU-S SAFÁ; or, Brothers of Purity. Translated from the Hindustani by Professor John Dowson, M R.A.S., Staff College, Sandhurst. Crown 8vo, pp. viii. and 156, cloth 1869. 7s.

INDIA.—ARCHÆOLOGICAL SURVEY OF WESTERN INDIA. See Burgess.

INDIA.—PUBLICATIONS OF THE ARCHÆOLOGICAL SURVEY OF INDIA. A separate list on application.

INDIA.—PUBLICATIONS OF THE GEOGRAPHICAL DEPARTMENT OF THE INDIA OFFICE, LONDON. A separate list, also list of all the Government Maps, on application.

INDIA.—PUBLICATIONS OF THE GEOLOGICAL SURVEY OF INDIA. A separate list on application.

INDIA OFFICE PUBLICATIONS :—

Aden, Statistical Account of. 5s
Assam, do. do. Vols. I. and II. 5s. each.
Baden Powell, Land Revenues, &c , in India. 12s.
Bengal, Statistical Account of. Vols I. to XX. 100s per set.
  Do. do. do. Vols. VI to XX 5s. each.
Bombay Code. 21s.
Bombay Gazetteer. Vol. II. 14s. Vol XIII. (2 parts), 16s
  Do. do. Vols III to VI., and X , XII, XIV. 8s. each.
Burgess' Archæological Survey of Western India. Vols. I and III 42s. each.
  Do. do do. Vol II. 63s.
  Do. do. do. Vols. IV. and V. 126s.
Burma (British) Gazetteer. 2 vols 50s
Catalogue of Manuscripts and Maps of Surveys. 12s.
Chambers' Meteorology (Bombay) and Atlas. 30s.
Cole's Agra and Muttra. 70s.
Cook's Gums and Resins 5s.
Corpus Inscriptionem Indicarum. Vol. I. 32s
Cunningham's Archæological Survey. Vols. I. to XV. 10s. and 12s. each.
  Do. Stupa of Bharut. 63s.

INDIA OFFICE PUBLICATIONS—*continued.*

Egerton's Catalogue of Indian Arms   2s. 6d.
Ferguson and Burgess, Cave Temples of India   42s.
      Do.   Tree and Serpent Worship.   105s.
Gamble, Manual of Indian Timbers.   10s
Hunter's Imperial Gazetteer.   9 vols.
Jaschke's Tibetan-English Dictionary.   30s
Kurz.   Forest Flora of British Burma.   Vols. I and II.   15s. each.
Liotard's Materials for Paper.   2s. 6d.
Markham's Tibet   21s.
    Do.   Memoir of Indian Surveys.   10s 6d.
    Do.   Abstract of Reports of Surveys.   1s. 6d
Mitra (Rajendralala), Buddha Gaya   60s.
Moir, Torrent Regions of the Alps.   1s.
Mysore and Coorg Gazetteer.   Vol. I and II.   10s. each.
    Do   do.   Vol. III.   5s.
N. W. P. Gazetteer.   Vols. I. and II.   10s. each.
    Do   do.   Vols. III to VI and X.   12s. each.
Oudh   do.   Vols. I. to III.   10s. each.
Pharmacopœia of India, The   6s.
People of India, The   Vols. I to VIII.   45s. each.
Raverty's Notes on Afghanistan and Baluchistan.   Sections I. and II.   2s.   Section III.   5s.
Rajputana Gazetteer   3 vols.   15s.
Saunders' Mountains and River Basins of India.   3s
Sewell's Amaravati Tope   3s.
Smith's (Brough) Gold Mining in Wynaad.   1s
Trigonometrical Survey, Synopsis of Great.   Vols I. to VI.   10s. 6d. each.
Trumpp's Adi Granth.   52s. 6d.
Watson's Cotton for Trials.   Boards, 10s. 6d.   Paper, 10s.
    Do   Rhea Fibre.   2s. 6d.
    Do   Tobacco.   5s.

INDIAN GAZETTEER.—See GAZETTEER.

INGLEBY.—See SHAKESPEARE.

INMAN.—NAUTICAL TABLES   Designed for the use of British Seamen.   By the Rev. James Inman, D.D., late Professor at the Royal Naval College, Portsmouth. Demy 8vo, pp xvi and 410, cloth   1877.   15s

INMAN.—HISTORY OF THE ENGLISH ALPHABET.   A Paper read before the Liverpool Literary and Philosophical Society   By T. Inman, M D   8vo, pp. 36, sewed. 1872.   1s.

IN SEARCH OF TRUTH.   Conversations on the Bible and Popular Theology, for Young People.   By A. M. Y.   Crown 8vo, pp. x and 138, cloth.   1875.   2s. 6d.

INTERNATIONAL NUMISMATA ORIENTALIA (THE) —Royal 4to, in paper wrapper. Part I. Ancient Indian Weights   By E Thomas, F.R.S.   Pp 84, with a Plate and Map of the India of Manu   9s. 6d.—Part II   Coins of the Urtukí Turkumáns. By Stanley Lane Poole, Corpus Christi College, Oxford.   Pp 44, with 6 Plates. 9s —Part III.   The Coinage of Lydia and Persia, from the Earliest Times to the Fall of the Dynasty of the Achæmenidæ   By Barclay V. Head, Assistant-Keeper of Coins, British Museum.   Pp. viii.-56, with 3 Autotype Plates   10s. 6d.— Part IV.   The Coins of the Tuluni Dynasty   By Edward Thomas Rogers.   Pp. iv.-22, and 1 Plate.   5s —Part V   The Parthian Coinage   By Percy Gardner, M.A   Pp. iv.-66, and 8 Autotype Plates   18s —Part VI.   The Ancient Coins and Measures of Ceylon   By T W Rhys Davids.   Pp. iv. and 60, and 1 Plate. 10s.—Vol. I., containing the first six parts, as specified above.   Royal 4to, half bound.   £3, 13s 6d.

INTERNATIONAL NUMISMATA—*continued*

Vol. II. COINS OF THE JEWS. Being a History of the Jewish Coinage and Money in the Old and New Testaments. By Frederick W. Madden, M.R A.S , Member of the Numismatic Society of London, Secretary of the Brighton College, &c., &c. With 279 woodcuts and a plate of alphabets. Royal 4to, pp. xii. and 330, Sewed. 1881. £2.

THE COINS OF ARAKAN, OF PEGU, AND OF BURMA. By Lieut.-General Sir Arthur Phayre, C.B., K.C.S.I., G C.M.G., late Commissioner of British Burma. Royal 4to, pp. viii. and 48, with Five Autotype Illustrations, wrapper. 1882. 8s. 6d.

JACKSON.—ETHNOLOGY AND PHRENOLOGY AS AN AID TO THE HISTORIAN. By the late J. W. Jackson. Second Edition. With a Memoir of the Author, by his Wife. Crown 8vo, pp xx and 324, cloth 1875. 4s. 6d.

JACKSON.—THE SHROPSHIRE WORD-BOOK. A Glossary of Archaic and Provincial Words, &c., used in the County. By Georgina F. Jackson. Crown 8vo, pp civ. and 524, cloth. 1881. 31s. 6d.

JACOB.—HINDU PANTHEISM. See Trübner's Oriental Series

JAGIELSKI.—ON MARIENBAD SPA, and the Diseases Curable by its Waters and Baths. By A. V. Jagielski, M.D., Berlin. Second Edition. Crown 8vo, pp. viii. and 186. With Map. Cloth. 1874 5s

JAMISON.—THE LIFE AND TIMES OF BERTRAND DU GUESCLIN. A History of the Fourteenth Century. By D. F Jamison, of South Carolina. Portrait. 2 vols. 8vo, pp. xvi., 287, and viii., 314, cloth. 1864. £1, 1s.

JAPAN.—MAP OF NIPPON (Japan): Compiled from Native Maps, and the Notes of most recent Travellers. By R. Henry Brunton, M.I C.E., F.R.G.S., 1880. Size, 5 feet by 4 feet, 20 miles to the inch. In 4 Sheets, £1, 1s ; Roller, varnished, £1, 11s. 6d ; Folded, in Case, £1, 5s. 6d.

JASCHKE. — A TIBETAN-ENGLISH DICTIONARY With special reference to the Prevailing Dialects. To which is added an English-Tibetan Vocabulary. By H. A. Jaschke, late Moravian Missionary at Kyèlang, British Lahoul. Imperial 8vo, pp. xxiv.-672, cloth. 1881 £1, 10s.

JASCHKE.—TIBETAN GRAMMAR. By H. A. Jaschke. Crown 8vo, pp. viii.-104, cloth. 1883. 5s.

JATAKA (THE), together with its COMMENTARY : being tales of the Anterior Births of Gotama Buddha. Now first published in Pali, by V. Fausböll. Text. 8vo. Vol. I , pp. viii. and 512, cloth. 1877 28s.—Vol. II., pp. 452, cloth. 1879. 28s.—Vol. III. *in preparation.* (For Translation see Trübner's Oriental Series, "Buddhist Birth Stories.")

JENKINS —A PALADIN OF FINANCE Contemporary Manners. By E Jenkins, Author of "Ginx's Baby." Crown 8vo, pp. iv and 392, cloth. 1882. 7s. 6d.

JENKINS.—VEST-POCKET LEXICON. An English Dictionary of all except familiar Words, including the principal Scientific and Technical Terms, and Foreign Moneys, Weights and Measures; omitting what everybody knows, and containing what everybody wants to know and cannot readily find. By Jabez Jenkins. 64mo, pp. 564, cloth. 1879 1s. 6d.

JOHNSON.—ORIENTAL RELIGIONS. See English and Foreign Philosophical Library, Extra Series, Vols. IV. and V.

JOLLY.—See NARADÍYA.

JOMINI —THE ART OF WAR. By Baron de Jomini, General and Aide-de-Camp to the Emperor of Russia. A New Edition, with Appendices and Maps. Translated from the French. By Captain G. H. Mendell, and Captain W. O Craighill. Crown 8vo, pp 410, cloth. 1879. 9s.

JORDAN.—ALBUM TO THE COURSE OF LECTURES ON METALLURGY, at the Paris Central School of Arts and Manufactures. By S. Jordan, C.E M.I. & S I. Demy 4to, paper. With 140 Plates, Description of the Plates, Numerical Data, and Notes upon the Working of the Apparatus. £4.

JOSEPH --RELIGION, NATURAL AND REVEALED. A Series of Progressive Lessons for Jewish Youth. By N. S. Joseph. Crown 8vo, pp. xii.-296, cloth. 1879. 3s.

JUVENALIS SATIRÆ. With a Literal English Prose Translation and Notes By J. D Lewis, M.A., Trin. Coll. Camb Second Edition. Two vols 8vo, pp xii. and 230 and 400, cloth. 1882. 12s.

KARCHER.—QUESTIONNAIRE FRANÇAIS Questions on French Grammar, Idiomatic Difficulties, and Military Expressions. By Theodore Karcher, LL B Fourth Edition, greatly enlarged. Crown 8vo, pp. 224, cloth. 1879. 4s. 6d. Interleaved with writing paper, 5s 6d.

KARDEC.—THE SPIRIT'S BOOK. Containing the Principles of Spiritist Doctrine on the Immortality of the Soul, &c., &c , according to the Teachings of Spirits of High Degree, transmitted through various mediums, collected and set in order by Allen Kardec. Translated from the 120th thousand by Anna Blackwell. Crown 8vo, pp. 512, cloth. 1875   7s 6d

KARDEC.—THE MEDIUM'S BOOK ; or, Guide for Mediums and for Evocations. Containing the Theoretic Teachings of Spirits concerning all kinds of Manifestations, the Means of Communication with the Invisible World, the Development of Medianimity, &c , &c. By Allen Kardec. Translated by Anna Blackwell. Crown 8vo, pp. 456, cloth. 1876. 7s. 6d.

KARDEC —HEAVEN AND HELL or, the Divine Justice Vindicated in the Plurality of Existences By Allen Kardec Translated by Anna Blackwell. Crown 8vo, pp. viii. and 448, cloth. 1878   7s 6d

KENDRICK.—GREEK OLLENDORFF A Progressive Exhibition of the Principles of the Greek Grammar. By Asahel C. Kendrick 8vo, pp 371, cloth. 1870. 9s.

KERMODE.—NATAL : Its Early History, Rise, Progress, and Future Prospects as a Field for Emigration. By W Kermode, of Natal. Crown 8vo, pp. xii. and 228, with Map, cloth. 1883   3s. 6d

KEYS OF THE CREEDS (THE). Third Revised Edition. Crown 8vo, pp. 210, cloth. 1876. 5s.

KINAHAN —VALLEYS AND THEIR RELATION TO FISSURES, FRACTURES, AND FAULTS. By G. H. Kinahan, M R.I.A , F R G S I.,&c Dedicated by permission to his Grace the Duke of Argyll. Crown 8vo, pp 256, cloth, illustrated. 7s. 6d.

KING'S STRATAGEM (The) ; OR, THE PEARL OF POLAND ; A Tragedy in Five Acts. By Stella. Second Edition. Crown 8vo, pp. 94, cloth. 1874. 2s. 6d

KINGSTON.—THE UNITY OF CREATION. A Contribution to the Solution of the Religious Question By F H. Kingston. Crown 8vo, pp. viii. and 152, cloth 1874. 5s.

KISTNER.—BUDDHA AND HIS DOCTRINES. A Bibliographical Essay. By Otto Kistner 4to, pp. iv. and 32, sewed. 1869. 2s. 6d.

KNOX —ON A MEXICAN MUSTANG. See under SWEET.

KLEMM —MUSCLE BEATING , or, Active and Passive Home Gymnastics, for Healthy and Unhealthy People By C. Klemm. With Illustrations. 8vo pp. 60, wrapper. 1878. 1s.

KOHL.—TRAVELS IN CANADA AND THROUGH THE STATES OF NEW YORK AND PENNSYLVANIA. By J. G Kohl Translated by Mrs Percy Sinnett Revised by the Author. Two vols. post 8vo, pp. xiv. and 794, cloth. 1861. £1, 1s.

KRAPF —DICTIONARY OF THE SUAHILI LANGUAGE. Compiled by the Rev Dr. L. Krapf, missionary of the Church Missionary Society in East Africa With an Appendix, containing an outline of a Suahili Grammar. Medium 8vo, pp. xl. and 434, cloth. 1882. 30s.

KRAUS.—CARLSBAD AND ITS NATURAL HEALING AGENTS, from the Physiological and Therapeutical Point of View. By J. Kraus, M.D. With Notes Introductory by the Rev. J. T. Walters, M.A. Second Edition. Revised and enlarged. Crown 8vo, pp. 104, cloth. 1880 5s.

KROEGER.—THE MINNESINGER OF GERMANY. By A. E. Kroeger. Fcap. 8vo, pp. 290, cloth 1873. 7s.

KURZ —FOREST FLORA OF BRITISH BURMA. By S Kurz, Curator of the Herbarium, Royal Botanical Gardens, Calcutta. 2 vols. crown 8vo, pp. xxx., 550, and 614, cloth. 1877. 30s.

LACERDA'S JOURNEY TO CAZEMBE in 1798. Translated and Annotated by Captain R F. Burton, F.R.G.S Also Journey of the Pombeiros, &c. Demy 8vo, pp. viii. and 272. With Map, cloth. 1873. 7s 6d

LANARI.—COLLECTION OF ITALIAN AND ENGLISH DIALOGUES. By A. Lanari. Fcap 8vo, pp viii. and 200, cloth. 1874. 3s. 6d.

LAND —THE PRINCIPLES OF HEBREW GRAMMAR. By J. P. N. Land, Professor of Logic and Metaphysics in the University of Leyden. Translated from the Dutch, by Reginald Lane Poole, Balliol College, Oxford. Part I. Sounds. Part II. Words. With Large Additions by the Author, and a new Preface. Crown 8vo, pp. xx. and 220, cloth. 1876. 7s. 6d.

LANE —THE KORAN. See Trübner's Oriental Series.

LANGE.—A HISTORY OF MATERIALISM. See English and Foreign Philosophical Library, Vols. I. to III.

LANGE —GERMANIA. A German Reading-book Arranged Progressively. By F. K. W. Lange, Ph.D. Part I. Anthology of German Prose and Poetry, with Vocabulary and Biographical Notes 8vo. pp. xvi. and 216, cloth, 1881, 3s. 6d. Part II Essays on German History and Institutions, with Notes. 8vo, pp. 124, cloth. Parts I. and II together 5s 6d.

LANGE,—GERMAN PROSE WRITING. Comprising English Passages for Translation into German Selected from Examination Papers of the University of London, the College of Preceptors, London, and the Royal Military Academy, Woolwich, arranged progressively, with Notes and Theoretical as well as Practical Treatises on themes for the writing of Essays. By F. K. W. Lange, Ph D., Assistant German Master, Royal Academy, Woolwich; Examiner, Royal College of Preceptors London. Crown 8vo, pp. viii. and 176, cloth. 1881. 4s.

LANGE —GERMAN GRAMMAR PRACTICE. By F K W. Lange, Ph.D. Crown 8vo, pp. viii and 64, cloth. 1882 1s. 6d

LANGE.—COLLOQUIAL GERMAN GRAMMAR. With Special Reference to the Anglo-Saxon Element in the English Language. By F. K. W. Lange, Ph.D , &c. Crown 8vo, pp. xxxii and 380, cloth. 1882. 4s. 6d.

LASCARIDES —A COMPREHENSIVE PHRASEOLOGICAL ENGLISH-ANCIENT AND MODERN GREEK LEXICON Founded upon a manuscript of G. P. Lascarides, and Compiled by L. Myriantheus, Ph D. 2 vols. 18mo, pp. xl. and 1338, cloth 1882. £1, 10s.

LATHE (THE) AND ITS USES; or, Instruction in the Art of Turning Wood and Metal, including a description of the most modern appliances for the Ornamentation of Plain and Curved Surfaces, &c Sixth Edition. With additional Chapters and Index. Illustrated. 8vo, pp. iv. and 316, cloth. 1883. 10s. 6d.

LE-BRUN.—MATERIALS FOR TRANSLATING FROM ENGLISH INTO FRENCH; being a short Essay on Translation, followed by a Graduated Selection in Prose and Verse. By L. Le-Brun. Seventh Edition Revised and corrected by Henri Van Laun. Post 8vo, pp xii. and 204, cloth. 1882. 4s. 6d.

LEE.—ILLUSTRATIONS OF THE PHYSIOLOGY OF RELIGION. In Sections adapted for the use of Schools Part I. By Henry Lee, F R C S., formerly Professor of Surgery, Royal College of Surgeons, &c. Crown 8vo, pp. viii. and 108, cloth. 1880. 3s. 6d.

LEES.—A PRACTICAL GUIDE TO HEALTH, AND TO THE HOME TREATMENT OF THE COMMON AILMENTS OF LIFE. With a Section on Cases of Emergency, and Hints to Mothers on Nursing, &c. By F. Arnold Lees, F L S. Crown 8vo, pp. 334, stiff covers. 1874. 3s.

LEGGE.—THE CHINESE CLASSICS. With a Translation, Critical and Exegetical, Notes, Prolegomena, and copious Indexes By James Legge, D D., of the London Missionary Society In 7 vols. Royal 8vo Vols. I.-V. in Eight Parts, published, cloth. £2, 2s. each Part.

LEGGE — THE CHINESE CLASSICS, translated into English With Preliminary Essays and Explanatory Notes Popular Edition. Reproduced for General Readers from the Author's work, containing the Original Text By James Legge, D.D. Crown 8vo. Vol. 1. The Life and Teachings of Confucius. Third Edition. Pp vi. and 338, cloth. 1872. 10s. 6d.—Vol. II. The Works of Mencius. Pp. x. and 402, cloth, 12s —Vol III. The She-King, or, The Book of Poetry. Pp. vi. and 432, cloth 1876 12s

LEGGE.—CONFUCIANISM IN RELATION TO CHRISTIANITY A Paper read before the Missionary Conference in Shanghai, on May 11th, 1877. By Rev. James Legge, D D., LL D, &c 8vo, pp 12, sewed. 1877. 1s 6d.

LEGGE —A LETTER TO PROFESSOR MAX MULLER, chiefly on the Translation into English of the Chinese Terms *Ti* and *Shang Ti* By James Legge, Professor of the Chinese Language and Literature in the University of Oxford. Crown 8vo, pp. 30, sewed. 1880. 1s

LEIGH —THE RELIGION OF THE WORLD. By H. Stone Leigh. 12mo, pp. xii. and 66, cloth. 1869. 2s. 6d.

LEIGH —THE STORY OF PHILOSOPHY. By Aston Leigh. Post 8vo, pp. xii. and 210, cloth. 1881. 6s.

LELAND —THE BREITMANN BALLADS The only authorised Edition Complete in 1 vol., including Nineteen Ballads, illustrating his Travels in Europe (never before printed), with Comments by Fritz Schwackenhammer. By Charles G Leland. Crown 8vo, pp. xxviii and 292. cloth 1872. 6s.

LELAND.—THE MUSIC LESSON OF CONFUCIUS, and other Poems. By Charles G. Leland. Fcap 8vo, pp viii. and 168, cloth. 1871. 3s. 6d.

LELAND.—GAUDEAMUS. Humorous Poems translated from the German of Joseph Victor Scheffel and others By Charles G. Leland. 16mo, pp. 176, cloth 1872. 3s. 6d.

LELAND —THE EGYPTIAN SKETCH-BOOK. By C. G Leland. Crown 8vo, pp. viii. and 316, cloth. 1873. 7s. 6d.

LELAND.—THE ENGLISH GIPSIES AND THEIR LANGUAGE. By Charles G. Leland. Second Edition. Crown 8vo, pp. xvi and 260, cloth. 1874 7s. 6d.

LELAND.—ENGLISH GIPSY SONGS IN ROMMANY, with Metrical English Translations. By Charles G. Leland, Professor E H. Palmer, and Janet Tuckey. Crown 8vo, pp. xii. and 276, cloth. 1875. 7s. 6d.

LELAND.—FU-SANG ; OR, THF DISCOVERY OF AMERICA by Chinese Buddhist Priests in the Fifth Century. By Charles G. Leland. Crown 8vo, pp. 232, cloth. 1875. 7s. 6d.

LELAND.—PIDGIN-ENGLISH SING-SONG ; or, Songs and Stories in the China-English Dialect. With a Vocabulary. By Charles G. Leland. Crown 8vo, pp. viii. and 140, cloth. 1876. 5s.

LELAND —THE GYPSIES. By C. G. Leland. Crown 8vo, pp 372, cloth 1882. 10s. 6d.

LEOPARDI.—See English and Foreign Philosophical Library, Vol. XVII.

LEO.—FOUR CHAPTERS OF NORTH'S PLUTARCH, Containing the Lives of Caius Marcius, Coriolanus, Julius Cæsar, Marcus Antonius, and Marcus Brutus, as Sources to Shakespeare's Tragedies ; Coriolanus, Julius Cæsar, and Antony and Cleopatra ; and partly to Hamlet and Timon of Athens. Photolithographed in the size of the Edition of 1595. With Preface, Notes comparing the Text of the Editions of 1579, 1595, 1603, and 1612 ; and Reference Notes to the Text of the Tragedies of Shakespeare Edited by Professor F. A. Leo, Ph.D , Vice-President of the New Shakespeare Society , Member of the Directory of the German Shakespeare Society ; and Lecturer at the Academy of Modern Philology at Berlin. Folio, pp. 22, 130 of facsimiles, half-morocco. Library Edition (limited to 250 copies), £1, 11s. 6d ; Amateur Edition (50 copies on a superior large hand-made paper), £3, 3s.

LERMONTOFF.—THE DEMON. By Michael Lermontoff. Translated from the Russian by A. Condie Stephen. Crown 8vo, pp. 88, cloth. 1881. 2s 6d.

LESLEY.—MAN'S ORIGIN AND DESTINY. Sketched from the Platform of the Physical Sciences. By. J. P. Lesley, Member of the National Academy of the United States, Professor of Geology, University of Pennsylvania Second (Revised and considerably Enlarged) Edition, crown 8vo, pp. viii and 142, cloth. 1881. 7s. 6d.

LESSING.—LETTERS ON BIBLIOLATRY. By Gotthold Ephraim Lessing. Translated from the German by the late H. H. Bernard, Ph.D. 8vo, pp 184, cloth 1862. 5s.

LESSING —See English and Foreign Philosophical Library, Extra Series, Vols. I. and II.

LETTERS ON THE WAR BETWEEN GERMANY AND FRANCE. By Mommsen, Strauss, Max Muller, and Carlyle. Second Edition. Crown 8vo, pp. 120, cloth. 1871. 2s. 6d.

LEWES —PROBLEMS OF LIFE AND MIND. By George Henry Lewes First Series : The Foundations of a Creed. Vol. I , demy 8vo. Third edition, pp. 488, cloth. 12s.—Vol. II., demy 8vo, pp. 552, cloth. 1875. 16s.

LEWES.—PROBLEMS OF LIFE AND MIND. By George Henry Lewes Second Series. THE PHYSICAL BASIS OF MIND. 8vo, with Illustrations, pp 508, cloth 1877. 16s. Contents.—The Nature of Life , The Nervous Mechanism , Animal Automatism ; The Reflex Theory.

LEWES.—PROBLEMS OF LIFE AND MIND. By George Henry Lewes. Third Series. Problem the First—The Study of Psychology : Its Object, Scope, and Method. Demy 8vo, pp. 200, cloth. 1879. 7s 6d.

LEWES.—PROBLEMS OF LIFE AND MIND. By George Henry Lewes Third Series. Problem the Second—Mind as a Function of the Organism. Problem the Third— The Sphere of Sense and Logic of Feeling. Problem the Fourth—The Sphere of Intellect and Logic of Signs. Demy 8vo, pp. x. and 500, cloth. 1879. 15s.

LEWIS — See JUVENAL and PLINY.

LIBRARIANS, TRANSACTIONS AND PROCEEDINGS OF THE CONFERENCE OF, held in London, October 1877. Edited by Edward B. Nicholson and Henry R. Tedder. Imperial 8vo, pp. 276, cloth. 1878. £1, 8s.

LIBRARY ASSOCIATION OF THE UNITED KINGDOM, Transactions and Proceedings of the Annual Meetings of the Imperial 8vo, cloth. FIRST, held at Oxford, October 1, 2, 3, 1878. Edited by the Secretaries, Henry R. Tedder, Librarian of the Athenæum Club, and Ernest C. Thomas, late Librarian of the Oxford Union Society. Pp. viii. and 192. 1879. £1, 8s —SECOND, held at Manchester, September 23, 24, and 25, 1879. Edited by H. R. Tedder and E. C. Thomas Pp x and 184 1880 £1, 1s —THIRD, held at Edinburgh, October 5, 6, and 7, 1880. Edited by E. C. Thomas and C. Welsh. Pp x. and 202. 1881 £1, 1s.

LIEBER —THE LIFE AND LETTERS OF FRANCIS LIEBER. Edited by T. S. Perry. 8vo, pp. iv. and 440, cloth, with Portrait. 1882. 14s.

LILLIE —BUDDHA AND EARLY BUDDHISM. By Arthur Lillie, late Regiment of Lucknow. With numerous Illustrations drawn on Wood by the Author Post 8vo, pp. xiv. and 256, cloth. 1881. 7s. 6d.

LITTLE FRENCH READER (THE) Extracted from " The Modern French Reader " Second Edition. Crown 8vo, pp. 112, cloth. 1872. 2s.

LLOYD AND NEWTON.—PRUSSIA'S REPRESENTATIVE MAN By F. Lloyd of the Universities of Halle and Athens, and W. Newton, F.R.G S. Crown 8vo, pp. 648, cloth 1875 10s. 6d.

LOBSCHEID.—CHINESE AND ENGLISH DICTIONARY, arranged according to the Radicals. By W. Lobscheid. 1 vol. imperial 8vo, pp. 600, cloth. £2, 8s.

LOBSCHEID —ENGLISH AND CHINESE DICTIONARY, with the Punti and Mandarin Pronunciation. By W. Lobscheid. Four Parts. Folio, pp viii. and 2016, boards. £8, 8s.

LONG.—EASTERN PROVERBS. See Trubner's Oriental Series.

LOVETT.—THE LIFE AND STRUGGLES OF WILLIAM LOVETT in his pursuit of Bread, Knowledge, and Freedom ; with some short account of the different Associations he belonged to, and of the Opinions he entertained 8vo, pp. vi. and 474, cloth. 1876. 5s.

LOVELY —WHERE TO GO FOR HELP : Being a Companion for Quick and Easy Reference of Police Stations, Fire-Engine Stations, Fire-Escape Stations, &c , &c., of London and the Suburbs. Compiled by W Lovely, R.N. Third Edition. 18mo, pp. 16, sewed. 1882 3d.

LOWELL —THE BIGLOW PAPERS. By James Russell Lowell. Edited by Thomas Hughes, Q C. A Reprint of the Authorised Edition of 1859, together with the Second Series of 1862 First and Second Series in 1 vol. Fcap., pp. lxviii.–140 and lxiv –190, cloth 1880. 2s. 6d.

LUCAS —THE CHILDREN'S PENTATEUCH : With the Hephterahs or Portions from the Prophets. Arranged for Jewish Children. By Mrs. Henry Lucas. Crown 8vo, pp. viii. and 570, cloth. 1878. 5s.

LUDEWIG.—THE LITERATURE OF AMERICAN ABORIGINAL LANGUAGES. By Hermann E. Ludewig. With Additions and Corrections by Professor Wm W. Turner. Edited by Nicolas Trübner. 8vo, pp. xxiv. and 258, cloth. 1858. 10s. 6d.

LUKIN.—THE BOY ENGINEERS : What they did, and how they did it. By the Rev. L. J. Lukin, Author of "The Young Mechanic," &c. A Book for Boys ; 30 Engravings. Imperial 16mo, pp. viii. and 344, cloth. 1877. 7s. 6d.

LUX E TENEBRIS ; OR, THE TESTIMONY OF CONSCIOUSNESS. A Theoretic Essay. Crown 8vo, pp. 376, with Diagram, cloth. 1874. 10s. 6d.

MACCORMAC.—THE CONVERSATION OF A SOUL WITH GOD : A Theodicy. By Henry MacCormac, M.D. 16mo, pp. xvi. and 144, cloth. 1877. 3s. 6d.

MACHIAVELLI.—THE HISTORICAL, POLITICAL, AND DIPLOMATIC WRITINGS OF NICOOLO MACHIAVELLI. Translated from the Italian by C E Detmold. With Portraits. 4 vols. 8vo, cloth, pp. xli., 420, 464, 488, and 472. 1882. £3, 3s.

MADDEN —COINS OF THE JEWS. Being a History of the Jewish Coinage and Money in the Old and New Testaments. By Frederick W Madden, M R A S. Member of the Numismatic Society of London, Secretary of the Brighton College, &c , &c. With 279 Woodcuts and a Plate of Alphabets. Royal 4to, pp. xii. and 330, cloth. 1881. £2, 2s.

MADELUNG.—THE CAUSES AND OPERATIVE TREATMENT OF DUPUYTREN'S FINGER CONTRACTION. By Dr Otto W. Madelung, Lecturer of Surgery at the University, and Assistant Surgeon at the University Hospital, Bonn. 8vo, pp. 24, sewed. 1876. 1s.

MAHAPARINIBBANASUTTA.—See CHILDERS.

MAHA-VIRA-CHARITA, or, The Adventures of the Great Hero Rama. An Indian Drama in Seven Acts. Translated into English Prose from the Sanskrit of Bhavabhuti. By John Pickford, M.A. Crown 8vo, cloth. 5s.

MALET.—INCIDENTS IN THE BIOGRAPHY OF DUST By H. P. Malet, Author of "The Interior of the Earth," &c. Crown 8vo, pp. 272, cloth. 1877. 6s.

MALET.—THE BEGINNINGS. By H. P. Malet. Crown 8vo, pp. xix. and 124, cloth. 1878. 4s. 6d.

MALLESON.—ESSAYS AND LECTURES ON INDIAN HISTORICAL SUBJECTS. By Colonel G. B. Malleson, C.S.I. Second Issue. Crown 8vo, pp. 348, cloth. 1876. 5s.

MANDLEY —WOMAN OUTSIDE CHRISTENDOM. An Exposition of the Influence exerted by Christianity on the Social Position and Happiness of Women. By J. G. Mandley. Crown 8vo, pp. viii. and 160, cloth. 1880. 5s.

MANIPULUS VOCABULORUM. A Rhyming Dictionary of the English Language. By Peter Levins (1570). Edited, with an Alphabetical Index, by Henry B. Wheatley. 8vo, pp. xvi. and 370, cloth. 1867. 14s.

MANŒUVRES.—A RETROSPECT OF THE AUTUMN MANŒUVRES, 1871. With 5 Plans. By a Recluse. 8vo, pp. xii. and 133, cloth 1872. 5s.

MARIETTE-BEY —THE MONUMENTS OF UPPER EGYPT: a translation of the "Itinéraire de la Haute Egypte" of Auguste Mariette-Bey. Translated by Alphonse Mariette. Crown 8vo, pp. xvi. and 262, cloth. 1877. 7s. 6d.

MARKHAM.—QUICHUA GRAMMAR AND DICTIONARY. Contributions towards a Grammar and Dictionary of Quichua, the Language of the Yncas of Peru. Collected by Clements R. Markham, F.S.A. Crown 8vo, pp. 223, cloth. £1, 11s. 6d.

MARKHAM.—OLLANTA : A Drama in the Quichua Language. Text, Translation, and Introduction. By Clements R. Markham, C.B. Crown 8vo, pp. 128, cloth. 1871. 7s. 6d.

MARKHAM.—A MEMOIR OF THE LADY ANA DE OSORIO, Countess of Chincon, and Vice-Queen of Peru, A D. 1629–39. With a Plea for the correct spelling of the Chinchona Genus. By Clements R. Markham, C.B., Member of the Imperial Academy Naturæ Curiosorum, with the Cognomen of Chinchon. Small 4to, pp. xii. and 100. With 2 Coloured Plates, Map, and Illustrations. Handsomely bound. 1874. 28s.

MARKHAM.—A MEMOIR ON THE INDIAN SURVEYS By Clements R. Markham, C B , F.R S., &c., &c. Published by Order of H. M. Secretary of State for India in Council. Illustrated with Maps. Second Edition. Imperial 8vo, pp. xxx. and 481, boards. 1878. 10s. 6d.

MARKHAM.—NARRATIVES OF THE MISSION OF GEORGE BOGLE TO TIBET, and of the Journey of Thomas Manning to Lhasa. Edited with Notes, an Introduction, and Lives of Mr Bogle and Mr. Manning. By Clements R. Markham, C.B , F R.S. Second Edition 8vo, pp. clxv. and 362, cloth. With Maps and Illustrations. 1879. 21s.

MARMONTEL.—BELISAIRE. Par Marmontel. Nouvelle Edition. 12mo, pp. xii. and 123, cloth. 1867. 2s. 6d.

MARTIN AND TRUBNER —THE CURRENT GOLD AND SILVER COINS OF ALL COUNTRIES, their Weight and Fineness, and their Intrinsic Value in English Money, with Facsimiles of the Coins. By Leopold C. Martin, of Her Majesty's Stationery Office, and Charles Truhner. In 1 vol. medium 8vo, 141 Plates, printed in Gold and Silver, and representing about 1000 Coins, with 160 pages of Text, handsomely bound in embossed cloth, richly gilt, with Emblematical Designs on the Cover, and gilt edges. 1863. £2, 2s.

MARTIN.—THE CHINESE : THEIR EDUCATION, PHILOSOPHY, AND LETTERS By W. A. P. Martin, D.D., LL.D., President of the Tungwen College, Pekin. 8vo, pp. 320, cloth. 1881 7s 6d.

MARTINEAU.—ESSAYS, PHILOSOPHICAL AND THEOLOGICAL. By James Martineau. 2 vols. crown 8vo, pp. iv. and 414—x. and 430, cloth. 1875 £1, 4s.

MARTINEAU.— LETTERS FROM IRELAND By Harriet Martineau. Reprinted from the *Daily News.* Post 8vo, pp. viii. and 220, cloth. 1852 6s 6d.

MATHEWS —ABRAHAM IBN EZRA'S COMMENTARY ON THE CANTICLES AFTER THE FIRST RECENSION. Edited from the MSS., with a translation, by H. J. Mathews, B.A., Exeter College, Oxford. Crown 8vo, pp. x., 34, and 24, limp cloth. 1874. 2s. 6d.

MAXWELL —A MANUAL OF THE MALAY LANGUAGE By W. E. MAXWELL, of the Inner Temple, Barrister-at-Law ; Assistant Resident, Perak, Malay Peninsula. With an Introductory Sketch of the Sanskrit Element in Malay. Crown 8vo, pp viii. and 182 cloth. 1882. 7s 6d

MAYER.—ON THE ART OF POTTERY : with a History of its Rise and Progress in Liverpool. By Joseph Mayer, F.S.A., F.R.S.N.A , &c. 8vo, pp. 100, boards. 1873. 5s.

MAYERS —TREATIES BETWEEN THE EMPIRE OF CHINA AND FOREIGN POWERS, together with Regulations for the conduct of Foreign Trade, &c. Edited by W. F. Mayers, Chinese Secretary to H B.M 's Legation at Peking. 8vo, pp. 246, cloth. 1877. 25s.

MAYERS —THE CHINESE GOVERNMENT: a Manual of Chinese Titles, categorically arranged and explained, with an Appendix By Wm. Fred Mayers, Chinese Secretary to H.B M.'s Legation at Peking, &c., &c. Royal 8vo, pp. viii. and 160, cloth. 1878. 30s.

M'CRINDLE.—ANCIENT INDIA, AS DESCRIBED BY MEGASTHENES AND ARRIAN; being a translation of the fragments of the Indika of Megasthenes collected by Dr. Schwanbeck, and of the first part of the Indika of Arrian By J. W. M'Crindle, M A., Principal of the Government College, Patna, &c. With Introduction, Notes, and Map of Ancient India. Post 8vo, pp. xi. and 224, cloth. 1877. 7s. 6d.

M'CRINDLE.—THE COMMERCE AND NAVIGATION OF THE ERYTHRÆAN SEA. Being a Translation of the Periplus Maris Erythræi, by an Anonymous Writer, and of Arrian's Account of the Voyage of Nearkhos, from the Mouth of the Indus to the Head of the Persian Gulf. With Introduction, Commentary, Notes and Index. By J. W. M'Crindle, M.A., Edinburgh, &c. Post 8vo, pp. iv. and 238, cloth. 1879 7s 6d.

M'CRINDLE.—Ancient India as Described by Ktesias the Knidian, being a Translation of the Abridgment of his "Indika" by Photios, and of the Fragments of that Work preserved in other Writers. With Introduction, Notes, and Index. By J. W. M'Crindle, M.A , M.R.S.A. 8vo, pp. viii. and 104, cloth. 1882. 6s.

MECHANIC (THE YOUNG) A Book for Boys, containing Directions for the use of all kinds of Tools, and for the construction of Steam Engines and Mechanical Models, including the Art of Turning in Wood and Metal. Fifth Edition. Imperial 16mo, pp. iv. and 346, and 70 Engravings, cloth. 1878. 6s.

MECHANIC'S WORKSHOP (AMATEUR). A Treatise containing Plain and Concise Directions for the Manipulation of Wood and Metals, including Casting, Forging, Brazing, Soldering, and Carpentry. By the Author of "The Lathe and its Uses." Sixth Edition. Demy 8vo, pp. iv. and 148. Illustrated, cloth. 1880. 6s.

MEDITATIONS ON DEATH AND ETERNITY. Translated from the German by Frederica Rowan. Published by Her Majesty's gracious permission 8vo, pp 386, cloth. 1862. 10s. 6d.
   DITTO. Smaller Edition, crown 8vo, printed on toned paper, pp. 352, cloth. 1863 6s.

MEDITATIONS ON LIFE AND ITS RELIGIOUS DUTIES. Translated from the German by Frederica Rowan. Dedicated to H.R H. Princess Louis of Hesse. Published by Her Majesty's gracious permission. Being the Companion Volume to "Meditations on Death and Eternity." 8vo, pp. vi. and 370, cloth. 1863. 10s. 6d.
   DITTO. Smaller Edition, crown 8vo, printed on toned paper, pp. 338. 1863. 6s.

MEDLICOTT.—A MANUAL OF THE GEOLOGY OF INDIA, chiefly compiled from the observations of the Geological Survey. By H. B. Medlicott, M.A., Superintendent, Geological Survey of India, and W. T. Blanford, A.R S M , F R.S , Deputy Superintendent. Published by order of the Government of India. 2 vols. 8vo, pp. xviii -lxxx.-818, with 21 Plates and large coloured Map mounted in case, uniform, cloth. 1879. 16s. (For Part III. see BALL.)

MEGHA-DUTA (THE). (Cloud-Messenger) By Kālidāsa. Translated from the Sanskrit into English Verse by the late H. H. Wilson, M.A., F.R S The Vocabulary by Francis Johnson. New Edition. 4to, pp. xi. and 180, cloth. 10s. 6d.

MENKE.—ORBIS ANTIQUI DESCRIPTIO : An Atlas illustrating Ancient History and Geography, for the Use of Schools ; containing 18 Maps engraved on Steel and Coloured, with Descriptive Letterpress.   By D. T. Menke.   Fourth Edition. Folio, half bound morocco.   1866.   5s.

MEREDYTH —ARCA, A REPERTOIRE OF ORIGINAL POEMS, Sacred and Secular.   By F. Meredyth, M A., Canon of Limerick Cathedral.   Crown 8vo, pp. 124, cloth. 1875.   5s.

METCALFE —THE ENGLISHMAN AND THE SCANDINAVIAN.   By Frederick Metcalfe, M.A., Fellow of Lincoln College, Oxford ; Translator of "Gallus" and "Charicles;" and Author of "The Oxonian in Iceland."   Post 8vo, pp. 512, cloth   1880   18s.

MICHEL —LES ÉCOSSAIS EN FRANCE, LES FRANÇAIS EN ÉCOSSE.   Par Francisque Michel, Correspondant de l'Institut de France, &c.   In 2 vols. 8vo, pp. vii., 547, and 551, rich blue cloth, with emblematical designs.   With upwards of 100 Coats of Arms, and other Illustrations.   Price, £1, 12s.—Also a Large-Paper Edition (limited to 100 Copies), printed on Thick Paper.   2 vols. 4to, half morocco, with additional Steel Engravings.   1862.   £3, 3s.

MICKIEWICZ. —KONRAD WALLENROD.   An Historical Poem.   By A. Mickiewicz. Translated from the Polish into English Verse by Miss M. Biggs.   18mo, pp. xvi. and 100, cloth.   1882.   2s. 6d

MILL.—AUGUSTE COMTE AND POSITIVISM.   By the late John Stuart Mill, M.P. Third Edition.   8vo, pp. 200, cloth.   1882.   3s. 6d.

MILLHOUSE.—MANUAL OF ITALIAN CONVERSATION.   For the Use of Schools.   By John Millhouse.   18mo, pp. 126, cloth.   1866.   2s.

MILLHOUSE.—NEW ENGLISH AND ITALIAN PRONOUNCING AND EXPLANATORY DICTIONARY.   By John Millhouse.   Vol. I. English-Italian. Vol II. Italian-English. Fourth Edition.   2 vols. square 8vo, pp. 654 and 740, cloth.   1867.   12s.

MILNE —NOTES ON CRYSTALLOGRAPHY AND CRYSTALLO-PHYSICS.   Being the Substance of Lectures delivered at Yedo during the years 1876–1877.   By John Milne, F.G.S.   8vo, pp. viii. and 70, cloth.   1879.   3s.

MINOCHCHERJI.—PAHLAVI, GUJARATI, AND ENGLISH DICTIONARY.   By Jamashji Dastur Minochcherji   Vol. I , with Photograph of Author.   8vo, pp. clxxii. and 168, cloth.   1877   14s.

MITRA.—BUDDHA GAYA : The Hermitage of Sákya Muni.   By Rajendralala Mitra, LL.D , C I.E , &c.   4to, pp. xvi and 258, with 51 Plates, cloth.   1879.   £3.

MOCATTA.—MORAL BIBLICAL GLEANINGS AND PRACTICAL TEACHINGS, Illustrated by Biographical Sketches Drawn from the Sacred Volume.   By J. L. Mocatta. 8vo, pp. viii. and 446, cloth.   1872.   7s.

MODERN FRENCH READER (THE) Prose.   Junior Course.   Sixth Edition.   Edited by Ch. Cassal, LL D , and Théodore Karcher, LL B.   Crown 8vo, pp. xiv. and 224, cloth.   1879.   2s. 6d.

    SENIOR COURSE.   Third Edition.   Crown 8vo, pp. xiv. and 418, cloth.   1880.   4s.

MODERN FRENCH READER —A GLOSSARY of Idioms, Gallicisms, and other Difficulties contained in the Senior Course of the Modern French Reader , with Short Notices of the most important French Writers and Historical or Literary Characters, and hints as to the works to be read or studied.   By Charles Cassal, LL.D., &c.   Crown 8vo, pp. viii. and 104, cloth.   1881.   2s. 6d.

MODERN FRENCH READER.—Senior Course and Glossary combined. 6s.

MORELET.—Travels in Central America, including Accounts of some Regions unexplored since the Conquest. From the French of A Morelet, hy Mrs. M. F. Squier. Edited by E. G. Squier. 8vo, pp. 430, cloth. 1871. 8s. 6d.

MORFIT.—A Practical Treatise on the Manufacture of Soaps. By Campbell Morfit, M.D., F.C S., formerly Professor of Applied Chemistry in the University of Maryland. With Illustrations. Demy 8vo, pp xii. and 270, cloth. 1871. £2, 12s. 6d.

MORFIT.—A Practical Treatise on Pure Fertilizers, and the Chemical Conversion of Rock Guanos, Marlstones, Coprolites, and the Crude Phosphates of Lime and Alumina generally into various valuable Products. By Campbell Morfit, M.D., F.C.S., formerly Professor of Applied Chemistry in the University of Maryland. With 28 Plates. 8vo, pp. xvi. and 547, cloth. 1873. £4, 4s.

MORRIS.—A Descriptive and Historical Account of the Godavery District, in the Presidency of Madras By Henry Morris, formerly of the Madras Civil Service, author of "A History of India, for use in Schools," and other works. With a Map. 8vo, pp. xii. and 390, cloth. 1878. 12s

MOSENTHAL.—Ostriches and Ostrich Farming. By J. de Mosenthal, late Member of the Legistive Council of the Cape of Good Hope, &c., and James E. Harting, F.L.S., F.Z.S , Member of the British Ornithologist's Union, &c. Second Edition. With 8 full-page illustrations and 20 woodcuts. Royal 8vo, pp. xxiv. and 246, cloth. 1879. 10s. 6d.

MOTLEY.—John Lothrop Motley : a Memoir. By Oliver Wendell Holmes. English Copyright Edition. Crown 8vo, pp. xii. and 275, cloth. 1878. 6s.

MUELLER.—The Organic Constituents of Plants and Vegetable Substances, and their Chemical Analysis. By Dr. G. C. Wittstein. Authorised Translation from the German Original, enlarged with numerous Additions, by Baron Ferd. von Mueller, K.C.M.G., M. & Ph. D., F.R.S. Crown 8vo, pp. xviii. and 332, wrapper. 1880. 14s.

MUELLER.—Select Extra-Tropical Plants readily eligible for Industrial Culture or Naturalisation With Indications of their Native Countries and some of their Uses By F. Von Mueller, K.C.M.G., M D , Ph.D., F R.S. 8vo, pp. x., 394, cloth. 1880. 8s.

MUHAMMED —The Life of Muhammed Based on Muhammed Ibn Ishak. By Abd El Malik Ibn Hisham. Edited by Dr. Ferdinand Wustenfeld. One volume containing the Arabic Text. 8vo, pp. 1026, sewed. £1, 1s. Another volume, containing Introduction, Notes, and Index in German. 8vo, pp. lxxii. and 266, sewed. 7s. 6d. Each part sold separately.

MUIR.—Extracts from the Coran. In the Original, with English rendering. Compiled by Sir William Muir, K C S I., LL.D., Author of "The Life of. Mahomet." Crown 8vo, pp. viii. and 64, cloth. 1880. 3s 6d.

MUIR.—Original Sanskrit Texts, on the Origin and History of the People of India, their Religion and Institutions. Collected, Translated, and Illustrated by John Muir, D.C.L., LL.D., Ph D., &c. &c.

Vol. I. Mythical and Legendary Accounts of the Origin of Caste, with an Inquiry into its existence in the Vedic Age. Second Edition, rewritten and greatly enlarged. 8vo, pp. xx. and 532, cloth. 1868. £1, 1s.

MUIR —ORIGINAL SANSKRIT TEXTS—*continued.*
Vol. II. The Trans-Himalayan Origin of the Hindus, and their Affinity with the Western Branches of the Aryan Race. Second Edition, revised, with Additions. 8vo, pp. xxxii and 512, cloth. 1871. £1, 1s.
Vol. III. The Vedas : Opinions of their Authors, and of later Indian Writers, on their Origin, Inspiration, and Authority. Second Edition, revised and enlarged. 8vo, pp. xxxii and 312, cloth. 1868. 16s.
Vol. IV. Comparison of the Vedic with the later representation of the principal Indian Deities. Second Edition, revised. 8vo, pp. xvi. and 524, cloth. 1873. £1, 1s.
Vol. V. Contributions to a Knowledge of the Cosmogony, Mythology, Religious Ideas, Life and Manners of the Indians in the Vedic Age. 8vo, pp xvi. and 492, cloth. 1870. £1, 1s.

MUIR.—TRANSLATIONS FROM THE SANSKRIT. See Trubner's Oriental Series.

MÜLLER.—OUTLINE DICTIONARY, for the Use of Missionaries, Explorers, and Students of Language. With an Introduction on the proper Use of the Ordinary English Alphabet in transcribing Foreign Languages. By F. Max Muller. M.A. The Vocabulary compiled by John Bellows. 12mo, pp. 368, morocco. 1867. 7s. 6d.

MÜLLER —LECTURE ON BUDDHIST NIHILISM. By F. Max Muller, M.A. Fcap. 8vo, sewed. 1869. 1s.

MÜLLER.—THE SACRED HYMNS OF THE BRAHMINS, as preserved to us in the oldest collection of religious poetry, the Rig-Veda-Sanhita Translated and explained, by F. Max Müller, M A , Fellow of All Souls' College, Professor of Comparative Philology at Oxford, Foreign Member of the Institute of France, &c , &c. Vol. I. Hymns to the Maruts or the Storm-Gods 8vo, pp. clii. and 264, cloth 1869. 12s 6d.

MÜLLER. —THE HYMNS OF THE RIG-VEDA, in the Samhita and Pada Texts. Reprinted from the Editio Princeps. By F. Max Muller, M A., &c. Second Edition, with the two Texts on Parallel Pages. In two vols. 8vo, pp 1704, sewed. £1, 12s.

MÜLLER.— A SHORT HISTORY OF THE BOURBONS. From the Earliest Period down to the Present Time. By R. M. Muller, Ph D., Modern Master at Forest School, Walthamstow, and Author of "Parallèle entre 'Jules César,' par Shakespeare, et 'Le Mort de César,' par Voltaire," &c. Fcap. 8vo, pp. 30, wrapper. 1882. 1s.

MÜLLER —ANCIENT INSCRIPTIONS IN CEYLON. By Dr Edward Muller. 2 Vols. Text, crown 8vo, pp. 220, cloth, and Plates, oblong folio, cloth. 1883. 21s.

MULLEY.—GERMAN GEMS IN AN ENGLISH SETTING. Translated by Jane Mulley. Fcap., pp. xii. and 180, cloth. 1877. 3s 6d

NÁGÁNANDA ; OR, THE JOY OF THE SNAKE WORLD A Buddhist Drama in Five Acts. Translated into English Prose, with Explanatory Notes, from the Sanskrit of Sri-Harsha-Deva, by Palmer Boyd, B A. With an Introduction by Professor Cowell. Crown 8vo, pp. xvi. and 100, cloth. 1872. 4s 6d.

NAPIER.—FOLK LORE ; or, Superstitious Beliefs in the West of Scotland within this Century. With an Appendix, showing the probable relation of the modern Festivals of Christmas, May Day, St. John's Day, and Hallowe'en, to ancient Sun and Fire Worship. By James Napier, F.R.S E., &c. Crown 8vo, pp. vii. and 190, cloth. 1878. 4s.

NARADÍYA DHARMA-SASTRA ; OR, THE INSTITUTES OF NARADA. Translated, for the first time, from the unpublished Sanskrit original. By Dr. Julius Jolly, University, Wurzburg. With a Preface, Notes, chiefly critical, an Index of Quotations from Narada in the principal Indian Digests, and a general Index. Crown 8vo, pp. xxxv. and 144, cloth. 1876. 10s. 6d.

NEVILL.—HAND LIST OF MOLLUSCA IN THE INDIAN MUSEUM, CALCUTTA. By Geoffrey Nevill, C.M.Z.S., &c., First Assistant to the Superintendent of the Indian Museum Part I. Gastropoda, Pulmonata, and Prosobranchia-Neuro-branchia. 8vo, pp. xvi. and 338, cloth. 1878. 15s.

NEWMAN.—THE ODES OF HORACE Translated into Unrhymed Metres, with Introduction and Notes. By F. W. Newman. Second Edition. Post 8vo, pp. xxi. and 247, cloth. 1876. 4s.

NEWMAN —THEISM, DOCTRINAL AND PRACTICAL; or, Didactic Religious Utterances. By F. W. Newman. 4to, pp. 184, cloth. 1858. 4s. 6d.

. NEWMAN.—HOMERIC TRANSLATION IN THEORY AND PRACTICE. A Reply to Matthew Arnold. By F. W. Newman. Crown 8vo, pp. 104, stiff covers. 1861. 2s. 6d.

NEWMAN —HIAWATHA: Rendered into Latin With Abridgment. By F. W. Newman. 12mo, pp. vii. and 110, sewed. 1862. 2s 6d.

NEWMAN —A HISTORY OF THE HEBREW MONARCHY from the Administration of Samuel to the Babylonish Captivity By F. W Newman. Third Edition. Crown 8vo, pp. x. and 354, cloth. 1865. 8s. 6d.

NEWMAN.—PHASES OF FAITH; or, Passages from the History of my Creed. New Edition, with Reply to Professor Henry Rogers, Author of the "Eclipse of Faith." Crown 8vo, pp. viii. and 212, cloth. 1881. 3s. 6d.

NEWMAN.—A HANDBOOK OF MODERN ARABIC, consisting of a Practical Grammar, with numerous Examples, Dialogues, and Newspaper Extracts, in European Type. By F. W. Newman Post 8vo, pp. xx. and 192, cloth. 1866. 6s.

NEWMAN.—TRANSLATIONS OF ENGLISH POETRY INTO LATIN VERSE. Designed as Part of a New Method of Instructing in Latin. By F. W. Newman. Crown 8vo, pp. xiv and 202, cloth. 1868. 6s.

NEWMAN.—THE SOUL: Her Sorrows and her Aspirations. An Essay towards the Natural History of the Soul, as the True Basis of Theology. By F. W. Newman. Tenth Edition. Post 8vo, pp. xii and 162, cloth. 1882. 3s. 6d.

NEWMAN.—MISCELLANIES; chiefly Addresses, Academical and Historical. By F. W. Newman. 8vo, pp. iv. and 356, cloth. 1869. 7s. 6d.

NEWMAN.—THE ILIAD OF HOMER, faithfully translated into Unrhymed English Metre, by F. W. Newman. Royal 8vo, pp. xvi. and 384, cloth 1871. 10s. 6d.

NEWMAN.—A DICTIONARY OF MODERN ARABIC. 1. Anglo-Arabic Dictionary 2. Anglo-Arabic Vocabulary. 3 Arabo-English Dictionary. By F. W. Newman. In 2 vols. crown 8vo, pp. xvi. and 376–464, cloth 1871. £1, 1s.

NEWMAN.—HEBREW THEISM. By F. W. Newman. Royal 8vo, pp. viii. and 172. Stiff wrappers. 1874. 4s. 6d.

NEWMAN.—THE MORAL INFLUENCE OF LAW. A Lecture by F. W. Newman, May 20, 1860. Crown 8vo, pp. 16, sewed. 3d.

NEWMAN.—RELIGION NOT HISTORY. By F. W. Newman. Foolscap, pp. 58, paper wrapper. 1877. 1s.

NEWMAN.—MORNING PRAYERS IN THE HOUSEHOLD OF A BELIEVER IN GOD. By F W. Newman. Second Edition. Crown 8vo, pp. 80, limp cloth. 1882. 1s. 6d.

NEWMAN.—REORGANIZATION OF ENGLISH INSTITUTIONS A Lecture by Emeritus Professor F. W. Newman. Delivered in the Manchester Athenæum, October 15, 1875. Crown 8vo, pp. 28, sewed. 1880. 6d.

NEWMAN.—WHAT IS CHRISTIANITY WITHOUT CHRIST? By F. W. Newman, Emeritus Professor of University College, London. 8vo, pp. 28, stitched in wrapper. 1881. 1s.

D

NEWMAN.—LIBYAN VOCABULARY. An Essay towards Reproducing the Ancient Numidian Language out of Four Modern Languages By F. W. Newman. Crown 8vo, pp. vi. and 204, cloth. 1882. 10s 6d

NEWMAN.—A CHRISTIAN COMMONWEALTH. By F W. Newman. Crown 8vo, pp. 60, cloth. 1883. 1s.

NEW SOUTH WALES, PUBLICATIONS OF THE GOVERNMENT OF. List on application.

NEW SOUTH WALES.—JOURNAL AND PROCEEDINGS OF THE ROYAL SOCIETY OF Published annually. Price 10s. 6d. List of Contents on application

NEWTON.—PATENT LAW AND PRACTICE. showing the mode of obtaining and opposing Grants, Disclaimers, Confirmations, and Extensions of Patents With a Chapter on Patent Agents. By A V. Newton. Enlarged Edition Crown 8vo, pp. xii. and 104, cloth. 1879. 2s. 6d.

NEW ZEALAND INSTITUTE PUBLICATIONS:—

  I. TRANSACTIONS AND PROCEEDINGS of the New Zealand Institute. Demy 8vo, stitched. Vols I to XIV., 1868 to 1881 £1, 1s each

  II. AN INDEX TO THE TRANSACTIONS AND PROCEEDINGS of the New Zealand Institute. Vols. I. to VIII Edited and Published under the Authority of the Board of Governors of the Institute. By James Hector, C.M.G., M D, F.R.S. Demy, 8vo, 44 pp, stitched. 1877. 2s 6d

NEW ZEALAND—GEOLOGICAL SURVEY. List of Publications on application.

NOIRIT.—A FRENCH COURSE IN TEN LESSONS. By Jules Noirit, B.A. Lessons I.–IV Crown 8vo, pp xiv and 80, sewed. 1870 1s 6d

NOIRIT—FRENCH GRAMMATICAL QUESTIONS for the use of Gentlemen preparing for the Army, Civil Service, Oxford Examinations, &c., &c. By Jules Noirit. Crown 8vo, pp. 62, cloth. 1870. 1s. Interleaved, 1s 6d.

NOURSE.—NARRATIVE OF THE SECOND ARCTIC EXPEDITION MADE BY CHARLES F. HALL. His Voyage to Repulse Bay; Sledge Journeys to the Straits of Fury and Hecla, and to King William's Land, and Residence among the Eskimos during the years 1864–69 Edited under the orders of the Hon Secretary of the Navy, by Prof J E Nourse, U.S.N. 4to, pp 1 and 644, cloth With maps, heliotypes, steel and wood engravings. 1880. £1, 8s.

NUGENT'S IMPROVED FRENCH AND ENGLISH AND ENGLISH AND FRENCH POCKET DICTIONARY. Par Smith. 24mo, pp. 489 and 320, cloth. 1873 3s.

NUTT.—TWO TREATISES ON VERBS CONTAINING FEEBLE AND DOUBLE LETTERS. By R Jehuda Hayug of Fez. Translated into Hebrew from the original Arabic by R. Moses Gikatilia of Cordova, with the Treatise on Punctuation by the same author, translated by Aben Ezra Edited from Bodleian MSS, with an English translation, by J. W. Nutt, M.A. Demy 8vo, pp. 312, sewed. 1870. 5s.

NUTT.—A SKETCH OF SAMARITAN HISTORY, DOGMA, AND LITERATURE. An Introtroduction to "Fragments of a Samaritan Targum" By J. W. Nutt, M A, &c, &c. Demy 8vo, pp. 180, cloth. 1874 5s.

OEHLENSCHLÄGER—AXEL AND VALBORG a Tragedy, in Five Acts, and other Poems. Translated from the Danish of Adam Oehlenschläger by Pierce Butler, M A., late Rector of Ulcombe, Kent Edited by Professor Palmer, M A., of St John's Coll, Camb. With a Memoir of the Translator. Fcap. 8vo, pp. xii. and 164, cloth. 1874. 5s.

OERA LINDA BOOK (THE)—From a Manuscript of the 13th Century, with the permission of the proprietor, C Over de Linden of the Helder. The Original Frisian Text as verified by Di J. O Ottema, accompanied by an English Version of Di. Ottema's Dutch Translation By W. R. Sandbach. 8vo, pp. xxv. and 254, cloth. 1876 5s.

OGAREFF.—ESSAI SUR LA SITUATION RUSSE. Lettres à un Anglais. Par N. Ogareff. 12mo, pp. 150, sewed 1862 3s.

OLCOTT—A BUDDHIST CATECHISM, according to the Canon of the Southern Church. By Colonel H S. Olcott, President of the Theosophical Society. 24mo, pp. 32. 1s.

OLCOTT.—THE YOGA PHILOSOPHY : Being the Text of Patanjali, with Bhojarajah's Commentary. A Reprint of the English Translation of the above, by the late Dr. Ballantyne and Govind Shastri Deva ; to which are added Extracts from Various Authors. With an Introduction by Colonel H. S. Olcott, President of the Theosophical Society The whole Edited by Tukaram Tatia, F.T.S. Crown 8vo, pp. xvi.-294, wrapper. 1882. 7s. 6d

OLLENDORFF.—METODO PARA APRENDER A LEER, escribir y hablar el Inglés segun el sistema de Ollendorff Por Ramon Palenzuela y Juan de la Carreño. 8vo, pp. xlvi. and 460, cloth. 1873. 7s. 6d.
KEY to Ditto. Crown 8vo, pp 112, cloth. 1873. 4s.

OLLENDORFF.—METODO PARA APRENDER A LEER, escribir y hablar el Frances, segun el verdadero sistema de Ollendorff ; ordenado en lecciones progresivas, consistiendo de ejercicios orales y escritos ; enriquecido de la pronunciacion figurada como se estila en la conversacion ; y de un Apéndice abrazando las reglas de la sintaxis, la formacion de los verbos regulares, y la conjugacion de los irregulares. Por Teodoro Simonné, Professor de Lenguas. Crown 8vo, pp. 342, cloth. 1873. 6s.
KEY to Ditto. Crown 8vo, pp. 80, cloth. 1873. 3s. 6d.

OPPERT.—ON THE CLASSIFICATION OF LANGUAGES A Contribution to Comparative Philology By Dr Gustav Oppert, Ph.D., Professor of Sanskrit, Presidency College, Madras 8vo, paper, pp. viii. and 146 1883. 7s 6d.

OPPERT—LISTS OF SANSKRIT MANUSCRIPTS in Private Libraries of Southern India, Compiled, Arranged, and Indexed by Gustav Oppert, Ph.D , Professor of Sanskrit, Presidency College, Madras. Vol. I. lex 8vo, pp. vii. and 620, cloth. 1883. £1, 1s

OPPERT—ON THE WEAPONS, ARMY ORGANISATION, AND POLITICAL MAXIMS OF THE ANCIENT HINDUS ; with special reference to Gunpowder and Firearms. By Dr. Gustav Oppert, Ph.D , Professor of Sanskrit, Presidency College, Madras. 8vo, paper, pp vi and 162. 1883. 7s. 6d.

ORIENTAL SERIES.—See TRUBNER'S ORIENTAL SERIES.

ORIENTAL TEXT SOCIETY'S PUBLICATIONS. A list may be had on application.

ORIENTAL CONGRESS.—REPORT OF THE PROCEEDINGS OF THE SECOND INTERNATIONAL CONGRESS OF ORIENTALISTS HELD IN LONDON, 1874. Royal 8vo, pp. viii. and 68, sewed. 1874 5s.

ORIENTALISTS.—TRANSACTIONS OF THE SECOND SESSION OF THE INTERNATIONAL CONGRESS OF ORIENTALISTS. Held in London in September 1874. Edited by Robert K Douglas, Hon. Sec. 8vo, pp. viii. and 456, cloth. 1876 21s.

OTTÉ—HOW TO LEARN DANISH (Dano-Norwegian) : a Manual for Students of Danish based on the Ollendorffian system of teaching languages, and adapted for self-instruction. By E C. Otté. Crown 8vo, pp. xx. and 338, cloth. 1879. 7s. 6d.
Key to above. Crown 8vo, pp 84, cloth. 3s.

OVERBECK.—CATHOLIC ORTHODOXY AND ANGLO-CATHOLICISM. A Word about the Intercommunion between the English and Orthodox Churches. By J. J. Overbeck, D.D. 8vo, pp. viii. and 200, cloth. 1866 5s.

OVERBECK—BONN CONFERENCE By J. J. Overbeck, D.D. Crown 8vo, pp. 48, sewed. 1876. 1s.

OVERBECK—A PLAIN VIEW OF THE CLAIMS OF THE ORTHODOX CATHOL O CHURCH AS OPPOSED TO ALL OTHER CHRISTIAN DENOMINATIONS. By J. J. Overbeck, D.D. Crown 8vo, pp iv and 138, wrapper. 1881. 2s. 6d.

OWEN.—FOOTFALLS ON THE BOUNDARY OF ANOTHER WORLD. With Narrative Illustrations. By R. D. Owen   An enlarged English Copyright Edition. Post 8vo, pp. xx. and 392, cloth. 1875. 7s. 6d.

OWEN.—THE DEBATABLE LAND BETWEEN THIS WORLD AND THE NEXT. With Illustrative Narrations.   By Robert Dale Owen. Second Edition. Crown 8vo, pp 456, cloth. 1874. 7s. 6d.

OWEN —THREADING MY WAY   Twenty-Seven Years of Autobiography   By R. D. Owen. Crown 8vo, pp. 344, cloth. 1874. 7s. 6d.

OYSTER (THE): WHERE, HOW, AND WHEN TO FIND, BREED, COOK, AND EAT IT. Second Edition, with a New Chapter, "The Oyster-Seeker in London." 12mo, pp viii and 106, boards. 1863. 1s.

PALESTINE —MEMOIRS OF THE SURVEY OF WESTERN PALESTINE.   Edited by W Besant, M.A , and E. H Palmer, M.A , under the Direction of the Committee of the Palestine Exploration Fund. Complete in seven volumes. Demy 4to, cloth, with a Portfolio of Plans, and large scale Map. Second Issue   Price Twenty Guineas.

PALMER.—LEAVES FROM A WORD-HUNTER'S NOTE-BOOK. Being some Contributions to English Etymology. By the Rev. A. Smythe Palmer, B.A., sometime Scholar in the University of Dublin. Crown 8vo, pp xii. and 316, cl. 1876   7s. 6d.

PALMER — A CONCISE DICTIONARY OF THE PERSIAN LANGUAGE. By E H. Palmer, M.A , of the Middle Temple, Barrister-at-Law, Lord Almoner's Reader, and Professor of Arabic, and Fellow of St. John's College in the University of Cambridge. Square royal 32mo, pp 726, cloth 1876   10s. 6d

PALMER.—THE SONG OF THE REED, AND OTHER PIECES. By E. H Palmer, M A., Cambridge. Crown 8vo, pp. 208, cloth. 1876. 5s.

PALMER.—HINDUSTANI, ARABIC, AND PERSIAN GRAMMAR. See Trubner's Collection

PALMER — THE PATRIARCH AND THE TSAR. Translated from the Russ by William Palmer, M A. Demy 8vo, cloth. Vol I. THE REPLIES OF THE HUMBLE NICON. Pp xl and 674. 1871. 12s —Vol II TESTIMONIES CONCERNING THE PATRIARCH NICON, THE TSAR, AND THE BOYARS. Pp lxxviii and 554. 1873 12s.—Vol III. HISTORY OF THE CONDEMNATION, OF THE PATRIARCH NICON. Pp. lxvi. and 558 1873. 12s —Vols. IV., V , and VI. SERVICES OF THE PATRIARCH NICON TO THE CHURCH AND STATE OF HIS COUNTRY, &c   Pp. lxxviii. and 1 to 660 ; xiv.-661-1028, and 1 to 254, xxvi -1029-1656, and 1-72. 1876. 36s.

PARKER—THEODORE PARKER'S CELEBRATED DISCOURSE ON MATTERS PERTAINING TO RELIGION. People's Edition. Crown 8vo, pp. 351. 1872 Stitched, 1s. 6d. , cloth, 2s

PARKER.—THEODORE PARKER. A Biography. By O. B. Frothingham. Crown 8vo, pp. viii. and 588, cloth, with Portrait. 1876 12s.

PARKER — THE COLLECTED WORKS OF THEODORE PARKER, Minister of the Twenty-eighth Congregational Society at Boston, U S   Containing his Theological, Polemical, and Critical Writings ; Sermons, Speeches, and Addresses ; and Literary Miscellanies. In 14 vols. 8vo, cloth   6s each.

Vol   I. Discourse on Matters Pertaining to Religion. Preface by the Editor, and Portrait of Parker from a medallion by Sauhni. Pp. 380.
Vol II. Ten Sermons and Prayers   Pp 360.
Vol III. Discourses of Theology. Pp. 318.
Vol. IV. Discourses on Politics. Pp. 312.
Vol. V. Discourses of Slavery. I. Pp 336.
Vol VI Discourses of Slavery. II Pp. 323
Vol. VII. Discourses of Social Science. Pp. 296.
Vol. VIII Miscellaneous Discourses. Pp. 230.
Vol IX. Critical Writings. I. Pp. 292.
Vol. X. Critical Writings. II Pp 308.
Vol. XI. Sermons of Theism, Atheism, and Popular Theology. Pp. 257.

PARKER.—COLLECTED WORKS—*continued.*

 Vol. XII. Autobiographical and Miscellaneous Pieces. Pp. 356
 Vol. XIII Historic Americans. Pp. 236
 Vol. XIV. Lessons from the World of Matter and the World of Man. Pp. 352.

PARKER.—MALAGASY GRAMMAR. See Trubner's Collection.

PATERSON—NOTES ON MILITARY SURVEYING AND RECONNAISSANCE. By Lieut.-Colonel William Paterson. Sixth Edition. With 16 Plates. Demy 8vo, pp. xii and 146, cloth. 1882. 7s. 6d.

PATERSON.—TOPOGRAPHICAL EXAMINATION PAPERS. By Lieut.-Col W. Paterson. 8vo, pp 32, with 4 Plates. Boards. 1882. 2s

PATERSON—TREATISE ON MILITARY DRAWING. With a Course of Progressive Plates. By Captain W. Paterson, Professor of Military Drawing at the Royal Military College, Sandhurst. Oblong 4to, pp. xii and 31, cloth. 1862 £1, 1s.

PATERSON—THE OROMETER FOR HILL MEASURING, combining Scales of Distances, Protractor, Clinometer, Scale of Horizontal Equivalents, Scale of Shade, and Table of Gradients. By Captain William Paterson. On cardboard. 1s

PATERSON—CENTRAL AMERICA. By W. Paterson, the Merchant Statesman. From a MS. in the British Museum, 1701 With a Map Edited by S. Bannister, M.A. 8vo, pp 70, sewed. 1857. 2s 6d.

PATON.—A HISTORY OF THE EGYPTIAN REVOLUTION, from the Period of the Mamelukes to the Death of Mohammed Ali; from Arab and European Memoirs, Oral Tradition, and Local Research. By A. A. Paton. Second Edition. 2 vols. demy 8vo, pp. xii. and 395, viii and 446, cloth. 1870. 7s. 6d.

PATON—HENRY BEYLE (otherwise DE STENDAHL). A Critical and Biographical Study, aided by Original Documents and Unpublished Letters from the Private Papers of the Family of Beyle. By A. A. Paton. Crown 8vo, pp. 340, cloth. 1874 7s. 6d.

PATTON.—THE DEATH OF DEATH; or, A Study of God's Holiness in Connection with the Existence of Evil, in so far as Intelligent and Responsible Beings are Concerned. By an Orthodox Layman (John M. Patton). Revised Edition, crown 8vo, pp. xvi and 252, cloth. 1881. 6s.

PAULI.—SIMON DE MONTFORT, EARL OF LEICESTER, the Creator of the House of Commons. By Reinhold Pauli. Translated by Una M. Goodwin. With Introduction by Harriet Martineau. Crown 8vo, pp xvi. and 340, cloth. 1876. 6s.

PETTENKOFER—THE RELATION OF THE AIR TO THE CLOTHES WE WEAR, THE HOUSE WE LIVE IN, AND THE SOIL WE DWELL ON. Three Popular Lectures delivered before the Albert Society at Dresden. By Dr. Max Von Pettenkofer, Professor of Hygiene at the University of Munich, &c. Abridged and Translated by Augustus Hess, M.D , M.R C.P , London, &c. Cr. 8vo, pp. viii. and 96, limp cl. 1873. 2s. 6d.

PETRUCCELLI.—PRELIMINAIRES DE LA QUESTION ROMAINE DE M ED ABOUT. Par F. Petruccelli de la Gattina 8vo, pp. xv. and 364, cloth. 1860. 7s. 6d.

PEZZI.—ARYAN PHILOLOGY, according to the most recent researches (Glottologia Aria Recentissima). Remarks Historical and Critical. By Domenico Pezzi. Translated by E. S Roberts, M A. Crown 8vo, pp xvi and 200, cloth. 1879 6s

PHAYRE—A HISTORY OF BURMA. See Trubner's Oriental Series.

PHAYRE.—THE COINS OF ARAKAN, OF PEGU, AND OF BURMA By Sir Arthur Phayre, C B., K.C.S I , G C M G , late Commissioner of British Burma. Royal 4to, pp.viii.-48, with Autotype Illustrative Plates. Wrapper. 1882. 8s. 6d.

PHILLIPS.—THE DOCTRINE OF ADDAI, THE APOSTLE, now first edited in a complete form in the Original Syriac, with English Translation and Notes. By George Phillips, D.D., President of Queen's College, Cambridge. 8vo, pp. xv. and 52 and 53, cloth. 1876. 7s. 6d.

PHILOLOGICAL SOCIETY, Transactions of, published irregularly. List of publications on application.

PHILOSOPHY (THE) OF INSPIRATION AND REVELATION By a Layman. With a preliminary notice of an Essay by the present Lord Bishop of Winchester, contained in a volume entitled "Aids to Faith" 8vo, pp. 20, sewed. 1875. 6d.

PICCIOTTO.—Sketches of Anglo-Jewish History. By James Picciotto. Demy 8vo, pp. xi and 420, cloth. 1875. 12s.

PIESSE —Chemistry in the Brewing-Room · being the substance of a Course of Lessons to Practical Brewers With Tables of Alcohol, Extract, and Original Gravity. By Charles H. Piesse, F.C.S., Public Analyst. Fcap , pp. viii. and 62, cloth. 1877. 5s.

PIRY.—Le Saint Édit, Étude de Litterature Chinoise. Préparée par A. Théophile Piry, du Service des Douanes Maritimes de Chine. 4to, pp xx and 320, cloth. 1879. 21s.

PLAYFAIR.—The Cities and Towns of China A Geographical Dictionary. By G M. H. Playfair, of Her Majesty's Consular Service in China. 8vo, pp. 506, cloth. 1879. £1, 5s.

PLINY.—The Letters of Pliny the Younger. Translated by J. D. Lewis, M A , Trinity College, Cambridge. Post 8vo, pp. vii. and 390, cloth. 1879. 5s.

PLUMPTRE —King's College Lectures on Elocution ; on the Physiology and Culture of Voice and Speech and the Expression of the Emotions by Language, Countenance, and Gesture. To which is added a Special Lecture on the Causes and Cure of the Impediments of Speech Being the substance of the Introductory Course of Lectures annually delivered by Charles John Plumptre, Lecturer on Public Reading and Speaking at King's College, London, in the Evening Classes Department. Dedicated by permission to H R H the Prince of Wales. Fourth, greatly Enlarged Illustrated, Edition. Post 8vo, pp xviii. and 494, cloth. 1883. 15s.

PLUMPTRE —General Sketch of the History of Pantheism By C E. Plumptre. Vol I , from the Earliest Times to the Age of Spinoza , Vol. II., from the Age of Spinoza to the Commencement of the 19th Century 2 vols demy 8vo, pp. viii and 395 ; iv and 348, cloth 1881. 18s.

POLE —The Philosophy of Music See English and Foreign Philosophical Library. Vol. XI.

PONSARD.—Charlotte Corday. A Tragedy. By F. Ponsard. Edited, with English Notes and Notice on Ponsard, by Professor C Cassal, LL D. 12mo, pp xi. and 133, cloth. 1867. 2s. 6d.

PONSARD.—L'Honneur et L'Argent. A Comedy By François Ponsard. Edited, with English Notes and Memoir of Ponsard, by Professor C. Cassal, LL D. Fcap. 8vo, pp xvi. and 172, cloth. 1869 3s 6d.

POOLE —An Index to Periodical Literature By W F. Poole, LL.D , Librarian of the Chicago Public Library Third Edition, brought down to January 1882 1 vol , royal 8vo, pp. xxviii and 1442, cloth 1883 £3, 13s. 6d Wrappers, £3, 10s.

PRACTICAL GUIDES :—

FRANCE, BELGIUM, HOLLAND, AND THE RHINE 1s.—ITALIAN LAKES 1s —WINTERING PLACES OF THE SOUTH 2s.—SWITZERLAND, SAVOY, AND NORTH ITALY. 2s 6d —GENERAL CONTINENTAL GUIDE. 5s —GENEVA. 1s —PARIS 1s —BERNESE OBERLAND. 1s —ITALY 4s.

PRATT.— A Grammar and Dictionary of the Samoan Language By Rev. George Pratt, Forty Years a Missionary of the London Missionary Society in Samoa. Second Edition Edited by Rev. S J. Whitmee, F.R.G S. Crown 8vo, pp. viii. and 380, cloth. 1878 18s.

PSYCHICAL RESEARCH, Society for, Proceedings. Published irregularly.

QUINET —THE RELIGIOUS REVOLUTION OF THE NINETEENTH CENTURY. From the French of Edgar Quinet. Fcap. 8vo, pp. xl. and 70, parchment. 1881. 1s. 6d.

QUINET. —EDGAR QUINET. See English and Foreign Philosophical Library, Vol. XIV.

RAM RAZ. —ESSAY ON THE ARCHITECTURE OF THE HINDUS. By Ram Raz, Native Judge and Magistrate of Bangalore, Corr. Mem. R. A S. With 48 Plates. 4to, pp. xiv. and 64, sewed. 1834 £2, 2s.

RAMSAY. —TABULAR LIST OF ALL THE AUSTRALIAN BIRDS AT PRESENT KNOWN TO THE AUTHOR, showing the distribution of the species. By E. P. Ramsay, F.L S , &c., Curator of the Australian Museum, Sydney. 8vo, pp. 36, and Map ; boards. 1878. 5s.

RAND, M'NALLY, & CO.'S BUSINESS ATLAS OF THE UNITED STATES, CANADA, AND WEST INDIAN ISLANDS. With a Complete Reference Map of the World, Ready Reference Index, &c., of all Post Offices, Railroad Stations, and Villages in the United States and Canada. With Official Census. 4to, pp. 212, cloth. 1881. £2, 12s. 6d.

RASK. —GRAMMAR OF THE ANGLO-SAXON TONGUE, from the Danish of Erasmus Rask. By Benjamin Thorpe. Third Edition, corrected and improved, with Plate. Post 8vo, pp vi. and 192, cloth. 1879. 5s 6d

RASK. —A SHORT TRACTATE on the Longevity ascribed to the Patriarchs in the Book of Genesis, and its relation to the Hebrew Chronology; the Flood, the Exodus of the Israelites, the Site of Eden, &c. From the Danish of the late Professor Rask, with his manuscript corrections, and large additions from his autograph, now for the first time printed. With a Map of Paradise and the circumjacent Lands. Crown 8vo, pp. 134, cloth. 1863. 2s. 6d.

RATTON. —A HANDBOOK OF COMMON SALT By J. J. L. Ratton, M.D , M.C., Surgeon, Madras Army. 8vo, pp. xviii. and 282, cloth. 1879. 7s. 6d

RAVENSTEIN —THE RUSSIANS ON THE AMUR ; its Discovery, Conquest, and Colonization, with a Description of the Country, its Inhabitants, Productions, and Commercial Capabilities, and Personal Accounts of Russian Travellers. By E. G. Ravenstein, F R.G S. With 4 tinted Lithographs and 3 Maps. 8vo, pp. 500, cloth. 1861. 15s.

RAVENSTEIN AND HULLEY —THE GYMNASIUM AND ITS FITTINGS. By E. G. Ravenstein and John Hulley. With 14 Plates of Illustrations. 8vo, pp 32, sewed. 1867. 2s. 6d.

RAVERTY. —NOTES ON AFGHANISTAN AND PART OF BALUCHISTAN, Geographical, Ethnographical, and Historical, extracted from the Writings of little known Afghan, and Tajyik Historians, &c., &c., and from Personal Observation By Major H. G. Raverty, Bombay Native Infantry (Retired). Foolscap folio. Sections I and II., pp. 98, wrapper. 1880. 2s. Section III., pp. vi. and 218. 1881. 5s.

READE. —THE MARTYRDOM OF MAN. By Winwood Reade. Fifth Edition. Crown 8vo, pp. viii. and 544, cloth. 1881. 7s. 6d.

RECORD OFFICE —A SEPARATE CATALOGUE OF THE OFFICIAL PUBLICATIONS OF THE PUBLIC RECORD OFFICE, on sale by Trübner & Co , may be had on application.

RECORDS OF THE HEART By Stella, Author of "Sappho," "The King's Stratagem," &c. Second English Edition. Crown 8vo, pp. xvi. and 188, with six steel-plate engravings, cloth. 1881. 3s 6d

REDHOUSE.—THE TURKISH VADE MECUM OF OTTOMAN COLLOQUIAL LANGUAGE: Containing a Concise Ottoman Grammar, a Carefully Selected Vocabulary Alphabetically Arranged, in two Parts, English and Turkish, and Turkish and English ; Also a few Familiar Dialogues and Naval and Military Terms. The whole in English Characters. the Pronunciation being fully indicated. By J. W Redhouse, M R A.S. Third Edition 32mo, pp. viii. and 372, cloth. 1882 6s.

REDHOUSE —ON THE HISTORY, SYSTEM, AND VARIETIES OF TURKISH POETRY. Illustrated by Selections in the Original and in English Paraphrase, with a Notice of the Islamic Doctrine of the Immortality of Woman's Soul in the Future State. By J. W. Redhouse, Esq., M.R A.S. 8vo, pp. 62, cloth, 2s. 6d ; wrapper, 1s. 6d. 1879.

REDHOUSE.—THE MESNEVĪ. See Trübner's Oriental Series.

REEMELIN —A CRITICAL REVIEW OF AMERICAN POLITICS. By C Reemelin, of Cincinnati, Ohio. Demy 8vo, pp. xxiv. and 630, cloth. 1881. 14s.

RENAN.—AN ESSAY ON THE AGE AND ANTIQUITY OF THE BOOK OF NABATHÆAN AGRICULTURE To which is added an Inaugural Lecture on the Position of the Shemitic Nations in the History of Civilisation. By Ernest Renan. Crown 8vo, pp. xvi. and 148, cloth. 1862 3s. 6d.

RENAN.—THE LIFE OF JESUS By Ernest Renan. Authorised English Translation. Crown 8vo, pp xii. and 312, cloth. 2s. 6d. , sewed, 1s. 6d.

RENAN —THE APOSTLES By Ernest Renan Translated from the original French. 8vo, pp viii. and 288, cloth. 1869. 7s. 6d.

REPORT OF A GENERAL CONFERENCE OF LIBERAL THINKERS, for the discussion of matters pertaining to the religious needs of our time, and the methods of meeting them. Held June 13th and 14th, 1878, at South Place Chapel, Finsbury, London 8vo, pp. 77, sewed. 1878. 1s.

RHODES.—UNIVERSAL CURVE TABLES FOR FACILITATING THE LAYING OUT OF CIRCULAR ARCS ON THE GROUND FOR RAILWAYS, CANALS, &c. Together with Table of Tangential Angles and Multiples. By Alexander Rhodes, C.E. Oblong 18mo, hand, pp. ix. and 104, roan. 1881. 5s

RHYS.—LECTURES ON WELSH PHILOLOGY. By John Rhys, M A., Professor of Celtic at Oxford, Honorary Fellow of Jesus College, &c., &c Second Edition, Revised and Enlarged. Crown 8vo, pp. xiv and 467, cloth 1879. 15s.

RICE —MYSORE AND COORG A Gazetteer compiled for the Government of India. By Lewis Rice, Director of Public Instruction, Mysore and Coorg. Vol I. Mysore in General. With 2 Coloured Maps. Vol II. Mysore, by Districts. With 10 Coloured Maps Vol. III Coorg With a Map 3 vols royal 8vo, pp. xii 670 and xvi. ; 544 and xxii. , and 427 and xxvii., cloth. 1878. 25s.

RICE.—MYSORE INSCRIPTIONS. Translated for the Government by Lewis Rice, 8vo, pp. xcii. and 336-xxx., with a Frontispiece and Map, boards. 1879. 30s.

RIDLEY.—KÁMILARÓI, AND OTHER AUSTRALIAN LANGUAGES. By the Rev. William Ridley, B A. Second Edition, revised and enlarged by the author ; with comparative Tables of Words from twenty Australian Languages, and Songs, Traditions, Laws, and Customs of the Australian Race. Small 4to, pp. vi. and 172, cloth. 1877. 10s. 6d.

RIG-VEDA-SANHITA. A Collection of Ancient Hindu Hymns Constituting the 1st to the 8th Ashtakas, or Books of the Rig-Veda; the oldest authority for the Religious and Social Institutions of the Hindus Translated from the Original Sanskrit. By the late H. H. Wilson, M A., F.R.S., &c., &c.

    Vol. I.   8vo, pp. lii. and 348, cloth. 21s.
    Vol. II. 8vo, pp. xxx. and 346, cloth. 1854. 21s.
    Vol. III. 8vo, pp. xxiv. and 525, cloth. 1857. 21s.
    Vol IV. Edited by E B. Cowell, M.A. 8vo, pp. 214, cloth. 1866. 14s.
    Vols. V. and VI. in the Press.

RILEY.—MEDIÆVAL CHRONICLES OF THE CITY OF LONDON. Chronicles of the Mayore and Sheriffs of London, and the Events which happened in their Days, from the Year A.D. 1188 to A.D. 1274. Translated from the original Latin of the "Liber de Antiquis Legibus" (published by the Camden Society), in the possession of the Corporation of the City of London; attributed to Arnold Fitz-Thedmar, Alderman of London in the Reign of Henry III —Chronicles of London, and of the Marvels therein, between the Years 44 Henry III., A.D. 1260, and 17 Edward III., A.D 1343. Translated from the original Anglo-Norman of the "Croniques de London," preserved in the Cottonian Collection (Cleopatra A. iv.) in the British Museum. Translated, with copious Notes and Appendices, by Henry Thomas Riley, M.A., Clare Hall, Cambridge, Barrister-at-Law. 4to, pp. xii and 319, cloth. 1863. 12s.

RIOLA.—How TO LEARN RUSSIAN: a Manual for Students of Russian, based upon the Ollendorffian System of Teaching Languages, and adapted for Self-Instruction. By Henry Riola, Teacher of the Russian Language With a Preface by W.R S. Ralston, M A. Crown 8vo, pp 576, cloth. 1878. 12s.
    KEY to the above. Crown 8vo, pp. 126, cloth 1878 5s

RIOLA.—A GRADUATED RUSSIAN READER, with a Vocabulary of all the Russian Words contained in it By Henry Riola, Author of "How to Learn Russian" Crown 8vo, pp. viii. and 314, cloth. 1879. 10s. 6d.

RIPLEY—SACRED RHETORIC; or, Composition and Delivery of Sermons. By Henry I. Ripley. 12mo, pp 234, cloth. 1858. 2s. 6d.

ROCHE.—A FRENCH GRAMMAR, for the use of English Students, adopted for the Public Schools by the Imperial Council of Public Instruction. By A. Roche. Crown 8vo, pp. xii and 176, cloth. 1869. 3s.

ROCHE.—PROSE AND POETRY. Select Pieces from the best English Authors, for Reading, Composition, and Translation By A. Roche. Second Edition. Fcap. 8vo, pp. viii. and 226, cloth. 1872 2s. 6d.

ROCKHILL—UDANAVARGA. See Trubner's Oriental Series

RODD.—THE BIRDS OF CORNWALL AND THE SCILLY ISLANDS. By the late Edward Hearle Rodd. Edited, with an Introduction, Appendix, and Memoir, by J. E. Harting 8vo, pp. lvi and 320, with Portrait and Map, cloth. 1880. 14s.

ROGERS—THE WAVERLEY DICTIONARY · An Alphabetical Arrangement of all the Characters in Sir Walter Scott's Waverley Novels, with a Descriptive Analysis of each Character, and Illustrative Selections from the Text. By May Rogers. 12mo, pp. 358, cloth. 1879. 10s.

ROSS—ALPHABETICAL MANUAL OF BLOWPIPE ANALYSIS, showing all known Methods, Old and New. By Lieut.-Colonel W. A. Ross, late R A., Member of the German Chemical Society (Author of "Pyrology, or Fire Chemistry"). Crown 8vo, pp xii. and 148, cloth. 1880. 5s.

ROSS.—PYROLOGY, OR FIRE CHEMISTRY; a Science interesting to the General Philosopher, and an Art of infinite importance to the Chemist, Metallurgist, Engineer, &c., &c. By W. A. Ross, lately a Major in the Royal Artillery. Small 4to, pp. xxviii. and 346, cloth. 1875. 36s.

ROSS.—CELEBRITIES OF THE YORKSHIRE WOLDS. By Frederick Ross, Fellow of the Royal Historical Society. 12mo, pp. 202, cloth. 1878. 4s.

ROSS —COREAN PRIMER · being Lessons in Corean on all Ordinary Subjects. Trans-literated on the principles of the "Mandarin Primer," by the same author. By Rev. John Ross, Newchwang. 8vo, pp 90, wrapper. 1877. 10s.

ROSS.—HONOUR OR SHAME? By R S. Ross 8vo, pp 183. 1878. Cloth. 3s. 6d; paper, 2s. 6d.

ROSS —REMOVAL OF THE INDIAN TROOPS TO MALTA. By R. S. Ross. 8vo, pp 77, paper. 1878. 1s. 6d.

ROSS —THE MONK OF ST. GALL. A Dramatic Adaptation of Scheffel's "Ekke-hard." By R S. Ross. Crown 8vo, pp. xii. and 218   1879.   5s

ROSS.—ARIADNE IN NAXOS By R S Ross. Square 16mo, pp. 200, cloth 1882. 5s.

ROTH.—NOTES ON CONTINENTAL IRRIGATION. By H. L. Roth. Demy 8vo, pp. 40, with 8 Plates, cloth. 1882. 5s.

ROUGH NOTES OF JOURNEYS made in the years 1868–1873 in Syria, down the Tigris, India, Kashmir, Ceylon, Japan, Mongolia, Siberia, the United States, the Sand-wich Islands, and Australasia Demy 8vo, pp 624, cloth. 1875   14s.

ROUSTAING.—THE FOUR GOSPELS EXPLAINED BY THEIR WRITERS. With an Appendix on the Ten Commandments Edited by J. B Roustaing. Translated by W E. Kirby. 3 vols. crown 8vo, pp 440-456-304, cloth 1881   15s.

ROUTLEDGE —ENGLISH RULE AND NATIVE OPINION IN INDIA From Notes taken in 1870-74. By James Routledge 8vo, pp. x. and 338, cloth. 1878. 10s. 6d.

ROWE.—AN ENGLISHMAN'S VIEWS ON QUESTIONS OF THE DAY IN VICTORIA. By C. J Rowe, M A. Crown 8vo, pp. 122, cloth. 1882   4s

ROWLEY —ORNITHOLOGICAL MISCELLANY. By George Dawson Rowley, M A., F Z S.
Vol. I. Part 1, 15s —Part 2, 20s —Part 3, 15s.—Part 4, 20s
Vol. II. Part 5, 20s —Part 6, 20s —Part 7, 10s. 6d —Part 8, 10s 6d —Part 9, 10s. 6d —Part 10, 10s 6d
Vol III Part 11, 10s 6d.—Part 12, 10s 6d —Part 13, 10s. 6d — Part 14, 20s.

ROYAL SOCIETY OF LONDON (THE).—CATALOGUE OF SCIENTIFIC PAPERS (1800-1863), Compiled and Published by the Royal Society of London. Demy 4to, cloth, per vol. £1 ; in half-morocco, £1, 8s. Vol. I. (1867), A to Clnzel pp. lxxix and 960; Vol II (1868), Coaklay—Graydon. pp iv and 1012 , Vol. III (1869), Greatheed—Leze pp. v and 1002 ; Vol IV. (1870), L'Héritier de Brutille—Pozzetti pp iv. and 1006 , Vol V. (1871), Plaag—Tizzam. pp iv. and 1000 ; Vol VI. (1872), Tkalec—Zylius, Anonymous and Additions. pp xi. and 763   Continuation of above (1864-1873) ; Vol. VII. (1877), A to Hyrtl pp. xxxi. and 1047 ; Vol VIII (1879), Ibañez—Zwicky pp 1310. A List of the Publications of the Royal Society (Separate Papers from the Philosophical Transactions), on application.

RUNDALL.—A SHORT AND EASY WAY TO WRITE ENGLISH AS SPOKEN. Méthode Rapide et Facile d'Ecrire le Français comme on le Parle. Kurze und Leichte Weise Deutsch zu Schreiben wie man es Spricht. By J. B. Rundall, Certificated Member of the London Shorthand Writers' Association. 6d. each

RUTHERFORD.—THE AUTOBIOGRAPHY OF MARK RUTHERFORD, Dissenting Minister. Edited by his friend, Reuben Shapcott. Crown 8vo, pp xii and 180, boards. 1881. 5s.

RUTTER.—See BUNYAN

SÂMAVIDHÂNABRÂHMANA (THE) (being the Third Brâhmana) of the Sâma Veda. Edited, together with the Commentary of Sâyana, an English Translation, Intro-duction, and Index of Words, by A. C Burnell. Vol I. Text and Commentary, with Introduction. Demy 8vo, pp xxxviii and 104, cloth 1873. 12s. 6d

SAMUELSON —HISTORY OF DRINK. A Review, Social, Scientific, and Political By James Samuelson, of the Middle Temple, Barrister-at-Law. Second Edition. 8vo, pp xxviii. and 288, cloth. 1880   6s.

SAND.—MOLIÈRE. A Drama in Prose. By George Sand. Edited, with Notes, by Th. Karcher, LL.B. 12mo, pp xx. and 170, cloth. 1868. 3s. 6d.

SARTORIUS.—MEXICO. Landscapes and Popular Sketches. By C. Sartorius. Edited by Dr Gaspey. With Engravings, from Sketches by M. Rugendas 4to, pp. vi and 202, cloth gilt. 1859. 18s.

SATOW—AN ENGLISH JAPANESE DICTIONARY OF THE SPOKEN LANGUAGE. By Ernest Mason Satow, Japanese Secretary to H M Legation at Yedo, and Ishibashi Masakata of the Imperial Japanese Foreign Office. Second Edition Imperial 32mo, pp xv. and 416, cloth. 1879. 12s. 6d

SAVAGE.—THE MORALS OF EVOLUTION By M J Savage, Author of "The Religion of Evolution," &c Crown 8vo, pp 192, cloth. 1880 5s

SAVAGE.—BELIEF IN GOD; an Examination of some Fundamental Theistic Problems By M J Savage. To which is added an Address on the Intellectual Basis of Faith By W H Savage 8vo, pp. 176, cloth. 1881. 5s.

SAVAGE—BELIEFS ABOUT MAN. By M. J. Savage Crown 8vo, pp. 130, cloth. 1882 5s.

SAYCE.—AN ASSYRIAN GRAMMAR for Comparative Purposes. By A. H Sayce, M.A., Fellow and Tutor of Queen's College, Oxford. Crown 8vo, pp. xvi. and 188, cloth. 1872. 7s. 6d.

SAYCE.—THE PRINCIPLES OF COMPARATIVE PHILOLOGY. By A. H Sayce, M.A. Crown 8vo, pp. 384, cloth. 1874. 10s. 6d.

SCHAIBLE.—AN ESSAY ON THE SYSTEMATIC TRAINING OF THE BODY. By C. H. Schaible, M.D , &c , &c. A Memorial Essay, Published on the occasion of the first Centenary Festival of Frederick L Jahn, with an Etching by H. Herkomer. Crown 8vo, pp. xviii and 124, cloth. 1878. 5s.

SCHEFFEL—MOUNTAIN PSALMS By J V. Von Scheffel. Translated by Mrs F. Brunnow. Fcap., pp 62, with 6 Plates after designs by A. Von Werner Parchment 1882. 3s. 6d.

SCHILLER.—THE BRIDE OF MESSINA Translated from the German of Schiller in English Verse. By Emily Allfrey. Crown 8vo, pp. viii. and 110, cloth 1876 2s.

SCHLAGINTWEIT.—BUDDHISM IN TIBET Illustrated by Literary Documents and Objects of Religious Worship. By Emil Schlagintweit, LL D With a folio Atlas of 20 Plates, and 20 Tables of Native Print in the Text. Roy. 8vo, pp. xxiv. and 404. 1863. £2, 2s.

SCHLEICHER—A COMPENDIUM OF THE COMPARATIVE GRAMMAR OF THE INDO-EUROPEAN, SANSKRIT, GREEK, AND LATIN LANGUAGES By August Schleicher. Translated from the Third German Edition, by Herbert Bendall, B.A., Chr. Coll., Camb. 8vo. Part I., Phonology. Pp.184, cloth. 1874 7s. 6d Part II., Morphology. Pp. viii. and 104, cloth. 1877. 6s.

SCHULTZ.—UNIVERSAL DOLLAR TABLES (Complete United States). Covering all Exchanges between the United States and Great Britain, France, Belgium, Switzerland, Italy, Spain, and Germany By C. W. H Schultz. 8vo, cloth. 1874. 15s.

SCHULTZ.—UNIVERSAL INTEREST AND GENERAL PERCENTAGE TABLES. On the Decimal System With a Treatise on the Currency of the World, and numerous examples for Self-Instruction. By C. W. H. Schultz. 8vo, cloth. 1874. 10s. 6d.

SCHULTZ—ENGLISH GERMAN EXCHANGE TABLES By C. W. H. Schultz With a Treatise on the Currency of the World. 8vo, boards 1874. 5s.

SCHWENDLER—INSTRUCTIONS FOR TESTING TELEGRAPH LINES, and the Technical Arrangements in Offices Written on behalf of the Government of India, under the Orders of the Director-General of Telegraphs in India. By Louis Schwendler Vol. I., demy 8vo, pp. 248, cloth. 1878. 12s. Vol. II., demy 8vo, pp. xi. and 268, cloth. 1880. 9s.

SCOONES —FAUST. A Tragedy By Goethe Translated into English Verse, by William Dalton Scoones. Fcap., pp. vi. and 230, cloth 1879 5s.

SCOTT —THE ENGLISH LIFE OF JESUS By Thomas Scott Crown 8vo, pp. xxviii. and 350, cloth. 1879. 2s 6d.

SCOTUS —A NOTE ON MR GLADSTONE'S "The Peace to Come." By Scotus. 8vo, pp 106 1878 Cloth, 2s. 6d; paper wrapper, 1s 6d.

SELL —THE FAITH OF ISLAM. By the Rev. E. Sell, Fellow of the University of Madras. Demy 8vo, pp. xiv. and 270, cloth. 1881. 6s 6d.

SELL.—IHN-I-TAJWID; OR, ART OF READING THE QURAN. By the Rev. E. Sell, B D. 8vo, pp. 48, wrappers. 1882. 2s. 6d.

SELSS —GOETHE'S MINOR POEMS. Selected, Annotated, and Rearranged By Albert M. Selss, Ph D Crown 8vo, pp xxxi. and 152, cloth 1875. 3s 6d.

SERMONS NEVER PREACHED. By Philip Phosphor. Crown 8vo, pp. vi and 124, cloth. 1878. 2s. 6d.

SEWELL —REPORT ON THE AMARAVATI TOPE, and Excavations on its Site in 1877. By Robert Sewell, of the Madras C.S., &c. With four plates. Royal 4to, pp. 70, boards 1880. 3s.

SHADWELL —A SYSTEM OF POLITICAL ECONOMY. By John Lancelot Shadwell. 8vo, pp 650, cloth. 1877. 7s. 6d.

SHADWELL.—POLITICAL ECONOMY FOR THE PEOPLE By John Lancelot Shadwell, Author of "A System of Political Economy." Reprinted from the "Labour News" Fcap., pp. vi and 154, limp cloth 1880. 1s 6d.

SHAKESPEARE'S CENTURIE OF PRAYSE; being Materials for a History of Opinion on Shakespeare and his Works, culled from Writers of the First Century after his Rise. By C. M. Ingleby. Medium 8vo, pp. xx. and 384. Stiff cover. 1874 £1, 1s. Large paper, fcap 4to, boards £2, 2s

SHAKESPEARE —HERMENEUTICS; OR, THE STILL LION Being an Essay towards the Restoration of Shakespeare's Text. By C. M. Ingleby. M.A., LL.D., of Trinity College, Cambridge Small 4to, pp 168, boards. 1875. 6s

SHAKESPEARE.—THE MAN AND THE BOOK. By C. M. Ingleby, M.A., LL.D. 8vo Part I. 6s.

SHAKESPEARE.—OCCASIONAL PAPERS ON SHAKESPEARE; being the Second Part of "Shakespeare: the Man and the Book" By C. M Ingleby, M.A., LL D, V P R.S L. Small 4to, pp. x and 194, paper boards. 1881. 6s

SHAKESPEARE —A NEW VARIORUM EDITION OF SHAKESPEARE. Edited by Horace Howard Furness. Royal 8vo. Vol. I. Romeo and Juliet Pp. xxiii and 480, cloth. 1871. 18s.—Vol. II. Macbeth. Pp. xix. and 492 1873. 18s.—Vols. III. and IV. Hamlet 2 vols pp. xx and 474 and 430. 1877. 36s.—Vol. V. King Lear. Pp. vi. and 504. 1880. 18s.

SHAKESPEARE.—CONCORDANCE TO SHAKESPEARE'S POEMS. By Mrs. H. H Furness Royal 8vo, cloth. 18s.

SHAKSPERE SOCIETY (THE NEW) —Subscription, One Guinea per annum List of Publications on application

SHERRING.—THE SACRED CITY OF THE HINDUS An Account of Benares in Ancient and Modern Times By the Rev M A. Sherring, M A, LL D.; and Prefaced with an Introduction by FitzEdward Hall, D.C L. With Illustrations. 8vo, pp. xxxvi. and 388, cloth. 21s.

SHERRING.—HINDU TRIBES AND CASTES; together with an Account of the Mohamedan Tribes of the North-West Frontier and of the Aboriginal Tribes of the Central Provinces By the Rev. M. A Sherring, M A, LL.B., Lond., &c. 4to. Vol II. Pp lxviii. and 376, cloth 1879. £2, 8s —Vol III., with Index of 3 vols. Pp. xii and 336, cloth. 1881 32s

SHERRING.—THE HINDOO PILGRIMS. By Rev. M. A. Sherring, M.A , LL.D. Crown 8vo, pp. 126, cloth. 1878. 5s.

SHIELDS —THE FINAL PHILOSOPHY , or, System of Perfectible Knowledge issuing from the Harmony of Science and Religion. By Charles W Shields, D.D., Professor in Princeton College. Royal 8vo, pp viii and 610, cloth. 1878. 18s

SIBREE —THE GREAT AFRICAN ISLAND. Chapters on Madagascar A Popular Account of Recent Researches in the Physical Geography, Geology and Exploration of the Country, and its Natural History and Botany ; and in the Origin and Divisions, Customs and Language, Superstitions, Folk-lore, and Religious Beliefs and Practices of the Different Tribes. Together with Illustrations of Scripture and Early Church History from Native Habits and Missionary Experience. By the Rev James Sibree, jun., F.R.G S , Author of "Madagascar and its People," -&c. 8vo, pp. xii. and 272, with Physical and Ethnological Maps and Four Illustrations, cloth. 1879. 12s.

SIBREE —FANCY AND OTHER RHYMES. With Additions. By John Sibree, M.A , London Crown 8vo, pp. iv. and 88, cloth 1882. 3s.

SIEDENTOPF. - THE GERMAN CALIGRAPHIST. Copies for German Handwriting. By E. Siedentopf. Obl. fcap. 4to, sewed 1869. 1s.

SIMCOX — EPISODES IN THE LIVES OF MEN, WOMEN, AND LOVERS By Edith Simcox. Crown 8vo, pp. 312, cloth. 1882. 7s. 6d.

SIMCOX —NATURAL LAW. See English and Foreign Philosophical Library, Vol. IV.

SIME —LESSING. See English and Foreign Philosophical Library, Extra Series, Vols. I. and II.

SIMPSON-BAIKIE —THE DRAMATIC UNITIES IN THE PRESENT DAY By E Simpson- Baikie. Third Edition. Fcap. 8vo, pp iv. and 108, cloth 1878 2s 6d.

SIMPSON-BAIKIE.—THE INTERNATIONAL DICTIONARY for Naturalists and Sportsmen in English, French, and German. By Edwin Simpson-Baikie. 8vo, pp. iv. and 284, cloth 1880. 15s.

SINCLAIR —THE MESSENGER : A Poem. By Thomas Sinclair, M.A. Foolscap 8vo, pp. 174, cloth. 1875. 5s.

SINCLAIR.—LOVES'S TRILOGY : A Poem. By Thomas Sinclair, M.A. Crown 8vo, pp 150, cloth 1876. 5s

SINCLAIR.—THE MOUNT : Speech from its English Heights By Thomas Sinclair, M.A. Crown 8vo, pp. viii. and 302, cloth. 1877. 10s.

SINGER.—HUNGARIAN GRAMMAR. See Trubner's Collection.

SINNETT —THE OCCULT WORLD. By A. P. Sinnett. Third Edition. 8vo, pp. xx. and 206, cloth. 1883. 3s. 6d.

SINNETT —ESOTERIC BUDDHISM. By A. P. Sinnett, Author of " The Occult World," President of the Simla Eclectic Philosophical Society. Second Edition. Crown 8vo, pp. xx.-216, cloth. 1883. 7s. 6d.

SMITH.—THE DIVINE GOVERNMENT. By S. Smith, M D. Fifth Edition. Crown 8vo, pp. xii and 276, cloth. 1866. 6s.

SMITH.—THE RECENT DEPRESSION OF TRADE. Its Nature, its Causes, and the Remedies which have been suggested for it. By Walter E Smith, B.A , New College Being the Oxford Cobden Prize Essay for 1879. Crown 8vo, pp. vi. and 108, cloth. 1880 3s

SMYTH.—THE ABORIGINES OF VICTORIA. With Notes relating to the Habits of the Natives of other Parts of Australia and Tasmania Compiled from various sources for the Government of Victoria. By R. Brough Smyth, F.L.S , F.G.S., &c., &c. 2 vols. royal 8vo, pp. lxxii -484 and vi -456, Maps, Plates, and Woodcuts, cloth 1878. £3, 3s.

SNOW—A THEOLOGICO-POLITICAL TREATISE. By G. D. Snow. Crown 8vo, pp. 180, cloth 1874 4s 6d.

SOLLING —DIUTISKA : An Historical and Critical Survey of the Literature of Germany, from the Earliest Period to the Death of Goethe. By Gustav Solling. 8vo, pp. xviii, and 368. 1863. 10s. 6d.

SOLLING.—SELECT PASSAGES FROM THE WORKS OF SHAKESPEARE. Translated and Collected. German and English By G. Solling. 12mo, pp. 155, cloth. 1866. 3s. 6d

SOLLING.—MACBETH. Rendered into Metrical German (with English Text adjoined) By Gustav Solling. Crown 8vo, pp. 160, wrapper. 1878. 3s. 6d.

SONGS OF THE SEMITIC IN ENGLISH VERSE. By G. E. W. Crown 8vo, pp. iv. and 134, cloth 1877 5s.

SOUTHALL.—THE EPOCH OF THE MAMMOTH AND THE APPARITION OF MAN UPON EARTH. By James C. Southall, A M.. LL D. Crown 8vo, pp. xii and 430, cloth Illustrated. 1878. 10s. 6d.

SOUTHALL —THE RECENT ORIGIN OF MAN, as illustrated by Geology and the Modern Science of Prehistoric Archæology. By James C. Southall. 8vo, pp. 606, cloth Illustrated. 1875. 30s.

SPANISH REFORMERS OF TWO CENTURIES FROM 1520 ; Their Lives and Writing, according to the late Benjamin B. Wiffen's Plan, and with the Use of His Materials. Described by E Boehmer, D D , Ph D. Vol. I. With B B. Wiffen's Narrative of the Incidents attendant upon the Republication of Reformistas Antiguos Españoles, and with a Memoir of B B Wiffen. By Isaline Wiffen. Royal 8vo, pp xvi and 216, cloth. 1874 12s 6d Roxburghe, 15s.—Vol II Royal 8vo, pp xii.-374, cloth. 1883. 18s.

SPEDDING —THE LIFE AND TIMES OF FRANCIS BACON. Extracted from the Edition of his Occasional Writings, by James Spedding. 2 vols post 8vo, pp. xx.-710 and xiv -708, cloth 1878 21s.

SPIERS —THE SCHOOL SYSTEM OF THE TALMUD By the Rev. B. Spiers. 8vo, pp. 48, cloth 1882. 2s 6d.

SPINOZA.—BENEDICT DE SPINOZA : his Life, Correspondence, and Ethics. By R. Willis, M D. 8vo, pp. xliv and 648, cloth. 1870 21s.

SPINOZA -—ETHIC DEMONSTRATED IN GEOMETRICAL ORDER AND DIVIDED INTO FIVE PARTS, which treat—1 Of God ; II Of the Nature and Origin of the Mind , III. Of the Origin and Nature of the Affects , IV. Of Human Bondage, or of the Strength of the Affects ; V. Of the Power of the Intellect, or of Human Liberty By Benedict de Spinoza Translated from the Latin by W. Hale White Post 8vo, pp. 328, cloth. 1883. 10s. 6d.

SPIRITUAL EVOLUTION, AN ESSAY ON, considered in its bearing upon Modern Spiritualism, Science, and Religion. By J. P. B. Crown 8vo, pp 156, cloth 1879 3s.

SPRUNER —DR KARL VON SPRUNER'S HISTORICO-GEOGRAPHICAL HAND-ATLAS, containing 26 Coloured Maps. Obl. cloth. 1861. 15s.

SQUIER —HONDURAS , Descriptive, Historical, and Statistical. By E. G. Squier, M.A., F.S A. Cr 8vo, pp viii. and 278, cloth 1870. 3s 6d

STATIONERY OFFICE —PUBLICATIONS OF HER MAJESTY'S STATIONERY OFFICE. List on application.

STEDMAN —OXFORD : Its Social and Intellectual Life With Remarks and Hints on Expenses, the Examinations, &c By Algernon M M. Stedman, B A., Wadham College, Oxford. Crown 8vo, pp. xvi and 309, cloth. 1878. 7s 6d.

STEELE.—AN EASTERN LOVE STORY. Kusa Játakaya : A Buddhistic Legendary Poem, with other Stories. By Th. Steele. Cr. 8vo, pp. xii. and 260, cl. 1871. 6s.

STENT.—THE JADE CHAPLET. In Twenty-four Beads A Collection of Songs, Ballads, &c. (from the Chinese). By G. C. Stent, M.N.C.B.R.A.S. Post 8vo, pp. viii. and 168, cloth. 1874. 5s.

STENZLER.—See AUCTORES SANSKRITI, Vol. II.

STOCK.—ATTEMPTS AT TRUTH. By St. George Stock. Crown 8vo, pp vi. and 248, cloth. 1882. 5s.

STOKES.—GOIDELICA—Old and Early-Middle Irish Glosses: Prose and Verse. Edited by Whitley Stokes. 2d Edition. Med 8vo, pp. 192, cloth 1872. 18s.

STOKES.—BEUNANS MERIASEK. The Life of Saint Meriasek, Bishop and Confessor. A Cornish Drama. Edited, with a Translation and Notes, by Whitley Stokes. Med. 8vo, pp. xvi. and 280, and Facsimile, cloth. 1872. 15s.

STOKES.—TOGAIL TROY, THE DESTRUCTION OF TROY. Transcribed from the Facsimile of the Book of Leinster, and Translated, with a Glossarial Index of the Rarer Words, by Whitley Stokes Crown 8vo, pp xvi. and 188, paper boards. 1882 18s.

STOKES.—THREE MIDDLE-IRISH HOMILIES ON THE LIVES OF SAINTS—PATRICK, BRIGIT, AND COLUMBA. Edited by Whitley Stokes. Crown 8vo, pp. xii and 140, paper boards. 1882. 10s 6d.

STRANGE —THE BIBLE ; is it "The Word of God"? By Thomas Lumisden Strange. Demy 8vo, pp. xii and 384, cloth. 1871. 7s.

STRANGE —THE SPEAKER'S COMMENTARY. Reviewed by T. L. Strange. Cr. 8vo, pp. viii. and 159, cloth. 1871. 2s 6d

STRANGE.—THE DEVELOPMENT OF CREATION ON THE EARTH. By T. L. Strange. Demy 8vo, pp. xii. and 110, cloth. 1874 2s. 6d.

STRANGE —THE LEGENDS OF THE OLD TESTAMENT. By T. L. Strange Demy 8vo, pp. xii. and 244, cloth. 1874. 5s

STRANGE.—THE SOURCES AND DEVELOPMENT OF CHRISTIANITY. By Thomas Lumisden Strange. Demy 8vo, pp. xx. and 256, cloth. 1875 5s

STRANGE.—WHAT IS CHRISTIANITY? An Historical Sketch. Illustrated with a Chart. By Thomas Lumisden Strange. Foolscap 8vo, pp. 72, cloth. 1880 2s. 6d.

STRANGE.—CONTRIBUTIONS TO A SERIES OF CONTROVERSIAL WRITINGS, issued by the late Mr. Thomas Scott, of Upper Norwood. By Thomas Lumisden Strange. Fcap. 8vo, pp. viii. and 312, cloth 1881. 2s 6d

STRANGFORD.—ORIGINAL LETTERS AND PAPERS OF THE LATE VISCOUNT STRANGFORD UPON PHILOLOGICAL AND KINDRED SUBJECTS. Edited by Viscountess Strangford. Post 8vo. pp. xxii. and 284, cloth. 1878. 12s. 6d.

STRATMANN.—THE TRAGICALL HISTORIE OF HAMLET, PRINCE OF DENMARKE. By William Shakespeare. Edited according to the first printed Copies, with the various Readings and Critical Notes. By F. H. Stratmann. 8vo, pp. vi. and 120, sewed. 3s. 6d.

STRATMANN.—A DICTIONARY OF THE OLD ENGLISH LANGUAGE. Compiled from Writings of the Twelfth, Thirteenth, Fourteenth, and Fifteenth Centuries. By F. H. Stratmann. Third Edition. 4to, pp. x. and 662, sewed. 1878. 30s.

STUDIES OF MAN. By a Japanese Crown 8vo, pp. 124, cloth. 1874. 2s. 6d.

SUYEMATZ.—GENJI MONOGATARI. The Most Celebrated of the Classical Japanese Romances. Translated by K. Suyematz. Crown 8vo, pp. xvi. and 254, cloth. 1882. 7s 6d.

SWEET —HISTORY OF ENGLISH SOUNDS, from the Earliest Period, including an Investigation of the General Laws of Sound Change, and full Word Lists. By Henry Sweet   Demy 8vo, pp. iv.-164, cloth. 1874. 4s. 6d.

SWEET —ON A MEXICAN MUSTANG THROUGH TEXAS FROM THE GULF TO THE RIO GRANDE. By Alex E Sweet and J. Armoy Knox, Editors of "Texas Siftings." English Copyright Edition. Demy 8vo, pp. 672. Illustrated, cloth. 1883. 14s.

SYED AHMAD.—A SERIES OF ESSAYS ON THE LIFE OF MOHAMMED, and Subjects subsidiary thereto. By Syed Ahmad Khan Bahadur, C.S.I.   8vo, pp. 532, with 4 Tables, 2 Maps, and Plate, cloth. 1870   30s.

TALBOT —ANALYSIS OF THE ORGANISATION OF THE PRUSSIAN ARMY. By Lieutenant Gerald F. Talbot, 2d Prussian Dragoon Guards.   Royal 8vo, pp 78, cloth. 1871. 3s.

TAYLER.—A RETROSPECT OF THE RELIGIOUS LIFE OF ENGLAND ; or, Church, Puritanism, and Free Inquiry. By J. J. Tayler, B A   Second Edition. Reissued, with an Introductory Chapter on Recent Development, by James Martineau, LL D., D D. Post 8vo, pp. 380, cloth. 1876   7s. 6d.

TAYLOR —PRINCE DEUKALION : A Lyrical Drama. By Bayard Taylor. Small 4to, pp. 172. Handsomely bound in white vellum. 1878. 12s.

TECHNOLOGICAL DICTIONARY of the Terms employed in the Arts and Sciences ; Architecture , Civil Engineering ; Mechanics ; Machine-Making ; Shipbuilding and Navigation ; Metallurgy ; Artillery ; Mathematics ; Physics ; Chemistry ; Mineralogy, &c. With a Preface by Dr K Karmarsch. Second Edition. 3 vols.
    Vol I. German-English-French.   8vo, pp. 646. 12s.
    Vol II English-German-French   8vo, pp 666. 12s.
    Vol. III. French-German-English.   8vo, pp. 618. 12s.

TECHNOLOGICAL DICTIONARY —A POCKET DICTIONARY OF TECHNICAL TERMS USED IN ARTS AND MANUFACTURES. English-German-French, Deutsch-Englisch-Franzosisch, Français-Allemand-Anglais.   Abridged from the above Technological Dictionary by Rumpf, Mothes, and Unverzagt. With the addition of Commercial Terms   3 vols. sq. 12mo, cloth, 12s.

TEGNER.—Esaias Tegnèr's Frithiof's Saga. Translated from the Swedish, with Notes, Index, and a short Abstract of the Northern Mythology, by Leopold Hamel. Crown 8vo, pp. vi. and 280, cloth. 1874. 7s 6d. With Photographic frontispiece, gilt edges, 10s.

THÉÂTRE FRANÇAIS MODERNE —A Selection of Modern French Plays. Edited by the Rev. P. H. E Brette, B.D , C. Cassal, LL.D., and Th. Karcher, LL.B.

    First Series, in 1 vol crown 8vo, cloth, 6s., containing—

CHARLOTTE CORDAY. A Tragedy. By F Ponsard   Edited, with English Notes and Notice on Ponsard, by Professor C. Cassal, LL D. Pp xii and 134. Separately, 2s 6d

DIANE A Drama in Verse By Emile Augier   Edited, with English Notes and Notice on Augier, by Th. Karcher, LL.B. Pp. xiv and 145. Separately, 2s. 6d.

LE VOYAGE À DIEPPE, A Comedy in Prose. By Wafflard and Fulgence. Edited, with English Notes, by the Rev. P. H. E. Brette, B.D. Pp 104. Separately, 2s. 6d.

    Second Series, crown 8vo, cloth, 6s., containing—

MOLIÈRE A Drama in Prose By George Sand. Edited, with English Notes and Notice of George Sand, by Th. Karcher, LL B. Fcap. 8vo, pp. xx and 170, cloth. Separately, 3s. 6d

LES ARISTOCRATIES A Comedy in Verse By Etienne Arago Edited, with English Notes and Notice of Etienne Arago, by the Rev. P. H. E Brette, B D. 2d Edition Fcap. 8vo, pp. xiv. and 236, cloth. Separately, 4s.

THEÁTRE FRANÇAIS MODERNE—*continued.*

Third Series, crown 8vo, cloth, 6s., containing—

LES FAUX BONSHOMMES. A Comedy. By Théodore Barrière and Ernest Capendu. Edited, with English Notes and Notice on Barrière, by Professor C. Cassal, LL D Fcap. 8vo, pp. xvi. and 304. 1868. Separately, 4s.

L'HONNEUR ET L'ARGENT. A Comedy. By François Ponsard. Edited, with English Notes and Memoir of Ponsard, by Professor C. Cassal, LL D. 2d Edition. Fcap. 8vo, pp. xvi. and 171, cloth. 1869. Separately, 3s. 6d.

THEISM —A CANDID EXAMINATION OF THEISM. By Physicus. Post 8vo, pp. xviii. and 198, cloth. 1878. 7s. 6d.

THEOSOPHY AND THE HIGHER LIFE; or, Spiritual Dynamics and the Divine and Miraculous Man By G. W , M D , Edinburgh President of the British Theosophical Society. 12mo, pp. iv. and 138, cloth. 1880. 3s.

THOM.—ST PAUL'S EPISTLES TO THE CORINTHIANS. An Attempt to convey their Spirit and Significance By the Rev. J. H. Thom. 8vo, pp. xii. and 408, cloth. 1851. 5s.

THOMAS —EARLY SASSANIAN INSCRIPTIONS, SEALS, AND COINS, illustrating the Early History of the Sassanian Dynasty, containing Proclamations of Ardeshir Babek, Sapor I., and his Successors. With a Critical Examination and Explanation of the celebrated Inscription in the Hájíábad Cave, demonstrating that Sapor, the Conqueror of Valerian, was a professing Christian. By Edward Thomas. Illustrated. 8vo, pp. 148, cloth. 7s. 6d.

THOMAS.—THE CHRONICLES OF THE PATHAN KINGS OF DEHLI. Illustrated by Coins, Inscriptions, and other Antiquarian Remains By E. Thomas, F.R.A.S. With Plates and Cuts. Demy 8vo, pp. xxiv. and 467, cloth. 1871. 28s.

THOMAS —THE REVENUE RESOURCES OF THE MUGHAL EMPIRE IN INDIA, from A.D. 1593 to A D. 1707 A Supplement to "The Chronicles of the Pathán Kings of Delhi." By E. Thomas, F.R.S. 8vo, pp. 60, cloth. 3s. 6d.

THOMAS.—SASSANIAN COINS. Communicated to the Numismatic Society of London. By E. Thomas, F.R.S. Two Parts, 12mo, pp. 43, 3 Plates and a Cut, sewed. 5s

THOMAS.—JAINISM; OR, THE EARLY FAITH OF ASOKA. With Illustrations of the Ancient Religions of the East, from the Pantheon of the Indo-Scythians. To which is added a Notice on Bactrian Coins and Indian Dates. By Edward Thomas, F R.S. 8vo, pp. viii.-24 and 82. With two Autotype Plates and Woodcuts. 1877. 7s. 6d.

THOMAS.—THE THEORY AND PRACTICE OF CREOLE GRAMMAR. By J. J. Thomas. 8vo, pp. viii. and 135, boards. 12s.

THOMAS.—RECORDS OF THE GUPTA DYNASTY. Illustrated by Inscriptions, Written History, Local Tradition, and Coins. To which is added a Chapter on the Arabs in Sind. By Edward Thomas, F.R.S. Folio, with a Plate, pp. iv. and 64, cloth. 14s.

THOMAS.—BOYHOOD LAYS. By William Henry Thomas. 18mo, pp. iv. and 74, cloth. 1877. 2s. 6d.

THOMPSON.—DIALOGUES, RUSSIAN AND ENGLISH. Compiled by A. R. Thompson. sometime Lecturer of the English Language in the University of St. Vladimir, Kieff. Crown 8vo, pp. iv. and 132, cloth. 1882. 5s.

THOMSON.—EVOLUTION AND INVOLUTION. By George Thomson, Author of " The World of Being," &c. Crown 8vo, pp. viii. and 206, cloth. 1880. 5s.

E

THOMSON —Institutes of the Laws of Ceylon By Henry Byerley Thomson Second Puisne Judge of the Supreme Court of Ceylon. In 2 vols. 8vo, pp. xx. and 647, pp. xx. and 713, cloth. With Appendices, pp 71. 1866 £2, 2s.

THORBURN —Bannú; or, Our Afghan Frontier. By S S Thorburn, F.C.S., Settlement Officer of the Bannú District 8vo, pp x. and 480, cloth 1876 18s.

THORPE.—Diplomatarium Anglicum Ævi Saxonici. A Collection of English Charters, from the reign of King Æthelberht of Kent, A D. DCV, to that of William the Conqueror. Containing : I Miscellaneous Charters II. Wills. III. Guilds. IV. Manumissions and Acquittances. With a Translation of the Anglo-Saxon. By the late Benjamin Thorpe, Member of the Royal Academy of Sciences at Munich, and of the Society of Netherlandish Literature at Leyden. 8vo, pp. xlii and 682, cloth. 1865. £1, 1s

THOUGHTS ON LOGIC; or, the S.N.I.X Propositional Theory. Crown 8vo, pp. iv. and 76, cloth. 1877 2s 6d.

THOUGHTS ON THEISM, with Suggestions towards a Public Religious Service in Harmony with Modern Science and Philosophy. Ninth Thousand Revised and Enlarged. 8vo, pp. 74, sewed. 1882. 1s.

THURSTON —Friction and Lubrication. Determinations of the Laws and Co-efficients of Friction by new Methods and with new Apparatus. By Robert H. Thurston, A M, C E, &c. Crown 8vo, pp. xvi and 212, cloth. 1879 6s 6d

TIELE —See English and Foreign Philosophical Library, Vol. VII. and Trubner's Oriental Series

TOLHAUSEN —A Synopsis of the Patent Laws of Various Countries. By A. Tolhausen, Ph D Third Edition. 12mo, pp. 62, sewed. 1870. 1s. 6d.

TONSBERG.—Norway Illustrated Handbook for Travellers. Edited by Charles Tonsberg. With 134 Engravings on Wood, 17 Maps, and Supplement. Crown 8vo, pp lxx, 482, and 32, cloth 1875. 18s

TOPOGRAPHICAL WORKS —A List of the various Works prepared at the Topographical and Statistical Department of the War Office may be had on application

TORRENS —Empire in Asia · How we came by it. A Book of Confessions. By W M. Torrens, M P. Med 8vo, pp. 426, cloth 1872. 14s.

TOSCANI —Italian Conversational Course. A New Method of Teaching the Italian Language, both Theoretically and Practically. By Giovanni Toscani, Professor of the Italian Language and Literature in Queen's Coll, London, &c. Fourth Edition. 12mo, pp xiv. and 300, cloth. 1872. 5s.

TOSCANI.—Italian Reading Course. By G. Toscani. Fcap. 8vo, pp. xii. and 160 With table Cloth 1875. 4s 6d.

TOULON —Its Advantages as a Winter Residence for Invalids and Others. By an English Resident. The proceeds of this pamphlet to be devoted to the English Church at Toulon. Crown 8vo, pp 8, sewed. 1873 6d.

TRADLEG —A Son of Belial Autobiographical Sketches. By Nitram Tradleg, University of Bosphorus. Crown 8vo, pp. viii.-260, cloth. 1882. 5s.

TRIMEN.—South-African Butterflies ; a Monograph of the Extra-Tropical Species By Roland Trimen, F L S., F.Z.S., M E.S, Curator of the South African Museum, Cape Town. Royal 8vo. [*In preparation.*

TRÜBNER'S AMERICAN, EUROPEAN, AND ORIENTAL LITERARY RECORD. A Register of the most Important Works published in America, India, China, and the British Colonies. With Occasional Notes on German, Dutch, Danish, French, Italian, Spanish, Portuguese, and Russian Literature. The object of the Publishers in issuing this publication is to give a full and particular account of every publication of importance issued in America and the East. Small 4to 6d. per number. Subscription, 5s. per volume.

TRÜBNER.—Trubner's Bibliographical Guide to American Literature : A Classed List of Books published in the United States of America, from 1817 to 1857. With Bibliographical Introduction, Notes, and Alphabetical Index. Compiled and Edited by Nicolas Trubner. In 1 vol. 8vo, half bound, pp. 750. 1859. 18s.

TRÜBNER'S Catalogue of Dictionaries and Grammars of the Principal Languages and Dialects of the World. Considerably Enlarged and Revised, with an Alphabetical Index. A Guide for Students and Booksellers. Second Edition, 8vo, pp. viii. and 170, cloth. 1882. 5s.

TRÜBNER'S Collection of Simplified Grammars of the Principal Asiatic and European Languages. Edited by Reinhold Rost, LL.D., Ph.D. Crown 8vo, cloth, uniformly bound.

    I.—Hindustani, Persian, and Arabic. By E. H. Palmer, M.A. Pp 112. 1882. 5s

    II.—Hungarian. By I Singer Pp. vi and 88. 1882. 4s 6d.

    III.—Basque By W. Van Eys Pp. xii. and 52 1883. 3s 6d.

    IV.—Malagasy. By G W. Parker Pp 66, with Plate 1883 5s

    V—Modern Greek By E M Geldart, M A. Pp. 68. 1883. 2s. 6d.

    VI—Roumanian By R. Torceanu. Pp . 1883.

    VII.—Tibetan Grammar. By H. A. Jaschke. Pp viii.–104. 1883. 5s.

TRÜBNER'S ORIENTAL SERIES —

    Post 8vo, cloth, uniformly bound.

Essays on the Sacred Language, Writings, and Religion of the Parsis. By Martin Haug, Ph.D., late Professor of Sanskrit and Comparative Philology at the University of Munich. Second Edition. Edited by E. W. West, Ph D. Pp xvi. and 428 1878. 16s.

Texts from the Buddhist Canon, commonly known as Dhammapada. With Accompanying Narratives. Translated from the Chinese by S. Beal, B A., Trinity College, Cambridge, Professor of Chinese, University College, London. Pp. viii and 176. 1878. 7s 6d.

The History of Indian Literature. By Albrecht Weber. Translated from the German by J Mann, M A, and Dr. T Zachariae, with the Author's sanction and assistance 2d Edition. Pp 368. 1882. 10s. 6d.

A Sketch of the Modern Languages of the East Indies. Accompanied by Two Language Maps, Classified List of Languages and Dialects, and a List of Authorities for each Language. By Robert Cust, late of H.M.I.C.S., and Hon. Librarian of R.A S. Pp. xii and 198. 1878. 12s.

The Birth of the War-God A Poem By Kálidasá Translated from the Sanskrit into English Verse, by Ralph T H Griffiths. M A., Principal of Benares College. Second Edition. Pp. xii. and 116 1879. 5s.

A Classical Dictionary of Hindu Mythology and History, Geography and Literature. By John Dowson, M.R.A.S., late Professor in the Staff College Pp. 432. 1879 16s.

Metrical Translations from Sanskrit Writers; with an Introduction, many Prose Versions, and Parallel Passages from Classical Authors By J. Muir, C.I.E, D.C.L, &c. Pp. xliv.–376. 1879. 14s.

Modern India and the Indians: being a Series of Impressions, Notes and Essays. By Monier Williams, D.C.L, Hon LL D. of the University of Calcutta, Boden Professor of Sanskrit in the University of Oxford. Third Edition, revised and augmented by considerable additions. With Illustrations and Map, pp. vii. and 368. 1879. 14s.

TRÜBNER'S ORIENTAL SERIES—*continued.*

THE LIFE OR LEGEND OF GAUDAMA, the Buddha of the Burmese. With Annotations, the Ways to Neibban, and Notice on the Phongyies, or Burmese Monks. By the Right Rev. P. Bigandet, Bishop of Ramatha, Vicar Apostolic of Ava and Pegu. Third Edition. 2 vols. Pp. xx.-368 and viii -326. 1880. 21s.

MISCELLANEOUS ESSAYS, relating to Indian Subjects. By B H Hodgson, late British Minister at Nepal. 2 vols., pp. viii.-408, and viii.-348. 1880. 28s.

SELECTIONS FROM THE KORAN By Edward William Lane, Author of an "Arabic-English Lexicon," &c. A New Edition, Revised, with an Introduction. By Stanley Lane Poole Pp cxii and 174 1879 9s

CHINESE BUDDHISM. A Volume of Sketches, Historical and Critical By J. Edkins, D D., Author of "China's Place in Philology," "Religion in China," &c , &c. Pp lvi and 454 1880. 18s

THE GULISTAN ; OR, ROSE GARDEN OF SHEKH MUSHLIU'D-DIN SADI OF SHIRAZ Translated for the first time into Prose and Verse, with Preface and a Life of the Author, from the Atish Kadah, by E. B Eastwick, F R S., M.R.A.S. 2d Edition. Pp. xxvi and 244. 1880 10s. 6d

A TALMUDIC MISCELLANY ; or, One Thousand and One Extracts from the Talmud, the Midrashim, and the Kabbalah Compiled and Translated by P. J. Hershon With a Preface by Rev. F. W. Farrar, D.D , F.R S., Chaplain in Ordinary to Her Majesty, and Canon of Westminster. With Notes and Copious Indexes. Pp. xxviii. and 362. 1880. 14s.

THE HISTORY OF ESARHADDON (Son of Sennacherib), King of Assyria, B C. 681-668. Translated from the Cuneiform Inscriptions upon Cylinders and Tablets in the British Museum Collection. Together with Original Texts, a Grammatical Analysis of each word, Explanations of the Ideographs by Extracts from the Bi-Lingual Syllabaries, and List of Eponyms, &c By E A Budge, B A , M R A.S , Assyrian Exhibitioner, Christ's College, Cambridge. Post 8vo, pp. xii. and 164, cloth. 1880 10s. 6d.

BUDDHIST BIRTH STORIES ; or, Jataka Tales The oldest Collection of Folk-Lore extant being the Jātakatthavannanā, for the first time edited in the original Pali, by V Fausböll, and translated by T. W. Rhys Davids. Translation. Vol. I. Pp. cxvi. and 348. 1880. 18s.

THE CLASSICAL POETRY OF THE JAPANESE. By Basil Chamberlain, Author of "Yeigio Henkaku, Ichiran." Pp. xii. and 228. 1880. 7s. 6d.

LINGUISTIC AND ORIENTAL ESSAYS. Written from the year 1846-1878. By R Cust, Author of "The Modern Languages of the East Indies." Pp. xii. and 484. 1880. 18s.

INDIAN POETRY Containing a New Edition of "The Indian Song of Songs,' from the Sanskrit of the Gita Govinda of Jayadeva , Two Books from "The Iliad of India" (Mahábhárata) ; "Proverbial Wisdom" from the Shlokas of the Hitopadesa, and other Oriental Poems. By Edwin Arnold, M.A., C.S I., &c , &c. Pp. viii. and 270 1881. 7s. 6d.

. THE RELIGIONS OF INDIA By A. Barth. Authorised Translation by Rev. J. Wood. Pp. xx. and 310. 1881. 16s.

HINDŪ PHILOSOPHY The Sānkhya Kārikā of Iswara Krishna. An Exposition of the System of Kapila With an Appendix on the Nyaya and Vaiseshika Systems. By John Davies, M.A , M.R.A.S. Pp vi. and 151. 1881. 6s.

TRÜBNER'S ORIENTAL SERIES—*continued.*

A MANUAL OF HINDU PANTHEISM. The Vedantasara. Translated with Copious Annotations. By Major G. A Jacob, Bombay Staff Corps, Inspector of Army Schools With a Preface by E. B. Cowell, M.A, Professor of Sanskrit in the University of Cambridge. Pp. x and 130. 1881. 6s

THE MESNEVĪ (usually known as the Mesnevīyi Sherīf, or Holy Mesnevī) of Mevlānā (Our Lord) Jelālu-'d-Din Muhammed, Er-Rūmī. Book the First. Together with some Account of the Life and Acts of the Author, of his Ancestors, and of his Descendants. Illustrated by a selection of Characteristic Anecdotes as collected by their Historian Mevlānā Shemsu-'d-Din Ahmed, El Eflākī El Arifī. Translated, and the Poetry Versified by James W. Redhouse, M.R.A.S., &c. Pp. xvi. and 136; vi. and 290. 1881. £1, 1s.

EASTERN PROVERBS AND EMBLEMS ILLUSTRATING OLD TRUTHS. By the Rev J. Long, Member of the Bengal Asiatic Society, F.R.G S. Pp. xv. and 280. 1881 6s.

THE QUATRAINS OF OMAR KHAYYÁM. A New Translation. By E. H. Whinfield, late of H.M. Bengal Civil Service. Pp. 96. 1881. 5s. THE PERSIAN TEXT, with an English Verse Translation Pp. xxxii.–335. 1883 10s 6d

THE MIND OF MENCIUS; or, Political Economy Founded upon Moral Philosophy. A Systematic Digest of the Doctrines of the Chinese Philosopher Mencius. The Original Text Classified and Translated, with Comments, by the Rev. E. Faber, Rhenish Mission Society. Translated from the German, with Additional Notes, by the Rev A B. Hutchinson, Church Mission, Hong Kong. Author in Chinese of "Primer Old Testament History," &c, &c. Pp xvi and 294. 1882 10s. 6d.

YÚSUF AND ZULAIKHA. A Poem by Jami. Translated from the Persian into English Verse. By R. T H. Griffith Pp xiv and 304. 1882 8s. 6d

TSUNI- || GOAM: The Supreme Being of the Khoi-Khoi By Theophilus Hahn, Ph.D, Custodian of the Grey Collection, Cape Town, Corresponding Member of the Geographical Society, Dresden; Corresponding Member of the Anthropological Society, Vienna, &c., &c. Pp. xii. and 154. 1882. 7s. 6d

A COMPREHENSIVE COMMENTARY TO THE QURAN. To which is prefixed Sale's Preliminary Discourse, with Additional Notes and Emendations. Together with a Complete Index to the Text, Preliminary Discourse, and Notes. By Rev E. M Wherry, M A, Lodiana. Vol. I Pp. xii. and 392. 1882. 12s 6d.

HINDU PHILOSOPHY. THE BHAGAVAD GĪTĀ; or, The Sacred Lay. A Sanskrit Philosophical Lay Translated, with Notes, by John Davies, M.A. Pp. vi and 208 1882 8s 6d

THE SARVA-DARSANA-SAMGRAHA; or, Review of the Different Systems of Hindu Philosophy. By Madhava Acharya Translated by E B. Cowell, M A., Cambridge, and A. E. Gough, M.A., Calcutta Pp. xii. and 282 1882 10s 6d

TIBETAN TALES. Derived from Indian Sources. Translated from the Tibetan of the Kay-Gyur By F Anton von Schiefner Done into English from the German, with an Introduction. By W R. S. Ralston, M A. Pp. lxvi and 368 1882 14s.

LINGUISTIC ESSAYS. By Carl Abel, Ph.D. Pp. viii. and 265 1882. 9s.

THE INDIAN EMPIRE: Its History, People, and Products. By W. W. Hunter, C.I.E., LL D. Pp. 568. 1882. 16s.

TRUBNER'S ORIENTAL SERIES—*continued.*

HISTORY OF THE EGYPTIAN RELIGION By Dr C P Tiele, Leiden. Translated by J. Ballingal. Pp xxiv. and 230. 1882. 7s. 6d.

THE PHILOSOPHY OF THE UPANISHADS. By A. E. Gough, M.A, Calcutta. Pp xxiv.-268. 1882 9s.

UDANAVARGA A Collection of Verses from the Buddhist Canon. Compiled by Dharmatrâta. Being the Northern Buddhist Version of Dhammapada. Translated from the Tibetan of Bkah-hgyur, with Notes, and Extracts from the Commentary of Pradjnavarman, by W. Woodville Rockhill Pp 240 1883 9s

A HISTORY OF BURMA, including Burma Proper, Pegu, Taungu, Tenasserim, and Arakan. From the Earliest Time to the End of the First War with British India By Lieut -General Sir Arthur P. Phayre, G C M G , K.C S I , and C.B. Pp. xii -312. 1883. 14s.

The following works are in preparation :—

MANAVA—DHARMA—CASTRA; or, Laws of Manu A New Translation, with Introduction, Notes, &c. By A C. Burnell, Ph.D , C I E , Foreign Member of the Royal Danish Academy, and Hon. Member of several learned societies.

THE APHORISMS OF THE SANKHYA PHILOSOPHY OF KAPILA. With Illustrative Extracts from the Commentaries By the late J. R Ballantyne. Second Edition, edited by Fitzedward Hall.

BUDDHIST RECORDS OF THE WESTERN WORLD, being the Si-Yu-Ki hy Hwen Thsang Translated from the original Chinese, with Introduction, Index, &c By Samuel Beal, Trinity College, Cambridge, Professor of Chinese, University College, London In 2 vols.

UNGER —A SHORT CUT TO READING · The Child's First Book of Lessons. Part I. By W. H. Unger. Fourth Edition Cr 8vo, pp. 32, cloth. 1873 5d. In folio sheets. Pp. 44. Sets A to D, 10d. each ; set E, 8d. 1873. Complete, 4s. SEQUEL to Part I and Part II Fourth Edition Cr 8vo pp 64, cloth. 1873. 6d. Parts I and II. Third Edition. Demy 8vo, pp. 76, cloth. 1873 1s 6d.

UNGER.—W. H UNGER'S CONTINUOUS SUPPLEMENTARY WRITING MODELS, designed to impart not only a good business hand, but correctness in transcribing. Oblong 8vo, pp. 40, stiff covers. 1874. 6d

UNGER THE STUDENT'S BLUE BOOK . Being Selections from Official Correspondence, Reports, &c. ; for Exercises in Reading and Copying Manuscripts, Writing, Orthography, Punctuation, Dictation, Précis, Indexing, and Digesting, and Tabulating Accounts and Returns. Compiled by W. H. Unger. Folio, pp. 100, paper. 1875. 4s

UNGER.—Two HUNDRED TESTS IN ENGLISH ORTHOGRAPHY, or Word Dictations. Compiled by W. H. Unger. Foolscap, pp viii. and 200, cloth. 1877. 1s. 6d. plain, 2s. 6d. interleaved.

UNGER —THE SCRIPT PRIMER · By which one of the remaining difficulties of Children is entirely removed in the first stages, and, as a consequence, a considerable saving of time will be effected In Two Parts. By W H. Unger. Part l. 12mo, pp xvi and 44, cloth. 5d Part II , pp 50, cloth 5d

UNGER.—PRELIMINARY WORD DICTATIONS ON THE RULES FOR SPELLING. By W H. Unger. 18mo, pp 44, cloth. 4d

URICOECHEA —MAPOTECA COLOMBIANA : Catalogo de Todos los Mapas, Planos, Vistas, &c., relativos a la América-Española, Brasil, e Islas adyacentes. Arreglada cronologicamente i precedida de una introduccion sobre la historia cartografica de América. Por el Doctor Ezequiel Uricoechea, de Bogóta, Nueva Granada. 8vo, pp. 232, cloth. 1860. 6s.

URQUHART —ELECTRO-MOTORS. A Treatise on the Means and Apparatus employed in the Transmission of Electrical Energy and its Conversion into Motivepower. For the Use of Engineers and Others. By J. W. Urquhart, Electrician. Crown 8vo, cloth, pp. xii. and 178, illustrated. 1882. 7s. 6d.

VAITANA SUTRA.—See AUCTORES SANSKRITI, Vol III.

VALDES —LIVES OF THE TWIN BROTHERS, JUÁN AND ALFONSO DE VALDÉS. By E. Boehmer, D D Translated by J. T Betts. Crown 8vo, pp. 32, wrappers. 1882. 1s.

VALDES —SEVENTEEN OPUSCULES. By Juán de Valdés. Translated from the Spanish and Italian, and edited by John T. Betts Crown 8vo, pp. xii and 188, cloth. 1882. 6s

VALDES —JUÁN DE VALDÉS' COMMENTARY UPON THE GOSPEL OF ST MATTHEW. With Professor Boehmer's "Lives of Juán and Alfonso de Valdés " Now for the first time translated from the Spanish, and never before published in English. By John T. Betts Post 8vo, pp xii and 512–30, cloth. 1882. 7s. 6d.

VALDES.—SPIRITUAL MILK ; or, Christian Instruction for Children. By Juán de Valdés Translated from the Italian, edited and published by John T Betts. With Lives of the twin brothers, Juán and Alfonso de Valdés. By E. Boehmer, D D Fcap 8vo, pp 60, wrappers 1882 2s.

VALDES —THREE OPUSCULES : an Extract from Valdés' Seventeen Opuscules. By Juán de Valdés. Translated, edited, and published by John T. Betts Fcap. 8vo, pp 58, wrappers. 1881 1s 6d

VALDES.—JUÁN DE VALDÉS' COMMENTARY UPON OUR LORD'S SERMON ON THE MOUNT. Translated and edited by J. T Betts With Lives of Juán and Alfonso de Valdés By E Boehmer, D D Crown 8vo, pp 112, boards. 1882 2s 6d

VALDES.—JUÁN DE VALDÉS' COMMENTARY UPON THE EPISTLE TO THE, ROMANS. Edited by J. T Betts Crown 8vo, pp. xxxii and 296, cloth. 1883. 6s.

VAN CAMPEN.—THE DUTCH IN THE ARCTIC SEAS. By Samuel Richard Van Campen, author of "Holland's Silver Feast." 8vo. Vol. I A Dutch Arctic Expedition and Route Third Edition. Pp. xxxvii. and 263, cloth. 1877. 10s. 6d. Vol. II. *in preparation.*

VAN DE WEYER.—CHOIX D'OPUSCULES PHILOSOPHIQUES, HISTORIQUES, POLITIQUES ET LITTÉRAIRES de Sylvain Van de Weyer, Précédés d'Avant propos de l'Editeur. Roxburghe style. Crown 8vo. PREMIÈRE SÉRIE. Pp 374 1863. 10s. 6d. – DEUXIÈME SÉRIE Pp. 502 1869 12s —TROISIÈME SÉRIE. Pp 391. 1875. 10s. 6d —QUATRIÈME SÉRIE. Pp. 366. 1876. 10s. 6d.

VAN EYS —BASQUE GRAMMAR. See Trübner's Collection.

VAN LAUN.—GRAMMAR OF THE FRENCH LANGUAGE By H. Van Laun. Parts I. and II. Accidence and Syntax 13th Edition Cr. 8vo, pp 151 and 120, cloth. 1874 4s. Part III. Exercises. 11th Edition. Cr. 8vo, pp. xii. and 285, cloth. 1873. 3s. 6d.

VAN LAUN.—LEÇONS GRADUÉES DE TRADUCTION ET DE LECTURE ; or, Graduated Lessons in Translation and Reading, with Biographical Sketches, Annotations on History, Geography, Synonyms and Style, and a Dictionary of Words and Idioms By Henri Van Laun. 4th Edition. 12mo, pp. viii. and 400, cloth. 1868. 5s.

VARDHAMANA'S GANARATNAMAHODADHI See AUCTORES SANSKRITI, Vol. IV.

VAZIR OF LANKURAN · A Persian Play. A Text-Book of Modern Colloquial Persian Edited, with Grammatical Introduction, Translation, Notes, and Vocabulary, by W. H Haggard, late of H.M Legation in Teheran, and G. le Strange. Crown 8vo, pp. 230, cloth. 1882. 10s. 6d.

VELASQUEZ AND SIMONNÉ'S NEW METHOD TO READ, WRITE, AND SPEAK THE SPANISH LANGUAGE. Adapted to Ollendorff's System   Post 8vo, pp. 558, cloth. 1880.   6s.

> KEY. Post 8vo, pp. 174, cloth.   4s.

VELASQUEZ.—A DICTIONARY OF THE SPANISH AND ENGLISH LANGUAGES.   For the Use of Young Learners and Travellers.   By M Velasquez de la Cadena. In Two Parts   I Spanish-English   II English-Spanish.   Crown 8vo, pp. viii. and 846, cloth   1878.   7s. 6d.

VELASQUEZ.—A PRONOUNCING DICTIONARY OF THE SPANISH AND ENGLISH LANGUAGES   Composed from the Dictionaries of the Spanish Academy, Terreos, and Salvá, and Webster, Worcester, and Walker   Two Parts in one thick volume. By M. Velasquez de la Cadena.   Roy. 8vo, pp. 1280, cloth.   1873.   £1, 4s.

VELASQUEZ.—NEW SPANISH READER : Passages from the most approved authors, in Prose and Verse   Arranged in progressive order.   With Vocabulary.   By M. Velasquez de la Cadena.   Post 8vo, pp. 352, cloth.   1866.   6s

VELASQUEZ.—AN EASY INTRODUCTION TO SPANISH CONVERSATION, containing all that is necessary to make a rapid progress in it.   Particularly designed for persons who have little time to study, or are their own instructors.   By M. Velasquez de la Cadena.   12mo, pp 150, cloth.   1863   2s. 6d.

VERSES AND VERSELETS.   By a Lover of Nature.   Foolscap 8vo, pp. viii. and 88, cloth.   1876   2s 6d

VICTORIA GOVERNMENT —PUBLICATIONS OF THE GOVERNMENT OF VICTORIA. *List in preparation.*

VOGEL —ON BEER.   A Statistical Sketch   By M. Vogel.   Fcap. 8vo, pp xii. and 76, cloth limp.   1874   2s.

WAFFLARD and FULGENCE.—LE VOYAGE À DIEPPE.   A Comedy in Prose.   By Wafflard and Fulgence.   Edited, with Notes, by the Rev. P H. E. Brette, B D Cr. 8vo, pp 104, cloth.   1867.   2s. 6d.

WAKE —THE EVOLUTION OF MORALITY.   Being a History of the Development of Moral Culture.   By C. Staniland Wake.   2 vols. crown 8vo, pp. xvi.–506 and xii –474, cloth   1878.   21s

WALLACE —ON MIRACLES AND MODERN SPIRITUALISM , Three Essays.   By Alfred Russel Wallace. Author of "The Malay Archipelago," "The Geographical Distribution of Animals," &c , &c.   Second Edition, crown 8vo, pp. viii. and 236, cloth.   1881   5s

WANKLYN and CHAPMAN.—WATER ANALYSIS   A Practical Treatise on the Examination of Potable Water.   By J A Wanklyn, and E T. Chapman.   Fifth Edition   Entirely rewritten. By J. A Wanklyn, M.R C S.   Crown 8vo, pp. x. and 182, cloth   1879   5s

WANKLYN.—MILK ANALYSIS ; a Practical Treatise on the Examination of Milk and its Derivatives, Cream, Butter, and Cheese.   By J. A Wanklyn, M R C.S., &c   Crown 8vo, pp. viii and 72, cloth.   1874.   5s.

WANKLYN —TEA, COFFEE, AND COCOA.   A Practical Treatise on the Analysis of Tea, Coffee, Cocoa, Chocolate, Maté (Paraguay Tea), &c   By J. A. Wanklyn, M R C.S , &c.   Crown 8vo, pp. viii. and 60, cloth.   1874.   5s.

WAR OFFICE — A LIST OF THE VARIOUS MILITARY MANUALS AND OTHER WORKS PUBLISHED UNDER THE SUPERINTENDENCE OF THE WAR OFFICE may be had on application.

WARD —ICE : A Lecture delivered before the Keswick Literary Society, and published by request   To which is appended a Geological Dream on Skiddaw.   By J. Clifton Ward, F.G.S.   8vo, pp. 28, sewed.   1870.   1s.

WARD.—ELEMENTARY NATURAL PHILOSOPHY; being a Course of Nine Lectures, specially adapted for the use of Schools and Junior Students. By J. Clifton Ward, F.G.S. Fcap. 8vo, pp. viii. and 216, with 154 Illustrations, cloth. 1871. 3s. 6d.

WARD—ELEMENTARY GEOLOGY. A Course of Nine Lectures, for the use of Schools and Junior Students By J Clifton Ward, F.G S. Fcap. 8vo, pp. 292, with 120 Illustrations, cloth. 1872. 4s. 6d.

WATSON.—INDEX TO THE NATIVE AND SCIENTIFIC NAMES OF INDIAN AND OTHER EASTERN ECONOMIC PLANTS AND PRODUCTS, originally prepared under the authority of the Secretary of State for India in Council. By John Forbes Watson, M.D. Imp. 8vo, pp 650, cloth. 1868. £1, 11s. 6d.

WEBER.—THE HISTORY OF INDIAN LITERATURE. By Albrecht Weber. Translated from the Second German Edition, by J. Mann, M.A., and T Zacharaiae, Ph D., with the sanction of the Author. Second Edition, post 8vo, pp xxiv. and 360, cloth. 1882. 10s. 6d.

WEDGWOOD.—THE PRINCIPLES OF GEOMETRICAL DEMONSTRATION, reduced from the Original Conception of Space and Form By H Wedgwood, M A. 12mo, pp 48, cloth. 1844. 2s.

WEDGWOOD—ON THE DEVELOPMENT OF THE UNDERSTANDING. By H. Wedgwood, A.M. 12mo, pp. 133, cloth. 1848. 3s.

WEDGWOOD.—THE GEOMETRY OF THE THREE FIRST BOOKS OF EUCLID. By Direct Proof from Definitions Alone. By H. Wedgwood, M A. 12mo, pp. 104, cloth. 1856. 3s.

WEDGWOOD.—ON THE ORIGIN OF LANGUAGE. By H. Wedgwood, M.A. 12mo, pp. 165, cloth. 1866. 3s 6d.

WEDGWOOD.—A DICTIONARY OF ENGLISH ETYMOLOGY. By H. Wedgwood. Third Edition, revised and enlarged. With Introduction on the Origin of Language 8vo, pp. lxxii. and 746, cloth. 1878. £1, 1s.

WEDGWOOD.—CONTESTED ETYMOLOGIES IN THE DICTIONARY OF THE REV. W. W. SKEAT. By H Wedgwood. Crown 8vo, pp. viii. and 194, cloth. 1882. 5s.

WEISBACH.—THEORETICAL MECHANICS: A Manual of the Mechanics of Engineering and of the Construction of Machines, with an Introduction to the Calculus. Designed as a Text-book for Technical Schools and Colleges, and for the use of Engineers, Architects, &c. By Julius Weisbach, Ph D, Oberbergrath, and Professor at the Royal Mining Academy at Freiberg, &c. Translated from the German by Eckley B. Coxe, A.M., Mining Engineer Demy 8vo, with 902 woodcuts, pp. 1112, cloth. 1877. 31s. 6d.

WELLER—AN IMPROVED DICTIONARY; English and French, and French and English. By E. Weller. Royal 8vo, pp. 384 and 340, cloth. 1864. 7s. 6d.

WEST and BUHLER—A DIGEST OF THE HINDU LAW OF INHERITANCE AND PARTITION, from the Replies of the Sástris in the Several Courts of the Bombay Presidency. With Introduction, Notes, and Appendix. Edited by Raymond West and J. G. Buhler. Second Edition. Demy 8vo, 674 pp, sewed. 1879. £1, 11s. 6d.

WETHERELL—THE MANUFACTURE OF VINEGAR, its Theory and Practice, with especial reference to the Quick Process. By C. M. Wetherell, Ph D., M D. 8vo, pp. 30, cloth. 7s. 6d.

WHEELDON—ANGLING RESORTS NEAR LONDON: The Thames and the Lea By J. P Wheeldon, Piscatorial Correspondent to "Bell's Life." Crown 8vo, pp. viii. and 218. 1878. Paper, 1s 6d.

WHEELER.—The History of India from the Earliest Ages. By J. Talboys Wheeler. Demy 8vo, cloth. Vol. I containing the Vedic Period and the Mahá Bhárata. With Map. Pp lxxv. and 576, cl. 1867, o. p. Vol. II. The Ramayana, and the Brahmanic Period. Pp lxxxviii. and 680, with 2 Maps, cl. 21s Vol. III. Hindu, Buddhist, Brahmanical Revival. Pp. xxiv.-500. With 2 Maps, 8vo, cl. 1874 18s. This volume may be had as a complete work with the following title, "History of India; Hindu, Buddhist, and Brahmanical" Vol. IV Part 1 Mussulman Rule. Pp xxvii.-320 1876 14s Vol IV, Part II., completing the History of India down to the time of the Moghul Empire. Pp. xxviii and 280 1881. 12s.

WHEELER —Early Records of British India . A History of the English Settlements in India, as told in the Government Records, the works of old Travellers, and other Contemporary Documents, from the earliest period down to the rise of British Power in India. By J. Talboys Wheeler, late Assistant Secretary to the Government of India in the Foreign Department Royal 8vo, pp. xxxii. and 392, cloth. 1878 15s

WHEELER.—The Foreigner in China. By L. N. Wheeler, D D With Introduction by Professor W. C. Sawyer, Ph.D. 8vo, pp. 268, cloth. 1881. 6s. 6d.

WHERRY —A Comprehensive Commentary to the Quran. To which is prefixed Sale's Preliminary Discourse, with additional Notes and Emendations. Together with a complete Index to the Text, Preliminary Discourse, and Notes By Rev E M Wherry, M.A , Lodiana. 3 vols post 8vo, cloth. Vol 1 Pp xii. and 392 1882. 12s. 6d

WHINFIELD —Quatrains of Omar Khayyam. See Trubner's Oriental Series.

WHINFIELD.—See Gulshan I. Raz.

WHIST.—Short Rules for Modern Whist, Extracted from the "Quarterly Review" of January 1871. Printed on a Card, folded to fit the Pocket. 1878. 6d.

WHITNEY —Language and the Study of Language · Twelve Lectures on the Principles of Linguistic Science. By W. D. Whitney. Third Edition. Crown 8vo, pp xii. and 504, cloth. 1870. 10s 6d

WHITNEY.—Language and its Study, with especial reference to the Indo-European Family of Languages Seven Lectures by W D Whitney, Instructor in Modern Languages in Yale College. Edited with Introduction, Notes, Tables, &c , and an Index, by the Rev R Morris, M A , LL.D. Second Edition. Crown 8vo, pp. xxii. and 318, cloth. 1880. 5s.

WHITNEY —Oriental and Linguistic Studies. By W. D Whitney. First Series. Crown 8vo, pp. x. and 420, cloth 1874 12s. Second Series. Crown 8vo, pp xii and 434 With chart, cloth. 1874. 12s.

WHITNEY —A Sanskrit Grammar, including both the Classical Language and the older Dialects of Veda and Brahmana By William Dwight Whitney, Professor of Sanskrit and Comparative Philology in Yale College, Newhaven, &c., &c. 8vo, pp. xxiv. and 486. 1879. Stitched in wrapper, 10s. 6d; cloth, 12s.

WHITWELL.—Iron Smelter's Pocket Analysis Book. By Thomas Whitwell, Member of the Institution of Mechanical Engineers, &c. Oblong 12mo, pp. 152, roan 1877. 5s

WILKINSON —The Saint's Travel to the Land of Canaan. Wherein are discovered Seventeen False Rests short of the Spiritual Coming of Christ in the Saints, with a Brief Discovery of what the Coming of Christ in the Spirit is By R. Wilkinson Printed 1648, reprinted 1874. Fcap. 8vo, pp 208, cloth. 1s. 6d.

WILLIAMS —THE MIDDLE KINGDOM. A Survey of the Geography, Government, Education, &c., of the Chinese Empire. By S. W. Williams. New Edition. 2 vols. 8vo. *[In preparation.*

WILLIAMS.—A SYLLABIC DICTIONARY OF THE CHINESE LANGUAGE; arranged according to the Wu-Fang Yuen Yin, with the pronunciation of the Characters as heard in Pekin, Canton, Amoy, and Shanghai. By S. Wells Williams, LL.D. 4to, pp. 1336. 1874. £5, 5s.

WILLIAMS.—MODERN INDIA AND THE INDIANS. See Trübner's Oriental Series.

WILSON.—WORKS OF THE LATE HORACE HAYMAN WILSON, M.A., F.R.S., &c.

Vols. I. and II. Essays and Lectures chiefly on the Religion of the Hindus, by the late H. H. Wilson, M.A., F.R.S., &c. Collected and Edited by Dr. Reinhold Rost 2 vols. demy 8vo, pp. xiii and 399, vi and 416, cloth. 21s.

Vols. III., IV., and V. Essays Analytical, Critical, and Philological, on Subjects connected with Sanskrit Literature Collected and Edited by Dr. Reinhold Rost. 3 vols. demy 8vo, pp. 408, 406, and 390, cloth. 36s.

Vols. VI , VII., VIII., IX , and X (2 parts). Vishnu Puráná, a System of Hindu Mythology and Tradition Translated from the original Sanskrit, and Illustrated by Notes derived chiefly from other Puránás By the late H. H. Wilson. Edited by FitzEdward Hall, M.A , D C L , Oxon. Vols. I. to V. (2 parts). Demy 8vo, pp. cxl. and 200, 344, 346, 362, and 268, cloth £3, 4s. 6d

Vols. XI. and XII. Select Specimens of the Theatre of the Hindus. Translated from the original Sanskrit. By the late H H. Wilson, M A , F.R.S Third corrected Edition. 2 vols demy 8vo, pp lxxi. and 384, iv. and 418, cloth. 21s.

WISE —COMMENTARY ON THE HINDU SYSTEM OF MEDICINE. By T. A. Wise, M.D. 8vo, pp. xx. and 432, cloth. 1845. 7s 6d.

WISE.—REVIEW OF THE HISTORY OF MEDICINE. By Thomas A Wise 2 vols. demy 8vo, cloth. Vol. I., pp. xcviii. and 397. Vol. II., pp. 574 10s.

WISE —FACTS AND FALLACIES OF MODERN PROTECTION. By Bernhard Ringrose Wise, B A , Scholar of Queen's College, Oxford (Being the Oxford Cobden Prize Essay for 1878) Crown 8vo, pp. vii. and 120, cloth. 1879 2s. 6d

WITHERS.—THE ENGLISH LANGUAGE AS PRONOUNCED. By G. Withers. Royal 8vo, pp. 84, sewed. 1874 1s.

WOOD.—CHRONOS Mother Earth's Biography. A Romance of the New School. By Wallace Wood, M D. Crown 8vo, pp. xvi. and 334, with Illustration, cloth. 1873 6s.

WOMEN.—THE RIGHTS OF WOMEN. A Comparison of the Relative Legal Status of the Sexes in the Chief Countries of Western Civilisation. Crown 8vo, pp. 104, cloth. 1875. 2s. 6d

WRIGHT.—FEUDAL MANUALS OF ENGLISH HISTORY, a series of Popular Sketches of our National History compiled at different periods, from the Thirteenth Century to the Fifteenth, for the use of the Feudal Gentry and Nobility. Now first edited from the Original Manuscripts. By Thomas Wright, M.A , F.S.A., &c. Small 4to, pp. xxix and 184, cloth. 1872. 15s.

WRIGHT.—THE HOMES OF OTHER DAYS. A History of Domestic Manners and Sentiments during the Middle Ages. By Thomas Wright, M A , F S.A. With Illustrations from the Illuminations in Contemporary Manuscripts and other Sources. Drawn and Engraved by F W. Fairholt, F.S.A. Medium 8vo, 350 Woodcuts, pp. xv. and 512, cloth. 1871. 21s.

WRIGHT.—A VOLUME OF VOCABULARIES, illustrating the Condition and Manners of our Forefathers, as well as the History of the forms of Elementary Education, and of the Languages Spoken in this Island from the Tenth Century to the Fifteenth. Edited by Thomas Wright, M A., F.S A., &c., &c. *[In the Press.*

WRIGHT.—THE CELT, THE ROMAN, AND THE SAXON; a History of the Early Inhabitants of Britain down to the Conversion of the Anglo-Saxons to Christianity. Illustrated by the Ancient Remains brought to light by Recent Research. By Thomas Wright, M.A, F S.A., &c., &c Third Corrected and Enlarged Edition. Cr. 8vo, pp. xiv. and 562. With nearly 300 Engravings. Cloth. 1875. 14s.

WRIGHT.—MENTAL TRAVELS IN IMAGINED LANDS. By H. Wright. Crown 8vo, pp. 184, cloth. 1878 5s.

WYLD —CLAIRVOYANCE; or, the Auto-Noetic Action of the Mind. By George Wyld, M D Edin. 8vo, pp. 32, wrapper. 1883. 1s

WYSARD.—THE INTELLECTUAL AND MORAL PROBLEM OF GOETHE'S FAUST. By A. Wysard. Parts I and II. Fcap. 8vo, pp. 80, limp parchment wrapper. 1883. 2s 6d.

YOUNG —LABOUR IN EUROPE AND AMERICA. A Special Report on the Rates of Wages, the Cost of Subsistence, and the Condition of the Working Classes in Great Britain, Germany, France, Belgium, and other Countries of Europe, also in the United States and British America. By Edward Young, Ph.D. Royal 8vo, pp vi. and 864, cloth. 1876 10s. 6d.

YOUNG MECHANIC (THE).—See MECHANIC.

ZELLER —STRAUSS AND RENAN An Essay by E. Zeller. Translated from the German. Post 8vo, pp. 110, cloth. 1866. 2s. 6d.

PERIODICALS

PUBLISHED AND SOLD BY TRUBNER & CO.

AMATEUR MECHANICAL SOCIETY'S JOURNAL —Irregular.

AMATEUR MECHANICS —Monthly, 6d.

ANTHROPOLOGICAL INSTITUTE OF GREAT BRITAIN AND IRELAND (JOURNAL OF) — Quarterly, 5s

ARCHITECT (AMERICAN) AND BUILDING NEWS —Contains General Architectural News, Articles on Interior Decoration, Sanitary Engineering, Construction, Building Materials, &c, &c. Four full-page Illustrations accompany each Number. Weekly. Annual Subscription, £1, 11s. 6d Post free

ASIATIC SOCIETY (ROYAL) OF GREAT BRITAIN AND IRELAND (JOURNAL OF).— Irregular.

BIBLICAL ARCHÆOLOGICAL SOCIETY (TRANSACTIONS OF).—Irregular.

BIBLIOTHECA SACRA —Quarterly, 4s. 6d. Annual Subscription, 18s. Post free.

BRITISH ARCHÆOLOGICAL ASSOCIATION (JOURNAL OF).—Quarterly, 8s.

BRITISH HOMŒOPATHIC SOCIETY (ANNALS OF).—Half-yearly, 2s. 6d.

BROWNING SOCIETY'S PAPERS —Irregular.

CALCUTTA REVIEW.—Quarterly, 8s. 6d. Annual Subscription, 34s. Post free.

CALIFORNIAN.—A Monthly Magazine devoted to the Literature, Art, Music, Politics, &c., of the West. 1s. 6d. Annual Subscription, 18s. Post free.

CAMBRIDGE PHILOLOGICAL SOCIETY (TRANSACTIONS OF).—Irregular.

ENGLISHWOMAN'S REVIEW.—Social and Industrial Questions. Monthly, 6d.

GEOLOGICAL MAGAZINE, or Monthly Journal of Geology, 1s. 6d. Annual Subscription, 18s. Post free.

GLASGOW, GEOLOGICAL SOCIETY OF (TRANSACTIONS OF).—Irregular.

INDEX MEDICUS —A Monthly Classified Record of the Current Medical Literature of the World. Annual Subscription, 30s. Post free.

INDIAN ANTIQUARY.—A Journal of Oriental Research in Archæology, History, Literature, Languages, Philosophy, Religion, Folklore, &c. Annual Subscription, £2. Post free.

LIBRARY JOURNAL.—Official Organ of the Library Associations of America and of the United Kingdom. Monthly, 1s. 6d. Annual Subscription, 20s. Post free.

MANCHESTER QUARTERLY.—1s. 6d.

MATHEMATICS (AMERICAN JOURNAL OF).—Quarterly, 7s. 6d. Annual Subscription, 24s. Post free.

ORTHODOX CATHOLIC REVIEW.—Irregular.

PHILOLOGICAL SOCIETY (TRANSACTIONS AND PROCEEDINGS OF).—Irregular.

PSYCHICAL RESEARCH (SOCIETY OF).—PROCEEDINGS.

PUBLISHERS' WEEKLY.—THE AMERICAN BOOK-TRADE JOURNAL. Annual Subscription, 18s. Post free.

SCIENTIFIC AMERICAN.—WEEKLY. Annual subscription, 18s. Post free.

SUPPLEMENT to ditto.—WEEKLY. Annual subscription, 24s. Post free.

SCIENCE AND ARTS (AMERICAN JOURNAL OF).—Monthly, 2s. 6d. Annual Subscription, 30s.

SPECULATIVE PHILOSOPHY (JOURNAL OF).—Quarterly, 4s. Annual Subscription, 16s. Post free, 17s.

SUNDAY REVIEW —Organ of the Sunday Society for Opening Museums and Art Galleries on Sunday.—Quarterly 1s. Annual Subscription, 4s. 6d. Post free.

TRUBNER'S AMERICAN, EUROPEAN, AND ORIENTAL LITERARY RECORD.—A Register of the most Important Works Published in America, India, China, and the British Colonies. With occasional Notes on German, Dutch, Danish, French, Italian, Spanish, Portuguese, and Russian Literature. Subscription for 12 Numbers, 5s. Post free.

TRUBNER & CO.'S MONTHLY LIST of New and Forthcoming Works, Official and other Authorised Publications, and New American Books Post free.

WESTMINSTER REVIEW.—Quarterly, 6s. Annual Subscription, 22s. Post free.

WOMAN'S SUFFRAGE JOURNAL —Monthly, 1d.

TRÜBNER & CO.'S CATALOGUES.

Any of the following Catalogues sent per Post on receipt of Stamps.

Agricultural Works. 2d.

Arabic, Persian, and Turkish Books, printed in the East. 1s.

Assyria and Assyriology. 1s.

1 ibliotheca Hispano-Americana. 1s. 6d.

Brazil, Ancient and Modern Books relating to. 2s. 6d

British Museum, Publications of Trustees of the. 1d.

Dictionaries and Grammars of Principal Languages and Dialects of the World. 5s

Educational Works. 1d.

Egypt and Egyptology. 1s.

Guide Books. 1d.

Important Works, published by Trubner & Co. 2d

Linguistic and Oriental Publications. 2d.

Medical, Surgical, Chemical, and Dental Publications. 2d

Modern German Books. 2d.

Monthly List of New Publications. 1d

Pali, Prakrit, and Buddhist Literature. 1s.

Portuguese Language, Ancient and Modern Books in the. 6d.

Sanskrit Books. 2s. 6d.

Scientific Works. 2d.

Semitic, Iranian, and Tatar Races. 1s.

TRÜBNER'S
COLLECTION OF SIMPLIFIED GRAMMARS
OF THE
PRINCIPAL ASIATIC AND EUROPEAN LANGUAGES.

EDITED BY REINHOLD ROST, LL.D., PH.D.

The object of this Series is to provide the learner with a concise but practical Introduction to the various Languages, and at the same time to furnish Students of Comparative Philology with a clear and comprehensive view of their structure. The attempt to adapt the somewhat cumbrous grammatical system of the Greek and Latin to every other tongue has introduced a great deal of unnecessary difficulty into the study of Languages. Instead of analysing existing locutions and endeavouring to discover the principles which regulate them, writers of grammars have for the most part constructed a framework of rules on the old lines, and tried to make the language of which they were treating fit into it. Where this proves impossible, the difficulty is met by lists of exceptions and irregular forms, thus burdening the pupil's mind with a mass of details of which he can make no practical use.

In these Grammars the subject is viewed from a different standpoint; the structure of each language is carefully examined, and the principles which underlie it are carefully explained; while apparent discrepancies and so-called irregularities are shown to be only natural euphonic and other changes. All technical terms are excluded unless their meaning and application is self-evident; no arbitrary rules are admitted; the old classification into declensions, conjugations, &c, and even the usual *paradigms* and tables, are omitted. Thus reduced to the simplest principles, the Accidence and Syntax can be thoroughly comprehended by the student on one perusal, and a few hours' diligent study will enable him to analyse any sentence in the language.

NOW READY.

Crown 8vo, cloth, uniformly bound.

I.—**Hindustani, Persian, and Arabic.** By the late E. H. Palmer, M.A. Pp. 112. 5s.

II.—**Hungarian.** By I. SINGER, of Buda-Pesth. Pp. vi. and 88. 4s. 6d.

III.—**Basque.** By W. VAN EYS. Pp. xii. and 52. 3s. 6d.

IV.—**Malagasy.** By G. W. PARKER. Pp. 66. 5s.

V.—**Modern Greek.** By E. M. GELDART, M.A. Pp 68. 2s. 6d.

VI.—**Roumanian.** By M. TORCEANU. Pp .

VII.—**Tibetan.** By H. A. JASCHKE. Pp. viii. and 104. 5s.

The following are in preparation ·—

SIMPLIFIED GRAMMARS OF

Russian, Polish, Bohemian, Bulgarian and **Serbian**, by Mr. MORFIL, of Oxford.

Assyrian, by Prof SAYCE

Hebrew, by Dr. GINSBURG.

Pali.

Danish, by Miss OTTÉ.

Cymric and **Gaelic,** by H. JENNER, of the British Museum.

Turkish, by J. W. REDHOUSE, M R A S.

Malay, by W. E MAXWELL, of the Inner Temple, Barrister-at-Law.

Finnic, by Prof. OTTO DONNER, of Helsingfors.

Swedish, by W. STURZEN-BECKER, of Stockholm.

Mr. Trübner is making arrangements with competent Scholars for the early preparation of Grammars of **Albanian, Siamese, Burmese, Japanese, Chinese,** *and* **Icelandic.**

LONDON : TRUBNER & CO., LUDGATE HILL.

PRINTED BY BALLANTYNE, HANSON AND CO.
EDINBURGH AND LONDON.

1000—27/9/83

Ingram Content Group UK Ltd.
Milton Keynes UK
UKHW021039280623
424151UK00005B/68